Sloterdijk Now

Theory Now

Series Editor: Ryan Bishop

Virilio Now, John Armitage
Baudrillard Now, Ryan Bishop
Sloterdijk Now, Stuart Elden

Sloterdijk Now

EDITED BY
STUART ELDEN

polity

Individual chapters © their authors 2012, this collection © Polity Press 2012

First published in 2012 by Polity Press

Polity Press
65 Bridge Street
Cambridge CB2 1UR, UK

Polity Press
350 Main Street
Malden, MA 02148, USA

ISBN-13: 978-0-7456-5135-4 (hardback)
ISBN-13: 978-0-7456-5136-1 (paperback)

A catalogue record for this book is available from the British Library.

Typeset in 11 on 13 pt Bembo
by Servis Filmsetting Ltd, Stockport, Cheshire
Printed and bound in Great Britain by MPG Books Group Limited, Bodmin, Cornwall

The publisher has used its best endeavours to ensure that the URLs for external websites referred to in this book are correct and active at the time of going to press. However, the publisher has no responsibility for the websites and can make no guarantee that a site will remain live or that the content is or will remain appropriate.

Every effort has been made to trace all copyright holders, but if any have been inadvertently overlooked the publisher will be pleased to include any necessary credits in any subsequent reprint or edition.

For further information on Polity, visit our website: www.politybooks.com

Contents

Acknowledgements

I would like to thank the contributors for their work in this volume and their advice at various stages, especially Eduardo Mendieta for his incisive and generous comments on the introduction. I am also grateful to Michael Eldred, Eliott Jarbe, Francisco Klauser, Sylvère Lotringer and Mario Wenning for their interest in Sloterdijk's work; Ryan Bishop as series editor; Keith-Ansell Pearson for his encouragement of the project at initial review stage; and the two anonymous reviewers of the full manuscript. I am grateful to Wieland Hoban for his translation of Sloterdijk's work for this volume, and advice on translation more generally. On behalf of all the contributors I also want to thank Emma Hutchinson and David Winters from Polity Press for their support, advice and interest in this project and to Clare Ansell and Susan Beer for their work on the production of the book.

Contributors

Babette Babich is Professor of Philosophy at Fordham University, and editor of the journal *New Nietzsche Studies*. Her books include *Words in Blood, Like Flowers: Philosophy and Poetry, Music and Eros in Hölderlin, Nietzsche, and Heidegger* (SUNY Press, 2006); *Eines Gottes Glück voller Macht und Liebe: Beiträge zu Nietzsche, Hölderlin, Heidegger* (Verlag der Bauhaus Universität Weimar, 2009) and *Nietzsches Wissenschaftsphilosophie: 'Die Wissenschaft unter der Optik des Künstlers zu sehn, die Kunst aber unter der des Lebens'* (Peter Lang, 2010).

Jean-Pierre Couture is Assistant Professor in the School of Political Studies at the University of Ottawa. He received his PhD in 2009 from the Université du Québec à Montréal on the political philosophy of Peter Sloterdijk. He is the author of several pieces on Sloterdijk's work, including articles in *Horizons Philosophiques*, *Society and Space*, and *Revue canadienne de science politique/Canadian Journal of Political Science*.

Stuart Elden is Professor of Political Geography at Durham University, and editor of the journal *Society and Space*. He is the author and editor of several books, including *Speaking Against*

Number: Heidegger, Language and the Politics of Calculation (Edinburgh University Press, 2006) and *Terror and Territory: The Spatial Extent of Sovereignty* (University of Minnesota Press, 2009). *The Birth of Territory* is forthcoming in 2012. He is currently beginning work on a book entitled *The Space of the World*.

Wieland Hoban is a British composer and translator resident in Germany. He has published essays on contemporary music in German and English in various academic journals and collections. He is the English translator of Sloterdijk's *God's Zeal* and *Derrida, an Egyptian* (both Polity Press, 2009), and is currently working on the translation of the *Sphären* trilogy for Semiotext(e). He has also translated work by Theodor Adorno, including his *Towards a Theory of Musical Reproduction* and volumes of his *Correspondence*.

Efraín Kristal is Professor and Chair of the Department of Comparative Literature at UCLA. He is author of several books including *Invisible Work: Borges and Translation* (Vanderbilt University Press 2002), and of the essay on Aesthetics and Literature for the *Blackwell Companion to Comparative Literature*. He is also editor of the *Cambridge Companion to the Latin American Novel* (2005) and associate editor of the *Blackwell Encyclopedia of the Novel* (2011).

Eduardo Mendieta is Professor of Philosophy at Stony Brook University. He has published translations of and interviews with Enrique Dussel, Angela Y. Davis, Jürgen Habermas, Richard Rorty and Karl-Otto Apel. His most recent book is entitled *Global Fragments: Globalizations, Latin Americanisms, and Critical Theory* (SUNY Press, 2007). He is currently working on a book entitled *Philosophy's War: Nomos, Topos, Polemos*.

Marie-Eve Morin is Assistant Professor of Philosophy at the University of Alberta. She is the author of *Jenseits der brüderlichen Gemeinschaft: Das Gespräch zwischen Jacques Derrida und Jean-Luc Nancy* (Ergon Press, 2006) and co-editor of *Jean-Luc Nancy and Plural Thinking: Expositions of World, Politics, Art, and Sense* (SUNY Press, forthcoming, with Peter Gratton). She is currently working on the Key Contemporary Thinkers volume on Nancy for Polity Press.

Peter Sloterdijk is Rektor and Professor of Philosophy and Media Theory at the Staatliche Hochschule für Gestaltung Karlsruhe. He currently co-hosts the German television show Im Glashaus: Das Philosophische Quartett. He is the author of over thirty books, including *Critique of Cynical Reason* (Suhrkamp 1983; University of Minnesota Press, 1989); *Sphären* (Suhrkamp, three volumes 1998–2004) and *Du mußt dein Leben ändern* (Suhrkamp, 2009).

Nigel Thrift is Vice Chancellor of the University of Warwick. He is the author, co-author and editor of numerous books, including *Cities: Reimaging the Urban* (Polity, 2002, with Ash Amin); *Non-Representational Theory: Space, Politics, Affect* (Routledge, 2007) and *Shaping the Day: A History of Timekeeping in England and Wales 1300–1800* (Oxford University Press, 2009, with Paul Glennie).

Sjoerd van Tuinen is Assistant Professor of Philosophy at Erasmus University Rotterdam. He is the author of *Peter Sloterdijk: Ein Profil* (Wilhelm Fink Verlag, 2006); and co-editor of *Die Vermessung des Ungeheuren: Philosophie nach Peter Sloterdijk* (Wilhelm Fink Verlag, 2009, with Marc Jongen and Koenraad Hemelsoet) and *Deleuze and The Fold: A Critical Reader* (Palgrave Macmillan, 2010, with Niamh McDonnell).

Abbreviations

Sloterdijk's Work

References to Sloterdijk's major works are made by the following abbreviations in parentheses in the text. So, for example, (LB 7; TA 9) refers to *Luftbeben*, p. 7; and *Terror from the Air*, p. 9. All of Sloterdijk's German works are published by Suhrkamp Verlag, Frankfurt am Main, unless otherwise noted. In large part these abbreviations are the same as those used by Sjoerd van Tuinen in *Peter Sloterdijk: Ein Profil*. The chapter authors have occasionally modified existing English translations. In the chapters, Sloterdijk's works are referred to by English titles where translations exist; to German titles where they do not. For the latter, English translations of the titles are provided in this reference list.

KZV   *Kritik der zynischen Vernunft*, 1983. English translation CCR.

ZB   *Der Zauberbaum. Die Entstehung der Psychoanalyse im Jahr 1785*, 1985. [The Magic Tree: The Emergence of Psychoanalysis in 1785]

DB   *Der Denker auf der Bühne. Nietzsches Materialismus*, 1986. English translation TS.

KMPA *Kopernikanische Mobilmachung und ptolmäische Abrüstung: Ästhetischer Versuch*, 1986. [Copernican Mobilization and Ptolemaic Disarmament: Aesthetic Essays]

ZWK *Zur Welt kommen – Zur Sprache kommen. Frankfurter Vorlesungen*, 1988. [To Come to World, to Come to Language]

ET *Eurotaoismus. Zur Kritik der politischen Kinetik*, 1989. [Eurotaoism: Towards a Critique of Political Kinetics]

VD *Versprechen auf Deutsch. Rede über das eigene Land*, 1990. [Promises in German: Speeches about the Own Land]

WF *Weltfremdheit*, 1993. [Unworldliness]

SB *Im selben Boot. Versuch über die Hyperpolitik*, 1993. [In the Same Boat: Essays on Hyperpolitics]

FEE *Falls Europa erwacht. Gedanken zum Programm einer Weltmacht am Ende des Zeitalters seiner politischen Absence*, 1994. [If Europe Awakes: Thoughts on the Programme of a World Power at the End of its Era of Political Absence]

SV *Selbstversuch, Ein Gespräch mit Carlos Oliveira*, 1996. [Self-Experiments: A Conversation with Carlos Oliviera]

SG *Der starke Grund zusammen zu sein. Erinnerungen an die Erfindung des Volkes*, 1998. [The Strong Reason to be Together: Reminders of the Invention of the People]

S I *Sphären I – Blasen, Mikrosphärologie*, 1998. [Spheres I – Bubbles, Microspherology]

S II *Sphären II – Globen, Makrosphärologie*, 1999. [Spheres II – Globes, Macrospherology]

RMP *Regeln für den Menschenpark. Ein Antwortschreiben zu Heideggers Brief über den Humanismus*, 1999. English translation RHZ.

VM *Die Verachtung der Massen. Versuch über Kulturkämpfe in der modernen Gesellschaft*, 2000. [Contempt of the Masses: Essays on the Culture-wars in Modern Society]

VGN *Über die Verbesserung der guten Nachricht. Nietzsches fünftes Evangelium. Rede zum 100. Todestag von Friedrich Nietzsche*, 2000. [On the Improvement of the Good News: Nietzsche's Fifth Gospel: A Speech on the 100th Anniversary of the Death of Friedrich Nietzsche]

MT   *Das Menschentreibhaus: Stichworte zur historischen und prophetischen Anthropologie. Vier große Vorlesungen*, 2001. [The Human Greenhouse: Keywords of Historical and Prophetic Anthropology: Four Major Lectures]

NG   *Nicht gerettet. Versuche nach Heidegger*, 2001. [Not Saved: Essays on Heidegger]

ST   *Die Sonne und der Tod: Dialogische Untersuchungen* with Hans-Jürgen Heinrichs, 2001. English translation NSND.

TB   *Tau von den Bermudas. Über einige Regime der Einbildungskraft*, 2001. [The Tau of Bermuda: On Some Regimes of the Imagination]

LB   *Luftbeben. An den Wurzeln des Terrors*, 2002. English translation TA.

S III   *Sphären III – Schäume, Plurale Sphärologie*, 2004. [Spheres III – Foam, Plural Spherology]

WK   *Im Weltinnenraum des Kapitals: Für eine philosophische Theorie der Globalisierung*, 2005.

ZZ   *Zorn und Zeit. Politisch-psychologischer Versuch*, 2006. English translation RT.

AI   *Der ästhetische Imperativ: Schriften zur Kunst*, edited by Peter Weibel, Hamburg: Philo and Philo Fine Arts, 2007. [The Aesthetic Imperative: Writings on Art]

DA   *Derrida Ein Ägypter: Über das Problem der jüdischen Pyramide*, 2007. English translation DA.

GE   *Gottes Eifer: Vom Kampf der drei Monotheismen*, Verlag Der Weltreligionen, 2007. English translation GZ.

TNKZ   *Theorie der Nachkriegszeiten: Bemerkungen zu den deutsch-französischen Beziehungen seit 1945*, 2008. English translation TPWP.

MLA   *Du mußt dein Leben ändern: Über Anthropotechnik*, 2009. [You Must Change Your Life: On Anthropotechnics]

PT   *Philosophische Temperamente: Von Platon bis Foucault*, München: Diedrichs, 2009. [Philosophical Temperaments: From Plato to Foucault]

SD   *Scheintod im Denken: Von Philosophie und Wissenschaft als Übung*, 2010. [Suspended Animation in Thought: Philosophy and Science as Exercises]

WSH   *Der Welt über die Straße helfen*, with Sven Völker, München: Wilhelm Fink Verlag, 2010. [Seeing the World Across the Road]

NHGS   *Die nehmende Hand und die gebende Seite: Beiträge zu einer Debatte über die demokratische Neubegründung von Steuern*, 2011. [The Taking Hand and the Giving Side: Contributions to a Debate on the Democratic Refounding of Taxation]

English Translations

CCR   *Critique of Cynical Reason*, translated by Michael Eldred, Minneapolis: University of Minnesota Press, 1988.

TS   *Thinker on Stage: Nietzsche's Materialism*, translated by Jamie Owen Daniel, Minneapolis: University of Minnesota Press, 1989.

LHTC   'Living Hot, Thinking Coldly: An Interview with Peter Sloterdijk', with Éric Alliez, translated by Chris Turner, *Cultural Politics*, Vol. 3 No. 3, 2007, pp. 307–26.

RHZ   'Rules for the Human Zoo', translated by Mary Varney Rorty, *Environment and Planning D: Society and Space*, Vol. 27 No. 1, 2009, pp. 12–28.

TPWP   *Theory of the Post-War Periods: Observations on Franco-German Relations since 1945*, translated by Robert Pain, Wien: Springer, 2009.

GZ   *God's Zeal: The Battle of the Three Monotheisms*, Cambridge: Polity, 2009, translated by Wieland Hoban.

DE   *Derrida, the Egyptian: On the Problem of the Jewish Pyramid*, Cambridge: Polity, 2009, translated by Wieland Hoban.

TA   *Terror from the Air*, translated by Amy Patton and Steve Corcoran, Los Angeles: Semiotext(e), 2009.

RT   *Rage and Time: A Psychopolitical Investigation*, translated by Mario Wenning, New York: Columbia University Press, 2010.

NSND   *Neither Sun nor Death*, translated by Steve Corcoran, Los Angeles: Semiotext(e), 2011.

There are also forthcoming English translations of VGN, S I, S II, S III, MLA, and WK.

Works by Friedrich Nietzsche

KSA   *Samtliche Werke: Kritische Studienausgabe*, edited by Giorgio Colli and Mazzino Montinari, Berlin and München: W. de Gruyter and Deutscher Taschenbuch Verlag, Fifteen Volumes, 1980 (cited by volume and page).

Individual works within it are cited by section to allow reference to the multiple English editions.

HH   *Human, All-too-Human*
GS   *The Gay Science*
TSZ   *Thus Spoke Zarathustra*
GM   *On the Genealogy of Morality*
TI   *Twilight of the Idols*
AC   *The Anti-Christ*
EH   *Ecce Homo*

Works by Martin Heidegger

SZ   *Sein und Zeit,* Tübingen: Max Niemeyer, Eleventh edition, 1967. Page references refer to the first edition of this text, which appear in the margins of subsequent German editions, and in the various English translations as *Being and Time*.

W   *Wegmarken,* Frankfurt am Main: Vittorio Klostermann, 1976. Page references refer to the first edition of this text, which appear in the margins of subsequent German editions, and in brackets in the text of the translation as *Pathmarks*, edited by William McNeill, Cambridge: Cambridge University Press, 1998. This text includes Heidegger's 'Letter on "Humanism"'.

1

Worlds, Engagements, Temperaments

Stuart Elden

Peter Sloterdijk is one of the most interesting, prolific and controversial thinkers currently working within European philosophy. Trained in philosophy, history and literature he was initially a freelance writer, but in the last decade has been Rektor of the Staatliche Hochschule für Gestaltung (State College of Design) in Karlsruhe, Germany where he has held a chair in philosophy and media theory since 1992. He first came to prominence with the philosophical bestseller *Kritik der zynischen Vernunft* in 1983, which was translated as *Critique of Cynical Reason* in 1988.[1] Since this time he has exercised a considerable influence over German and other European thought, especially French and Spanish. In Germany he is a well-known media figure, co-hosting the television show 'In the Glasshouse: Philosophical Quartet', on the German ZDF channel, with Rüdiger Safranski since 2002. He is a regular newspaper columnist.

Yet in the English-speaking world his stature has been considerably less, in large part down to the lack of translations of his work. While the majority of his works are in Spanish and French translations, in English only *Critique of Cynical Reason*, *Thinker on Stage: Nietzsche's Materialism* and some shorter pieces were translated in the 1980s and 1990s. The lack of translations of some of his most important works has made it difficult to get a handle on Sloterdijk's overall project and specific books. He is in danger of becoming more talked about than read. Yet even his critics recognize that he has something to say. In *First as Tragedy, Then as Farce*, for example, Žižek described him as 'definitely not one of our side, but also not a complete idiot';[2] and in *Living in the End Times* as 'the liberal-conservative *enfant terrible* of contemporary German thought'.[3] Žižek has sought fit to attend to his writings in a number of places, also devoting pages to him in *The Parallax View* and *Violence*.[4]

This lack of translations has begun to be remedied over the past few years, with translations of several of his works, and many more to come. 2009 saw translations of five shorter books – *God's Zeal*; *Derrida, an Egyptian*; *Theory of the Post-War Periods*; *Terror from the Air*; and *Rules for the Human Zoo*; with the more substantial *Rage and Time* and *Neither Sun Nor Death* following in the next couple of years. Translations are in progress for the three volumes of *Sphären*; *Im Weltinnenraum des Kapitals*; and *Du mußt dein Leben ändern*.[5] Rights to many of his other works have been sold. In just a few years then, Sloterdijk has become a major figure in Anglophone engagements with continental theory, quickly moving from a peripheral position to one of the most visible contemporary philosophers. He shares conference platforms with thinkers such as Bruno Latour and Jacques Rancière, and his standing has increased with a number of high profile lectures across the world, including visiting posts in New York, Paris and Zürich.

Yet Sloterdijk is a difficult, and even at times infuriating, thinker. His ideas can appear immediately accessible and applicable, only to prove difficult to pin down. He writes two main kinds of books – short, often polemical, interventions; and much longer, wide-ranging and often digressive examinations of large topics from a variety of angles. Kusters has tellingly likened Sloterdijk's works to 'the stations of the London Underground; easy to enter, to find your way through, and to exit again, but hard to conceive in groundwork or overall idea'.[6] This is surely something anyone who has spent time with his work would agree with: it can be hard to discern an overall intention to his writings; much less a system that binds them all together. In part this is because many of his books – think *Critique of Cynical Reason*, *Im Weltinnenraum des Kapitals, Rage and Time, Sphären* and *Du mußt dein Leben ändern* – take a particular topic as a lens through which to view human history and thought. Another book, another lens. This inevitably leads to the nagging feeling that the learning on display, while vast, is sometimes superficial. Another book, another angle that is seemingly crucial. Yet this is perhaps asking him to be something he would oppose. Sloterdijk privileges the literary over the structural; *poesis* over rigour. He is often more of a cultural critic than a mainstream philosopher, trading on a literary and intellectual tradition that has more in common with an earlier generation of German thought and post-war French theorists than recent Anglo-American philosophy. Sloterdijk arguably signs up to the claim of Deleuze and Guattari in *What is Philosophy?* that the task of the thinker is to generate concepts. These concepts can then be deployed. Indeed, many of Sloterdijk's later works are developments of themes and ideas outlined in schematic form in earlier writings.

His influences can similarly be difficult to trace. Explicitly indebted to, and engaging with, Nietzsche and Heidegger, he has also a profound debt to French thought. This included Foucault in his earlier works, although somewhat displaced by Deleuze and Derrida in more recent ones. He also stresses the importance of the work of Sartre (SV 45–8). But in his references he is closer to an intellectual magpie, taking ideas and inspiration from a wide range of sources, and arranging them in intriguing ways. Crucially these inspirations are not only from the European tradition but also outside, including the years he spent studying in India.[7] Sloterdijk is perhaps best understood not as a philosopher in a narrow, academic sense, but as closer to a man of letters, a humanist and intellectual. To come to the world, as the title of one of his early books suggests, is to come to language (ZWK). Philosophy, for Sloterdijk, is a form of literature. He is often critical of the academic style of contemporary philosophy, and its lack of contemporary commitment. Nonetheless, his own modes of engagement can be peculiar. A charismatic and engaging lecturer, he sometimes acts in a deliberately provocative way – witness his recent arguments with Axel Honneth concerning taxation and the welfare state, not to mention the furor over his 1999 lecture on genetics where he crossed swords with Jürgen Habermas – only to feign astonishment at the reactions that followed.

This brief introduction provides an overview of Sloterdijk's work, beginning with the engagement with Nietzsche and the work on the cynics; touching on his critique of political kinetics and the role of Europe; before saying rather more about the spheres project and the metaphysics of globalization; and then finally turning to the notion of anthropotechnics. These are not exhaustive, and do not entirely fit into neatly chronological categories, but the intention is to outline the main contours of his thought, before situating the chapters that follow.

Sloterdijk's *Critique of Cynical Reason* parodied Kant's critical project, but the title was one that many others, Sartre included, had appropriated. In his final lecture course on the cynics from 1984, Foucault tells his audience that he's been told about Sloterdijk's recently published book. Foucault confesses that he's not yet read it, but remarks that 'no critique of reason will be spared us', as there have been pure, dialectical, political and now cynical. He notes that he's been given some rather differing assessments of the book's interest.[8] Foucault was in a sense right, as the book provoked widely divergent reactions.[9] Sloterdijk's project was to retrieve a more critical form of cynicism that would be faithful to original cynics like Diogenes, a form he calls *kynicism*. This differs from the disillusioned modern variant of cynicism which has sunk into a malaise, a state of enlightened false consciousness. It might appear to be comfortable but is in reality impoverished. Like many of Sloterdijk's books it is wildly digressive, encyclopaedic and seemingly disordered.

Sloterdijk claimed that the book was situated on the left, but this was not the left dominated by the cultural Marxism of the then dominant Frankfurt school. Indeed, Sloterdijk proposed that instead the true critical theory in Germany came out of Freiburg, the place where Husserl and Heidegger had spent most of their careers (ET 143). Yet rather than Husserl, alongside Heidegger was another controversial German philosopher, Nietzsche. Neither Nietzsche nor Heidegger would have been considered left-leaning, yet Sloterdijk, in common with French thinkers of a slightly earlier generation, thought they could be appropriated in more progressive ways. In the *Critique* he raises the prospect of 'an existential Left, a neokynical Left – I risk the expression: a Heideggerian Left' (KZV 395; CCR 209); and elsewhere talks of a 'Nietzschean Left'.[10] Sloterdijk's work is clearly a break with orthodox Left thought, and increasingly seems to bear little relation to that part of the political spectrum. As such, the kind of relation he has with other major contemporary European thinkers such as Žižek and Badiou with their return to Lenin and Mao is inevitably highly charged and fractious.

Sloterdijk's writings have always had a profound debt to the arts, something he shared with Heidegger and Nietzsche and the first generation Frankfurt school of Adorno and Horkheimer, rather than the more rigid approach of the school's post-war thinkers. Indeed, after the *Critique*, Sloterdijk's next book was a novel, *Der Zauberbaum*, which in itself was a challenge to Habermas's injunction to keep philosophy and literature separate, and the academic book that followed was explicitly on Nietzsche, ranging across his works but focused as a study of his *Birth of Tragedy* (DB; TS).[11] Sloterdijk has periodically returned to Nietzsche's work seeing him as a prophet of the human yet to come (ET; VGN; MT), a project which explicitly links to his interest in self-fashioning and anthropotechnics discussed below. Sloterdijk's contribution is thus more in the way of reopening critical theory to a vibrancy that he felt was missing from the post-war tradition of the Frankfurt school. As both Babich and Couture below note, Sloterdijk felt that 'the masochistic element has outdone the creative element' in critical theory (CCR xxxv). His aim, in part, is to reverse this.

Rather than the claim that Sloterdijk is the 'most French of the German philosophers' (LHTC 320–1), he would doubtless describe himself as, like Nietzsche, a 'good European'. A number of books followed over the next few years, including *Eurotaoismus*, which was subtitled 'towards a critique of political kinetics'. He suggests that we need to move towards a politics, not of infinite movement or mobilization, but of lightness or levity, the conundrum of how beings who are condemned to act can be 'still in the storm' (ET 54).[12] At the beginning of the 1990s he published a sequence of books that picked up these political or geopolitical themes, including *Im Selben Boot* and *Falls Europa erwacht*. The last was a rallying call for Europe, taken as a whole, to reclaim its place on the world stage, in the wake of the end of the Cold War. Both books proclaim a worldly or cosmopolitan ethics, suggesting that the world as a whole has to be taken seriously as the place of our mutual co-existence. This is a call for a post-imperial Europe, as one power among others on a global stage. This theme is picked up as a major theme in *Weltfremdheit*, especially the last chapter on cosmopolitan citizenship.

Many commentators on his work, authors in this volume including the editor among them, see Sloterdijk's *magnum opus* as the three-volume *Sphären*.[13] Žižek described it as the 'monumental *Spheres* trilogy', and suggests that 'far from advocating a return to pre-modern containment, Sloterdijk was the first to propose what one can call a "provincialism for the global era"'.[14] Like the *Critique* and some of Sloterdijk's other works it is broadly conceived and the arguments supported by a wide range of references, texts and illustrations. The book can be seen in many lights, but one which has become common is to take Sloterdijk seriously when he contends that it should be understood as the counterpart to Heidegger's *Being and Time*, as *Being and Space* (S I 345) which he later describes as 'the great unwritten book of Western Philosophy' (S II 59 n. 17). The spatial aspects of Heidegger's thought have received periodic attention,[15] but in *Sphären* Sloterdijk engages directly with Heidegger's own texts only occasionally (S I 336–45; and see NG). Instead his focus is to take inspiration from the ideas and to work that through in extraordinary breadth and detail.[16]

For Sloterdijk, in distinction to Heidegger, the key concern is not so much being, *das Sein*, but rather being-with or being-together, *Mit-sein*. This is a question both of our relation to the world of things that do not share our mode of being, and the world of other humans, who do.[17] Sloterdijk takes the Heideggerian idea of being-in-the-world and analyses the 'in' the way Heidegger expressly denied, as a spatial term, as a question of location, of where we are (WK 308; NSND 175–6).[18] As Oosterling suggests, for Sloterdijk '*Dasein* is *design*', and the focus becomes the interiors we inhabit.[19] In an interview with Bettina Funcke, Sloterdijk suggests that when he began writing in the 1990s that there was 'a voluntary spatial blindness because to the extent that temporal problems were seen as progressive and cool, the questions of space were thought to be old-fashioned and conservative, a matter for old men and shabby imperialists'.[20] He suggests that the work of Foucault and Deleuze and Guattari, while now recognized as pioneering in these respects, did not initially have the impact that they have today. Gaston Bachelard's *Poetics of Space* was inspirational, and is frequently cited in *Sphären*, though he suggests that he resisted this influence.[21] In this interview he suggests that Heidegger was the spark for his reflections.

> I was also fascinated by a chalkboard drawing Martin Heidegger made around 1960, in a seminar in Switzerland, in order to help psychiatrists better understand his ontological theses. As far as I know, this is the only time that Heidegger made use of visual means to illustrate logical facts; he otherwise rejected such anti-philosophical aids. In the drawing, one can see five arrows, each of which is rushing toward a single semicircular horizon – a magnificently abstract symbolization of the term *Dasein* as the state of being cast in the direction of an always-receding world horizon (unfortunately, it's not known how the psychiatrists reacted to it). But I still recall how my antenna began to buzz back then, and during the following years a veritable archaeology of spatial thought emerged from this impulse.[22]

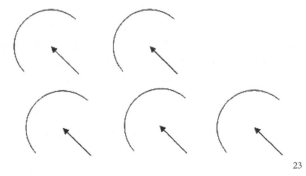

23

Being is being-with; being-with is always to be in a world. Being-in-a-sphere, then, is the primary thought he seeks to examine in the project. Spheres come in a range of sizes. The book moves from the bubbles of the first volume, where the first sphere is that of the womb, to the globes of the second volume, working through the family home, architecture, the *polis*, the nation and other spaces and environs. These two volumes are subtitled micro-spherology and macro-spherology, and there is a somewhat rudimentary scalar sense at play here (S I 631), although they should not be simply reduced to a set of nested hierarchies. If the first is a critique of subjectivity, and its interrelation with an environment; the second proposes a way to offer a properly philosophical theory of globalization. The third treats what he calls plural-spherology, where the model is that of foam, an interlocking and multiple set of cells, to understand connection and relation. Klauser has highlighted four attributes of foam: it is made up of variable shapes and sizes; it lacks a clear centre; it is both fragile and interconnected in its fragility; and part of a process of creation.[24] As Sloterdijk and Éric Alliez discuss, this is a concept that bears relation to Deleuze and Guattari's rhizome (LHTC 322–3). Yet rhizomes are sometimes reduced to complex networks, which for Sloterdijk fails to grasp the three dimensional aspect of connection, what we might call the volumetric. Foams are loosely structured, whose bubbles are connected, but separate, with the walls of one the walls of the next, stabilizing over time (S III 48–51).

Sloterdijk has described the 'foam city' as the life of living in an apartment, both connected to others but also isolated (S III 604–7). He draws on the work of the architect Thom Mayne who coined the phrase 'connected isolation' (S III 255), which he suggests could be a Heideggerian concept.[25] One of the key developments of the twentieth century, contends Sloterdijk, was that instead of targeting individuals, warfare and punishment began to target the atmosphere. This, for him, links the poison gas attacks of the First World War, judicial execution in gas chambers, the extermination of the Jews, nuclear bombs and the firebombing of the Second World War (LB; TA).

Sloterdijk developed ideas from this project in another major work that appeared only one year after the final volume of *Sphären*, *Im Weltinnerraum des Kapitals*. Like the second volume of *Sphären*, and especially developing the long final chapter of that book (S II 801–1005), it offers a philosophical theory of globalization, an alternative chronology of the world. He suggests three key epochs. First there is the metaphysical or mathematical globalization of the Greeks, with the geometricization of the enormous, the monstrous or colossal (*Ungeheuren*) (S II 47). This is followed almost two thousand years later with the terrestrial globalization of European colonialism and commerce. He provocatively claims that modern history effectively begins in 1492 and stretches to the period between 1944–1974: from Columbus and the Behaim globe to Bretton Woods and Portuguese decolonization (WK 21, 30, 246, 248–9; FEE 9; NG 371, this volume, p. 168). Sloterdijk suggests that the fundamental figure of modernity was provided not by Copernicus, but by Magellan: it was 'not that the earth orbits the sun, but that money circumnavigates the earth' (S II 56; see 856; WK 79); and the final, contemporary, globalization of saturation, with simultaneity and proximity leading to the end of spatio-temporal distantiation. He finds anticipations of this in the *loco*-motives (literally movements of place) that ran on the railroads, and the telegraph cables that ran alongside them that dissolved space (WK 60), or Captain Nemo's motto of *mobilis in mobili* (mobility in the mobile) (WK 145–6). This schema fits with his earlier claims of an old, modern and post-modern world, that can be understood through changes in movement, or what he calls a political kinetics (ET 30; see also KMPA). As Sloterdijk suggests, 'the theory of the globe [*Kugel*] is, at the same time, the first analysis of power' (S II 56).

In the first half of *Im Weltinnerraum des Kapitals* Sloterdijk recounts a pre-history of globalization, but with a strong emphasis on maritime navigation, colonization and the imaginary of water. One of his key sources is Hermann Melville's *Moby Dick*. The key architectural and thought-figure in the second half of *Im Weltinnerarum des Kapitals* is that of the Crystal Palace, the name given to the 1851 Great Exhibition centre in London, but seen now a model for global capitalism.[26] The Crystal Palace had been the object of critique for an earlier generation of thinkers, including Dostoevsky in *Notes from the Underground* (WK 26).[27] Sloterdijk sees these 'final spheres' as effectively a museum or an art installation, and would be tempted to use the phrase *Gesamtkunstwerk* – a total work of art – if that phrase had not already been taken over by an 'aesthetic ideology' (S III 811), notably Richard Wagner. The Crystal Palace, Sloterdijk suggests, is the link between the arcades that Walter Benjamin analysed and the modern shopping mall.[28] He suggests that the Palace has today become generalized, and that we spend our lives inside this huge container of boredom. Inside the Palace, the 'interior world' of capitalism, all needs are catered for, politics gets replaced by consumer preferences, and the military support and environmental degradation that makes this all possible is kept safely out of view.

Taken together with *Sphären* itself this is a remarkable out-pouring of ideas, though it is hard not to agree with Oosterling's view that 'Sloterdijk's spherological project is monstrous indeed! More adequate a qualification cannot be found for his trilogy-plus *Sphären*-project. The number of pages is enormous, the use of neologisms excessive, the conceptual avalanche overwhelming, the historically embedded, methodological legitimization over-powering.'[29] Indeed, Sloterdijk describes modernity as monstrous in both spatial and temporal form and in its objects (NG 380, this volume, p. 167). Yet 'monstrous' should not be construed only as a criticism: rather monstrous can mean a range of things from pro-digious, marvellous, to vast, and derives from the Latin *monstrum*, a wonder or potent. As Sloterdijk notes, it should be traced not to the late Latin *monstrare*, to show, but to the classical Latin *monere*, to warn or admonish.[30]

Almost immediately, Sloterdijk followed this enormous project with another attempt at a broad overview of Western history. This was the book *Zorn and Zeit*, translated as *Rage and Time*. The trans-lation's title inevitably misses the playful allusion to Heidegger's *Sein und Zeit*. Sloterdijk points out that the first noun of Western tradition, in Homer's *Iliad*, is *menis*, anger or rage: 'Of the anger of Achilles son of Peleus, Sing o Goddess.'[31] In the book Sloterdijk is both serious and light-hearted, offering a detailed reading of theology both in terms of human anger and divine wrath. These themes are developed in *God's Zeal*, which discusses the three great monotheisms of Judaism, Christianity and Islam, and looks at the conflicts between them. Especially in *Rage and Time* the clash between *eros* and *thymos*, between appetite and pride, courage, anger and ambition, is a central theme.[32] Sloterdijk situates a whole range of political-social movements of the last hundred or so years, including communism, in the broader context of two millennia of monotheism. Most global emancipatory projects, Sloterdijk contends, are motivated by rage, a barely concealed *ressentiment*.

Sloterdijk is no stranger to controversy. The first wave of this came in the wake of his controversial lecture at the Elmau institute in Germany in 1999 (RMP; RHZ). The lecture was entitled 'Rules for the Human Zoo', and was framed as a response to Heidegger's famous 'Letter on "Humanism"'. Sloterdijk mourned the demise of traditional letter writing as a means of communication, and contrasted this with the letters of our DNA.[33] He framed parts of the lecture in biological terms, including terms that had become tainted by Nazi connotations such as *Selektion* (selection) and *Züchtung* (breeding). The lecture – which only appeared in English translation in 2009 (RHZ) – was more talked about than read, sparking charged exchanges between Sloterdijk and figures associated with Habermas.[34] The work should be seen within his broader work on the notion of anthropotechnics, and as Žižek has pointed out, to argue that changes in gene technology require us to reflect again on ethics is not an unreasonable proposition.[35]

This theme has returned to his work in recent years, with his most recent major book *Du mußt dein Leben ändern* perhaps best understood as an engagement with the aesthetics of self-fashioning. This is a project that in the late twentieth century was exemplified by the late work of Michel Foucault. While Sloterdijk does pay attention to Foucault here, a range of rather different, and often surprising thinkers are brought to the project. Rilke, Kafka, Nietzsche and Heidegger receive some discussion, but Wittgenstein, in particular, is given a challenging and very distinctive reading. Indeed, Foucault is described as 'Wittgensteinian' at one point (MLA 234). It is provocative in that it challenges the dominant, analytic, reading of Wittgenstein in order to retrieve the ascetic, cultural, even existential elements of his work. It is from Wittgenstein that Sloterdijk takes one of his most powerful motifs: culture is an *Ordensregel* (MLA 210), a monastic rule or observance; or at least it presupposes an observance. The idea of a select culture being a separation from the norm through codes and modes of behaviour is at the heart of his project.

The idea of the book lies in its title, that where there is a clash between the life of the individual and the life of the society they are in, it is within our power to change our life. Changing the life will allow a better fit which will remove the clash. Self-fashioning or discipline is crucial. This, it is suggested, is crucial to the entire chronology of Western philosophy, although Sloterdijk, as often in his works, makes links to Eastern thought (especially Indian) as well. He discusses the importance of Indian influences on his thought in a recently translated collection of interviews (NSND 16–17). Sloterdijk is therefore tapping into a major current of contemporary thought: the project of making (and remaking) ourselves through our actions. It therefore ranges from the field occupied by popular accounts of philosophy as means of changing your life (such as the works of Alain de Botton) to debates about the ethics of gene technology, thereby picking up on earlier themes. The book offers a fundamental challenge to religion, because it sees it as merely one of many possible spiritual practices. Various mental and physical training regimes are available, a process of remaking the human, through the notion of an exercise (*Übung*) (see also SD). Žižek has suggested that the book 'provides elements for a materialist theory of religion, conceiving religion as an effect of material practices of self-training and self-change – one can even claim that he thereby contributes to a Communist theory of culture'.[36] As with many of his works there are a wide range of discussions, including those of army, biopolitics, psychology, verticality, Greek thought, the Church of Scientology, art, ethics and the state.

Since that book, which appeared in 2009, Sloterdijk has published a shorter contribution on design aesthetics (in WSH); a collection of pen-portraits of some of the major thinkers of the tradition from Plato to Foucault entitled *Philosophische Temperamente*; and an expansion of his arguments concerning the welfare state (NHGS). By the time this book appears two more are scheduled to have been published: an A–Z of his metanarratives, *Die Großen Erzählungen – Ein Lesebuch* (Grandnarratives – A Reader); and a collection of his interviews, *Lesen in den Eingeweiden des Zeitgeistes* (Reading the Entrails of the Zeitgeist).[37] His productivity is relentless and astonishing; a wealth of ideas are there to be discovered, engaged with, and employed.

The chapters that follow provide a wide-ranging overview of and engagement with these ideas. Babette Babich's contribution sets Sloterdijk's work on cynicism in the context of wider debates within German critical theory, and his work as a whole in relation to his debt to Nietzsche. The focus is on the different readings of the Greek philosopher Diogenes, and in particular Sloterdijk's embrace of his irreverence. Babich's chapter showcases the same kinds of attributes that make Sloterdijk's work so appealing; learned and digressive in about equal measure. Towards the end Babich raises the question of how Sloterdijk accounts for women, highlighting one of the blind spots of his work.

Sjoerd van Tuinen, author of the essential study *Peter Sloterdijk: Ein Profil*,[38] focuses on a related theme; Sloterdijk's thinking of *ressentiment*. In Nietzsche's *On the Genealogy of Morality*, *ressentiment* is the central category of slave morality. For Sloterdijk it is something that must be overcome. Van Tuinen ranges widely across Sloterdijk's works, especially focusing on *Rage and Time*, *God's Zeal* and *Du mußt dein Leben ändern*. Van Tuinen is particularly good in suggesting the way that these works of what might be called psychopolitics link to the cosmopolitics of the *Sphären* trilogy and *Im Weltinnenraum des Kapitals*.

In his chapter, Eduardo Mendieta offers a discussion of Sloterdijk's thinking of the question of humanism, and what might come in its wake as a replacement or alternative. Mendieta reads Sloterdijk in relation to Heidegger's thought on humanism and technology, suggesting that 'if Gadamer urbanized Heidegger, Sloterdijk has modernized him'. Providing a brief overview of traditional, Renaissance humanism, Mendieta outlines how Sloterdijk proposes what might be called a 'hyperhumanism', discussing his works on anthropotechnics and the aesthetics of self-fashioning.

Marie-Eve Morin takes up the relation of Sloterdijk's work to that of Heidegger, but focuses much more on Sloterdijk's appropriation and critique of the early Heidegger. While Morin shows that in places Sloterdijk's claims cannot be reconciled with Heidegger's text, her concern is much more with what Sloterdijk does with these readings. She is particularly interested in the way that Sloterdijk uses anthropology to develop claims about the notions of worlds, and the way that the human-comes-to-be-world through their engagement with an environment. This provides the basis for a discussion of spatial relations such as the complex interplay of distance and proximity; a concern which runs through Sloterdijk's *Sphären* project. The final part of the chapter directly engages that work, and his wider concerns with globalization and technology.

In mid 2009 Sloterdijk's provocative remarks on the welfare state appeared in the German newspaper *Frankfurt Allgemeine Zeitung*. In a piece entitled 'The Revolution of the Giving Hand', Sloterdijk suggested that this was a form of institutionalized kleptocracy, taking from its most productive citizens.[39] The current director of the Frankfurt School, Axel Honneth, responded, as did many others.[40] The next two chapters use this debate as the basis for their reflections. First Jean-Pierre Couture uses it as a way of engaging with Sloterdijk's position as a public intellectual in Germany and beyond. One of Couture's most telling points is to contrast Sloterdijk and Honneth's modes of engagement: the former throwing down challenges to provoke debate and bring about changes in thinking; the later wedded to ideas of ethics in public discussions and the role of intellectual responsibility.

Wieland Hoban then uses the same debate as a way into thinking about Sloterdijk's mode of engagement in his writing more generally. As one of Sloterdijk's key English translators, responsible for *God's Zeal*, *Derrida, an Egyptian* and currently working on the monumental *Sphären* trilogy, Hoban is ideally placed to focus on Sloterdijk's style. Using the give and take idea from Sloterdijk's recent polemics, he discusses the way he uses and manipulates language and empirical evidence to suit his positions. Hoban rightly steers a path between outright critique and appreciation of Sloterdijk's virtues as a writer.

Nigel Thrift develops a similar theme in his contribution, looking at the relation between philosophy and social science through the status of evidence. For Thrift, Sloterdijk offers the potential for a different way of engaging with the world. While he is critical of some of Sloterdijk's more journalistic excursions and of his playing fast and loose with facts, in *Sphären* Thrift finds the distillation of what he admires in Sloterdijk's work. He suggests that the empirical examples, photographs, artworks and diagrams are part of a wider movement away from simply analysis of texts within continental philosophy. He locates this combination of philosophy, social sciences and the creative arts as a mode of world-making, a theme he has been developing in his own recent work.

In the penultimate chapter, Efraín Kristal offers a focus on the question of literature in Sloterdijk's work, showing that Sloterdijk's indebtedness to the novel in particular is something that runs deep through his writings. Through a reading of Sloterdijk's own novel, *Der Zauberbaum*, and drawing on his use of Thomas Mann's *Joseph and his Brothers* and Jorge Luis Borges' *Book of Sand*, Kristal demonstrates how Sloterdijk's use of fiction, narrative and metaphor are crucial elements of his writing style. As such this analysis reinforces one of this book's central messages: that whatever Sloterdijk's limitations as a 'conventional' philosopher, he is quite remarkable as a literary, cultural and social theorist. As he states: 'as far as I can, I will defend myself against the obligation to choose between philosophy and poetry' (NSND 158).

The book closes with Sloterdijk himself, with a translation of one of the chapters of his book *Nicht Gerettet*. The book is a series of essays on Heidegger, and in this piece, Sloterdijk develops ideas about art, the artificial and monstrosity. In distinction to some of the more political-polemical writings that have recently been translated such as *Rage and Time* and *God's Zeal*, this piece finds Sloterdijk engaging with some of his most influential predecessors, and on some of his favourite themes: the question of art, the figure of the sphere or globe, and the interrelations of space and time.

This book as a whole has the aim of introducing his work for English-language audiences; setting an agenda for the engagement with his ideas; and relating his writings to a range of political, theoretical and practical contexts. It joins the special issues of the journals *Cultural Politics* and *Society and Space* as an important moment in the interpretation, mediation and use of his work in English.[41] The contributors range across disciplines, languages and locations, and between them give a broad overview of the scope of Sloterdijk's work; assess it both in relation to the tradition and his contemporary importance; and discuss what they find inspirational and intriguing, problematic and provocative in his ideas. In considering Sloterdijk's work we should perhaps relate to him in the way that he suggests we should read the tradition in *Philosophische Temperamente*. That book is revealing because it shows that he does not consider philosophy to be simply the arguments and proofs of the great thinkers, but their temperaments or moods, their mode of engagement with the world. We would repay Sloterdijk badly if we simply listed his errors, staked out our differences, and disputed his claims. We should also engage with his ideas, follow his paths, and take inspiration from his tireless intellectual energy and breadth of engagements. In his prodigious writings he opens up many worlds to explore.

2

Sloterdijk's Cynicism: Diogenes in the Marketplace

Babette Babich

Der Cyniker warnt dich – cave canem . . .

Nietzsche, *Der Fall Wagner*

Whose Diogenes?

Peter Sloterdijk's *Kritik der zynischen Vernunft* was published in 1983, a few years after Jean François Lyotard's 1979 *La Condition Postmoderne* and nearly four decades after the appearance of Max Theodor Horkheimer's and Adorno's 1944 *Dialektik der Aufklärung*. It would take five years for an English translation to appear. Inasmuch as Sloterdijk worked for a time as a journalist (with academic work as a sideline) before he became an academic (with at least television journalism as a sideline), he continues to have a journalist's breadth, even if he tends to be known more for his provocative lecture, *Rules for the Human Zoo*, than for his *Critique of Cynical Reason* or for his work on architecture, politics, ecology or for a recent book borrowing its title from Rilke's iconic poem to the force of art, *Du mußt dein Leben ändern*.

A critical book would seem to be one that wants to be taken

seriously and this is not easy with Sloterdijk. Here there is a parallel with Slavoj Žižek who was among the first to invoke Sloterdijk's *The Critique of Cynical Reason* in *The Sublime Object of Ideology*,[1] and, as in Žižek's case, it has been even more difficult for many readers to parse Sloterdijk's humour. Not quite as elusive as Hegel with his jokes, Sloterdijk confuses us, rather as Nietzsche confuses us by transposing his Diogenes from the Athenian polis, lodged by the porch of Cybele's temple, to a more northern locus, a German town, by a church, on market day. And we need not wait for Nietzsche: with Diogenes we are already confused. In addition to the barrel, in addition to his public masturbation, there is also the question of revaluing values, devaluing the coin of the times.

Thus Diogenes was an honest man but only *faute de mieux*. And we could have guessed this, we good readers of Plato, remembering as philosophers do the importance of money for Plato (did you inherit it? did you earn it?) who himself resolved the problems of cupidity and corruption by abolishing money – at least for the rulers. As Žižek says of Marx and the phantasms of ideology, which phantasms are always about money when it comes to Lacan (and not only Lacan), 'When individuals use money, they know very well that there is nothing magical about it – that money, in its materiality, is simply an expression of social relations. The everyday spontaneous ideology reduces money to a simple sign giving the individual possessing it a right to a certain part of the social product.'[2] The problem is that knowing this does not affect what individuals do in practice. Thus they act 'as if money, in its material reality, is the immediate embodiment of wealth as such'.[3] And the money issue, 'in its material reality', bears on Diogenes who began life as a banker's son who, as it were, suffered the 'price of truth'. Trading false coins for true, presumably after a certain 'antiquing process' (recall, if you will, Mark Twain's *Adventures of Huckleberry Finn* which includes among other useful practical advice, Jim's trick for aging a counterfeit quarter with a potato 'so anybody in town would take it in a minute'). Thus we are informed by Diogenes Laertius that Diogenes (of Sinope) was forced 'into exile because his father was entrusted with the money of the state and adulterated the coinage'.[4] This is not only a sin of the father, as Diogenes himself travelled to the oracle at Delphi and was there told to 'adulterate the coin'. The story is an old and complicated one,[5] worth noting both for Sloterdijk's attention to cynicism and for Nietzsche's programmatic notion of the 'revaluation of values'.

Nietzsche sets his cynical madman in the marketplace with a lantern in the full light of morning not only to remind us that today we would regard Diogenes as a lunatic (as we could already have learned from Jonathan Swift's *Tale of a Tub*).[6] And as Zarathustra descends from his hermit cave to preach, his prototype, Nietzsche's crazed spokesman, goes to the market to proclaim, 'I seek God! I seek God!'

Diogenes found his barrel – or oversize amphora – in a temple dedicated to Cybele, the Phyrgian mother goddess. As in Empedocles' *Katharmoi*, Cybele is associated with love and Diogenes was reputed to have enjoyed the favours of her temple's priestesses or prostitutes. And nothing is more seductive to seductresses than the ascetic, as both Lacan and Nietzsche remind us that denial is the original discourse of mastery.

It is not for what Kirkegaard liked to call 'the erotic' but the tension with the market that animates the madman. As Kierkegaard describes the contrast between the worldly aesthetic and the religious interior to the latter: 'In the magnificent cathedral the Honorable and Right Reverend *Geheime-General-Ober-Hof-Prädikant*, the elect favourite of the fashionable world, appears before an elect company and preaches with emotion upon the text he himself elected: "God hath elected the base things of the world and the things that are despised." And nobody laughs.'[7] Nietzsche invokes the same economic tension or horizon and it is the reason our madman appears in the 'bright morning hours' (KSA III, 480; GS 125). Morning, the hour with 'gold in its mouth', is still the best time for going to market, the vendors are freshly eager, the best goods have not yet been picked over, and no one is yet thinking of packing up. With time on their hands, the market at morning is the best place to meet worldly, *enlightened* men: *cynical* by contrast with Sloterdijk's *kynic* and cynical for the same reasons we might be. Thus they laugh at the madman in their midst, as we might laugh at Diogenes with his lantern, full of decently enlightened false consciousness about religion, in the face of the only things that matter. We enough, recognize ourselves. Sloterdijk's

point is that we can get cynicism wrong (it's been so long since
we read ancient philosophy) *and* that we are animated by the same
values. Thus we deny in advance any consideration of even the
idea of changing our practices. Not possible we say: think of the
cost! Today's scholars (that would be today's enlightened knights
of false consciousness) just happen to take corporate viewpoints as
their own, complete with the plural pronoun to go with it. *We*
cannot afford to stop fishing the oceans dry, *we* cannot afford to
renounce genetically modified seeds (how will farmers live if they
cannot buy seed from Monsanto?), *we* cannot afford to stop the
devastations of mining or to stop drilling for oil, exploiting shale
fields, coal fields, *we* cannot stem the forces of deforestation, *we*
cannot change factory farming practices, and so on and on.

Academic readers, we can take his point; ah, cynically, and to
help us here, Sloterdijk uses the oh so critical orthographical distinction between kynic and cynic. But even if we get the point,
here with Žižek's help – 'Kynicism represents the popular, plebeian rejection of the official culture by means of irony and sarcasm'[8]
– we can yet, we *should still*, ask: who was Diogenes?

But we think we know. Thus Nietzsche's Diogenes Laertius
tells us about Diogenes of Sinope, also called the cynic. But who
was Diogenes, son of a state banker, money changer, revaluer of
values, exile who became a kynic for his pains and died a slave but
of the kind who sold himself as one who could rule men – who
was Diogenes?

It is worth noting that we think we know cynicism because we
have interiorized it, in the same way that we think we know the
ironic, the parodic, the tragic and the comic. Just so, we suppose
we know something of the cynical-satirical tradition as we recall
Milton's very Aristotelian admonition:

> for a Satyr as it was born out of a Tragedy, so ought to resemble
> his parentage, to strike high and adventure dangerously at the most
> eminent vices among the greatest persons.[9]

Thus we can suppose we know the cynics and not Zeno, Cleanthes,
Chrysippus but Diogenes of Sinope and not as related satirical authors,
as we recall Mennipus (nothing to read), Lucian (too much to read)
but not less from Nietzsche and his specialty, Diogenes Laertius.

In other centuries (and this is why, whether we like it or not, we need the word post-modern: this is why I cited Milton above and it is why Žižek cites not only Lacan and Marx but Umberto Eco's *The Name of the Rose*), it is satire that teaches us about our Diogenes, Diogenes the dog, Diogenes the kynic. In just this way Swift's *Tale of a Tub* illuminates Diogenes, writing satirically as Swift does from his own position as dean of St. Patrick's. The close connection of religion and satire is also the connection between kynic and cynic. Thus Sloterdijk hums Heine's 'I know the style, I know the text / And also their lordships, the authors. / I know they secretly drank wine / and publically preached water.'[10]

Shall we go back to ancients to understand Sloterdijk? We worry that we may miss too much of his current interests if we do so. Thus and in general, there are dangers when we attempt to breathe new life into dead words: to give 'blood to the ghosts', as Hugh Lloyd-Jones would say. Still what is the significance of Sloterdijk's *Critique of Cynical Reason*? Why invoke the cynic? In slightly more contemporary language, as Sloterdijk favours the postwar epoch of Vanevar Bush and company, we echo Warren McCulloch, the cybernetician: 'Don't bite my finger, look where I am pointing.'[11]

By following the classical philosopher Heinrich Niehues-Pröbsting on cynicism (CCR lx),[12] Sloterdijk's *Critique of Cynical Reason* takes us back to our dog Diogenes not by way of Nietzsche (although he is first among the many pictures in Sloterdijk's text: 'Neo-"Cyniker"', Nietzsche, the thinker of ambivalence' [CCR xxviii]) but and much rather by the way of the enlightenment as such including Adorno along with Kant as well as Žižek's (and Lacan's) all-time favourite, the Marquis de Sade, and Marx and Freud, and numerous other authors.[13] Indeed, the point for Sloterdijk is to go beyond not only Kant but also Adorno. As he tells us, Sloterdijk intends to offer 'a theory of consciousness with flesh and blood (and teeth)' (CCR xxxi).

Thus we meet the 'philosophizing town bum' countering 'Plato's subtle theory of eros by masturbating in public' (CCR 101). We recognize his 'Majesty, the Baby',[14] and note the gender specificity of the spoiled boy central to the whole of theory and not just Sloterdijk's reading. Here, Sloterdijk writes,

the kynic farts, shits, pisses, masturbates on the street, before the
eyes of the Athenian market. He shows contempt for fame, ridicules
the architecture, refuses respect, parodies the stories of the gods and
heroes, eats raw meat and vegetables, lies in the sun, fools around with
the whores and says to Alexander the Great that he should get out of
his sun. (CCR 103–4)

The kynic's project claims sovereignty: 'The excluded lower
element goes to the market place and challenges the higher
element. Feces, urine, sperm.' (CCR 104).

Sloterdijk's list of bodily functions, celebrating the noises that
go with them, conspicuously upturning or shocking social convention, corresponds to the sentimental conviction (held by most
boys) that these indeed are the funniest and best and most enjoyable things ever, peeing mighty streams in competition with the
gods (or just one's friends), shitting (or even just talking about it),
and then there is farting and then, if a boy waits long enough, there
is sperm, just the word all by itself, and the ecstatic salaciousness of
its production, a kind of sublimated anal phase, we can let nose-
picking in for a lesser or second place. Nor do I fail to recognize
that most men, especially those in the military industrial complex,
remain persuaded of such adolescent insights as the truth of the
world.[15]

Sloterdijk emphasizes the 'cynical' focus on urination as an
'achievement'. Perhaps our author has once upon a time laughed
himself to pieces over the Belgo-Flemish *Manneken pis* and now
grown up, finds himself a more robust yet similarly simple image,
similarly voyeuristic and similarly silly (I am thinking of the
'squints' or satires or *silloi* as I say this, although one should not as
the connection is metonymic). It is not for nothing that Sloterdijk
gives us the image of 'Hercules pissing' (CCR 105), immortalized
in stone, to illustrate the existentialist dialectic of such '"dirty"
materialism' as a kind of self-presentation and 'argumentation'.

If Sloterdijk refers to bodily functions, he goes further than
Nietzsche (if he also happens to favour urination as Nietzsche
did,[16] but also like Freud – to recall Freud's enthusiasm for
Hercules' Augean efforts).

As a child of the 1968 generation, Sloterdijk takes the modality

of shock – even his important concluding reference to Thomas
Mann's 'pleural shock' (CCR 529 ff) – with a naive trust that only
a child of the 1960s (even the 1960s in Germany) could muster.
This is not theory, it is life, lived in the spirit of a generation persuaded that simply by changing one's clothes (or going without
them) or flouting sexual conventions (and going without them), or
transcendental meditation and yoga, and natural food, and above
all by way of certain musical choices, a folk could for the first and
really change the world.

Pissing as world-changing? Why ever not? It's something
anyone can do (and it is a loss of vitality when, due to illness or
age, this is not so) and of course, urination is also, classically speaking, the very Freudian origin of the fantasy of penis envy. Boys
and men are mightily persuaded (and will not be disabused of this
faith) that women long for nothing but this very floppy append-
age and its marvellous powers. Thus Swift emphasizes Gulliver's
'making water' as an 'event' and part of his adventures among the
Lilliputians, not just once[17] but again and no less and to save the
day, whereby Swift has his Gulliver go on – and what more could
Freud's heart have desired? – to make a capital case of it: complain-
ing that because of such a saving gesture he is subsequently and
thus unfairly brought up on charges.[18]

Again, Sloterdijk emphasizes for us: 'But urine in the academy!
That would be the total dialectic tension, the art of pissing against
the idealist wind.' (CCR 105). The sentence is incomplete.
Diogenes, wiry and tough as he may be, is no Hercules and pissing,
like spitting, into the wind is messy.

Which is the point for Sloterdijk. We are to rehabilitate sexuality (so long as we don't ask *whose* sexuality we will be rehabilitating
here) and to celebrate laughter, once again, as long as we don't ask
who is laughing. As Nietzsche muses, 'even laughter may yet have
a future' even as Nietzsche reminds us that 'for the meantime, the
comedy of existence has not yet "become conscious" of itself'
(KSA I, 370; GS 1). For Sloterdijk as for Odo Marquard, Steffen
Dietzsch, and many others, our suspicious lack of laughter has little
to do with the sufficiency 'of truth' as Nietzsche here all-too-epis-
temologically insists but and much rather with all the spoilsports
who conspire to hold us back. For otherwise, of that we are sure,

we'd all be laughing. Yet Sloterdijk worries: people laugh to death; what is it that happens when one splits one's sides? Liberation has its risks and first in line would seem to be Sloterdijk himself, with all his learning, dangerously beyond the average scholar, like Adorno, or even more accurately like the Menippean satirist, as Northrop Frye had analysed such a display of intellectual prowess or kynical self-presentation, showing 'his exuberance in intellectual ways, by piling up an enormous mass of erudition about his theme or in overwhelming his pedantic targets with an avalanche of their own jargon'.[19]

So many allusions, so little understanding.

Minima Amoralia and the Sloterdijk Affair: Technology and Fascism

Our popularly ongoing moral–ethical objections to Heidegger will explain for some readers the 'Sloterdijk Affair' following Sloterdijk's Elmau lecture, *Rules for the Human Zoo*, a scandal that, had nothing else assured this, also brought Sloterdijk an excess of intellectual notoriety. And fame is fame, as Oscar Wilde observed in a parallel context. Sloterdijk himself locates the problem on the side of a certain lack of manliness, with which deficiency of course our boy hero cannot be associated:

> I wasn't unaware, either, that this 'materialist' terminology was going to create definite unease among Heideggerians of a neo-pietist persuasion. Having proposed an iconoclastic – and 'Left-wing' – reading of Heidegger's work in *Critique of Cynical Reason*, I didn't at any cost wish to be confused with that de-virilized, conservative Heideggerianism. (LHTC 320)

Central here is Sloterdijk's *framing* of the issue of (this is not the same as *questioning*) technology.[20]

Formulaically placing himself on the other side of a 'de-virilized' Heideggerianism, Sloterdijk makes it plain that he reads his Nietzsche with the right thinkers, that would also be to say in the right tonality: if not what I elsewhere call 'analytic' thinkers (mainstream given their power in the academy) then certainly not gelded thinkers either. Sloterdijk's Nietzsche is a 'hard Nietzsche', a kind of 'systems' Nietzsche, a rhizomatic or biopower Nietzsche (here Sloterdijk reserves the ecologist's word, *bioculture*, for himself): Nietzsche à la 'Deleuze, Foucault, Derrida, Luhmann' (LHTC 318). Well, Luhmann anyway.

Thus Sloterdijk rewrites the materialism of his earlier title, *Thinker on Stage* alongside what some (perhaps captivated by the language of gravitational singularity in cosmological physics – do, please, think of black holes) have called the *technological singularity*.[21]

For Sloterdijk (although he does not mention them as such in his *Critique of Cynical Reason*), techno-futurists of the sort that have only continued to proliferate (between Ray Kurzweil, to be located on the rapturous side of the future with Jaron Lanier, say, on the kynical side) are only late comers to the very 'modern' future, following not only (Hegel's!) Friedrich Dessauer and Adrien Turel but also other representatives of the fascism that grew out of the Weimar Republic.

And arguably because the literal bioculture of genetic engineering has not been going as well as anticipated (given pesky technical details, i.e. the organism, and that cloning adults seems to produce organisms that senesce and thus die markedly faster than ordinarily bred organisms do, be they sheep or Korean Saluki puppies or mice, seemingly to recover their origins) the new enthusiasm for the coming technological rapture seems to be growing. The 'faith' in science, especially industrial, corporate, capitalist technology has been with us, here according to Sloterdijk, since the interregnum between the two wars, and such a vision is fascist through and through. Nor, thanks to the already mentioned Vanevar Bush, did techno-science fall from grace or power in the wake of the Second World War. And we all know the rest.

Gadgets, as Günther Anders already warned in 1956,[22] are what it is all about. Hot in the fifties, the hype about the latest gadget (iPad anyone?) is no less so today. If critics of technological rapturists charge that we simply or factually lack the technology supposed by the theorizing or speculation, the reply is simply that there is a curve that shows that the technology will come, a nice manifestation of the cargo cult confidence that continues to be our own vision of techno-scientific salvation. As iPhone commercials chirpily proclaim and without needing to ask what we might have in mind: *there's an app for that*. And of this we have no doubt – which is the way faith works.

Yet there is nothing new under the sun, and Sloterdijk reminds us that this was *already* an issue and *already* imagined as *resolved* for the crippled military victims after the First World War. Thus he cites Brecht's *Interjection*, from which we need repeat only the line relevant for the techno-futurists of today: 'Here this evening, a man will be reassembled like a car / Without losing anything in the process' (CCR 441). Sloterdijk thus cites Brecht's own uncanny anticipation:

> To accommodate himself to the course of the world
> And to let his private fish swim away
> And no matter what he is remodeled into,
> In doing so no mistake is made. (CCR 442)

Like Brecht, Nietzsche also emphasized the usually unsung dangers of large-scale or grand 'politics' reviewed on the terms of ordinary political or everyday social life.[23] The great issue of war for Nietzsche is what it wreaks on everyday things, here and now. Nietzsche's aphorism 'Great Politics and What They Cost' [*Grosse Politik und Ihre Einbussen*] contextualizes an often ill-understood concept.[24] Here Nietzsche neither highlights destruction nor denounces the subtle stimulus such a negative impulse is imagined to engender for a depleted social system of jaded productivity and stale surplus but laments the dispersal of the 'capital' of heart and mind [*Kopf- und Herz-Capitale*] – this would be Brecht's 'private fish' – as the 'cost' of technological modernity as this is always and inevitably a military undertaking, the 'cost involved in the extraction, year in, year out, of an extraordinary number of its most efficient and industrious men from their proper professions and occupations so that they become soldiers' (KSA II, 315; HH I, 481).

Sloterdijk's invocation of Brecht's '*remodeling* of the civilian as a soldier' (CCR 442) as prelude to his chapter on 'Artificial Limbs' should be read with a view to the 'reassembling' (i.e. the rehabilitation) of the victims of war, citing Erich Kästner's 1931 *Fabian*, to remind the reader that 'fifteen years after the war, its victims still lay in endless agonies' (CCR 443). The connection with today's fascination with the trans-human of the coming technological singularity plays itself out beyond mere flesh and blood humanity. And isn't that flesh and blood humanity 'obsolete' anyway – as Kurzweil optimistically suggests and as Anders already challenged (in a cynical, critical tone) as far back as 1956? We vote for optimism with our cynicism, avoiding criticism in order to bracket its pessimism (especially when it comes to authors like Anders). Thus Sloterdijk reads the conceptual disconnect of the recommendations to the handicapped as it served the purposes of both political and spiritual (re-)deployment. 'Two things were recommended to the mutilated survivors by the standard psychotechnical textbooks; a will to live as *hard as* steel and the training of the body to handle artificial limbs' (CCR 444). And we know all about post-war physical therapy in America, or better said: we know nothing of it although it is all around us, as an array of statistics are there for the searching – which is to say that these same facts and their implications are only occasionally an open or overt theme for public discourse – to tell us that more grievously wounded soldiers have survived the still-ongoing wars in Afghanistan (and still Iraq) than ever before.

> In the textbooks on the maimed and the writings of the medical-technical industry, a highly apposite image of the human being emerges: *Homo prostheticus*, who is supposed to say a wildy joyful Yes to everthing that says No to the 'individuality' of 'individuals' (CCR 446).

This is the prosthesis still associated with fascism. We recognize Dr. Strangelove as German not by his Kissinger-like accent but by his obviously prosthetic hand (and seemingly programmed or automatic Hitler salute), already a trans-human by way of his wheelchair. For Sloterdijk the move is immediately made in the direction of the Kurzweilian *singularity*: 'Personality amputated? No problem – we have another for you in stock' (CCR 449).

Essential here is the quiescence of any technological anxiety after the fashion of a Jacques Ellul or a Herbert Marcuse or indeed and more agitatedly yet: the Günther Anders already cited. And we do not read such authors – they are not 'hot' enough. Indeed most us are confident that talk of technological autonomy is so much philosophical blather, as Sloterdijk explains this as a logical consequence of its already consummate autonomy in the society of the machine, that is 'the society of labor and war' (CCR 448). Nothing like cynical distance, as Žižek had explained this move for us. Thus, technology in its ultimate alliance with humanism

> takes the 'upper hand'; it threatens to degrade human beings; it wants to make us into robots. But if we pay attention and keep our souls in shape, nothing will happen to us. For technology is, after all, there for people and not people for technology. (CCR 448)

Sloterdijk goes on to cite Dessauer, 'In the fourth realm (*Reich*), we enter a new land that opens up technology to us',[25] explaining that the Fourth Reich 'is that of inventions, those things that have been brought into existence only by human beings, the immeasurable potential of what can still be invented and realized' (CCR 455.) This may sound like trans-humanism, soon to be raptured up into the 'clouds' of Kurzweil's anticipated techno-singularity, but for Sloterdijk this is the world *already* and fully fleshed out in Dessauer. It is 'as if technology reached over into the sphere of the *Ding an sich* . . . which according to Kant is inaccessible to us, in order to create out of this sphere previously nonexisting objects of experience, machines' (CCR 455). It is this ontico-ontological consummation that intrigues Sloterdijk: 'Inventions of this quality are ontological enrichments in the inventory of existence – whereby humanity is allotted the role of coauthor of the existing' (CCR 456).

Thus it is unimportant that the technology requisite for the machine-consciousness and machine-human-mind-meld rapture of which Kurzweil speaks is not really close to existing. More pedestrianly regarded – and it is pedestrian – Kurzweil's ultimate reference is the achievement of a search engine (Google!) and an iPhone: in this sense, neither cynical nor kynical, the singularity turns out to be already here.

This is like finding out that you are a cyborg because you have contact lenses or, this is Ray Kurzweil's example: you have an iPhone. How underwhelming for those of us who might have hoped for more from cyborg life. And for the rest of what does not exist or for those predictions previously named pesky, the ones that have not panned out – these too are of little consequence: trivial details. Like the drugstore magazine that tells us what event about to happen confirms what prediction Nostradamus is supposed to have once predicted, the passage of time and the failure of that event to transpire according to plan is always as irrelevant as historical hermeneutics of the actual text. One shrugs and updates the date. Like 'jam tomorrow', the future is a course that hasn't yet been set: *to be arranged*. The point is to believe: rather like 'manifesting' wealth or a 'life-partner'.

But the implications are not as banal as most new-age ideas. Technology 'appears as the promise of a total solution to problems' and will, 'one day' according to Kurzweil as 'already' for Dessauer, as Sloterdijk cites him, 'work out all misery' (CCR 456). The sophisticated move of today's Kurzweil (go ahead: *be* the machine) is not one that would have been wasted on Dessauer or, in a different sense, Sloterdijk, who goes on to observe of Dessauer as we might also observe of Kurzweil: 'In an astoundingly shortsighted way [Dessauer/Kurzweil] overlooks the destructive aspect of "invention." . . . At the heart of this theory stands a subject who can no longer suffer because it has become wholly prosthesis' (CCR 457).

And Sloterdijk chides us for our enthusiasm for such a totalizing solution and he includes Heidegger as he does so, noting that Heidegger's early so-called existential theory, his account of *das Man*,[26] could only be 'an excuse for the cheapest kind of outrage' (CCR 202). Thus Sloterdijk locates *Being and Time* in the historical period in which it was formed:

> No thought is so intimately embedded in its time as that of being-unto-death: it is the philosophical key word in the age of imperialist and Fascist world wars. Heidegger's theory falls in the breathing space between the First and the Second World Wars, the first and the second modernization of mass death. (CCR 202)

Key for Sloterdijk's media reflections here and elsewhere, Heidegger's *Being and Time* 'stands midway between the first triumvirate of the destruction industry: Flanders, Tannenberg, Verdun, and the second Stalingrad, Auschwitz, Hiroshima' (CCR 202). Note that Sloterdijk's second trio of names illuminates Heidegger's irritating identification of Germany with Europe and of Europe itself as a kind of captive butterfly, impaled between America and its capitalism and Russia and its Bolsheviks: 'Europe lies in a pincers between Russia and America, which are metaphysically the same, namely in regard to their world character and their relation to the spirit.'[27] The cynic identifies Germany at the heart of Europe with all its historical consquences as we always invert the order of history as we write it. As Sloterdijk cites Gustav Regler's awful ditty: 'There was once a Communist / who didn't know what a Nazi is, / he went into a brown house, / and without any bones, he came out! Hahahaha!'[28]

Historio-critically, Sloterdijk links Adorno and Heidegger: 'without death industry, no distraction industry' (CCR 202). Political in this sense, 'Heidegger's theory of death harbors the greatest critique by this century of the last' (CCR 202). Thus the conceptual accomplishments of the nineteenth century depends upon 'formal' equations or

> equivalences between the idea of evolution, the concept of revolution, the concept of selection, the struggle for existence and the survival of the fittest, the idea of progress and the myth of race. In all these concepts, an optics is tested out that objectifies the downfall of others. . . . Viewed superficially only the personal pronoun is altered: 'One dies' becomes 'I die.' (CCR 202)

In 'conscious being-unto-death Heideggerian existence revolts against the "constant reassurance about death" on which an excessively destructive society necessarily depends' (CCR 202).

Dämmerung: The Twilight of False Consciousness

Once again, we recall the year: 1981. The echoes resound. We hear Nietzsche and Heidegger to be sure, as we hear Adorno and

Benjamin but above all perhaps we hear Marcuse. We do not hear Lyotard though we might have and the term post-modernism could be substituted for cynicism. But that would be to make it too easy. And we think we know what it is to be modern (Bruno Latour rightly disputes this,[29] as did, of course, Foucault). We do not 'know' the cynics, yet all of us 'know' what the word means: just as all of us are cynics – already and in advance.

It is in this context of already knowing that Sloterdijk gives us Diogenes in his barrel: 'In the picture book of social characters he has always appeared as a distance-creating mocker, as a biting and malicious individualist who acts as though he needs nobody and who is loved by nobody because nobody escapes his crude unmasking gaze uninjured' (CCR 3–4).

And one cannot but draw a parallel to Sloterdijk's suggestion in his *Rules for the Human Zoo* that one imagine what a society composed solely of Levinas scholars might look or feel like (RMP 29; RHZ 19). At the same time, like Habermas and like Levinas, Sloterdijk himself cannot be accused of '*over*much' (where would that leave us?) sympathy for animals or for nature – and it has rightly been observed that he is not quite up to the task of thinking about women even where, maybe especially where he speaks of the body, masturbation, pornography.

Indeed, those women who are present in Sloterdijk's text are there only as objects of fairly conventional desire.[30] Nor does it occur to Sloterdijk to wonder about the woman who might be reading the text or the desires that she might (or might not) have for her own part. And to explain this, we cannot return to the Greeks – not quite. But it might be argued that Sloterdijk excludes women for the same reason, *ceteris paribus*, that Levinas is compelled to exclude women, which in Levinas' case means that woman is not the Other. Levinas is an observant Jew and religion justifies a myriad of sexist sins. And maybe we can argue similarly that Sloterdijk is thinking kynically.

Nor can it do to say that there were no women 'cynics' (there were) – which is perhaps and among other things, the most disconcerting aspect of the cynic doctrine, as women 'profit' (however this 'profit' is to be understood) but even more so, as women suffer (but as Nietzsche reminds us these are the same) from convention, be it traditional or otherwise. Thus Hipparchia of Maroneia had to put up with more than Kierkegaard's child-bride-qua-intended Regina Olsen, but the difference between Hipparchia and Regina was one of practical *askesis* – which would, at least for some readers, make Regina the feminist hero. The same difference makes Hipparchia a cynic or, better said, *kynic* philosopher, just to retain Sloterdijk's distinction here.

It is with Adorno (not Habermas) that Sloterdijk's sympathies are free to find expression, out in the open, and, not surprisingly, women and the question of virility is involved. 'Critical Theory', so we read, categorically rejects 'the masculine world' (CCR xxxiv). Beyond Lacan, it 'is inspired by an archaic No to the world of the fathers, legislators, and profiteers' (CCR xxxiv). And Sloterdijk is not done: 'The masochistic element has outdone the creative element' (CCR xxxv), adding the condemnation of the 'sensitive', expressed as 'paralyzing resentment' nourished upon 'an archaic rage against "masculinity", that cynical sense for facts exhibited by political as well as scientific "positivists"' (CCR xxxv). And we are then hardly surprised to read that it 'took refuge in the realm of the mother, in the arts, and encoded longings' (CCR xxxv). Oh, can we add deconstruction too? Why ever not? 'With Adorno, the denial of the masculine went so far that he retained only one letter from his father's name, W' (CCR xxxv).

Thus we get to hear about Adorno's sex life but not in detail just the gossip. The year is 1981 and we have already been there and done that. Adorno we are told is reduced, done to ground by nakedness, not just nakedness, naked *breasts* (CCR xxxvii). And Sloterdijk recalls these words in the body of the text (nothing like self-reference):

> Does the reader remember the episode in the lecture hall described in the Preface? The disturbance of the lecture and the female student's naked breasts? Now their baring was no run-of-the-mill erotic-cheeky argument with female skin. They were, almost in the ancient sense, cynically bared bodies, bodies as arguments, bodies as weapons. (CCR 109)

Fascinating, so that is where the women are.

Now having spent time in German lecture halls, as a student and as a visiting professor, I myself recall wondering (just to myself) how the women students were able to take notes so assiduously while they were knitting (and this was 1984 and decades after the 'cynical' moment of encounter with Adorno). Perhaps, so I wondered then, Germans of both sexes are simply *Übermenschen* (or more currently said: *ÜbermenschInnen*). And it is not otherwise in American-style academic practice, I have students of both sexes, who use computers or 'text' just as assiduously today. A certain self-induced autism covers over the return to the sexism that never really left.

Ah well. Kynic or cynic?

Sloterdijk who moves between analyzing the claims of objectivity and analysis and claiming the same for himself concludes his introduction: 'A mixture of cynicism, sexism, "matter-of-factness," and psychologism constitutes the mood of the superstructure in the West, a twilight mood, good for owls and philosophy' (CCR xxxviii).

It is not only that Sloterdijk, to be sure: like most of us, has his blind spots. For it remains significant that only women *have* to learn, this would be the great philosophical advantage of oppressed consciousness, to take the viewpoint of others. What can work to make Sloterdijk elusive here is his insistence on maleness or virility, a Falstaff-style modus that is hard to refuse because it insists upon itself – like a man sitting in a New York subway car with his legs spread as wide as possible in order to take up two or three or four seats, he's a man, a displaying primate, and he needs those seats. But more than this is at work.

Here Sloterdijk borrows a leaf from Nietzsche (his translator misses the allusion but it's not too direct anyway), where Nietzsche talks about his own stupidities 'down deep' – and this is relevant after Sloterdijk's *Critique of Transparency* in psychoanalysis, contra Freud's self-serving insistence on patenting the technique solely and only in his own name by naming himself the discoverer of the unconscious despite antecedents, Sloterdijk goes in for historical Mesmerism. But and of course, this is a critique after all, we recall that the unconscious is already announced in Kant (this is the substance of the allusion to the 'dear little self', and it is why subjective intentions fail to suffice as proof of conformity to moral law as they offer no assurance that some other self-interest may not have been in play). Thus we read Sloterdijk's *Critique of the Illusions of Privacy* of 'artful stupefaction' or better said (stupefaction is far too kind) 'stupidification' [*Verdummung*] as this 'manifests itself in a whole range of modern naturalisms: racism, sexism, fascism, vulgar biologism and egoism' (CCR 59).

Critics, according to Sloterdijk

> have long since blended together with what is to be criticized, and that distance that would be created by morality has been lost through a general muddling in immorality, semimorality, and the morality of lesser evils. Cultivated and informed people of today have become aware of the essential model of critique and the procedure of unmasking without having been shaken. (CCR 88)

And in the two decades that have come and gone between the time of this reflection, even before the world changed and references to the GDR ceased to make any sense, and before the shock of invoking Marx becomes something else again, Sloterdijk asks in a Nietzschean voice, 'Who today is still an enlightener? The question is almost too direct to be decent' (CCR 88). And he does answer with a directness that lets the reader know that we do not have to do with an ordinary critical text, or any kind of merely academic context.

What is certain, for my own part, is that when I am hit up for cash on a NY city sidewalk, I pay up and, at the same time, I happen to know that I am using the best expedient to assure my imperturbability. The same may be said for the email that implores me to add my 'voice' to 'halt' the destruction of the rainforest, to preventing the death of polar bears, wolves, seals, coyotes, and horses and kittens too. I always hit a key to respond and I do so although I know better than to think that it makes any bit of difference. Our civilization shrugs: so what about wild animals, domestic animals, so what about the fish, so what about the dolphins, the turtles, the whales, so what about the sharks? Let us not even begin to think of trees and rocks. Who's kidding who?

Nor does it end there: America is now in its longest war. It is hard to think of anyone who is not a European who is not disappointed in Obama just because of the war(s) if not because of his clear collusion with the banks (the bailout) and the wealthy (it was not for nothing that Obama extended Bush's tax cuts for the rich at the same time as he extended unemployment benefits as a distracting palliative for a dysfunctional economy and to blur the most immediate effects of the same cuts), and in the case of health care, his collusion with the insurance companies (so-called health care, so it has transpired, is nothing but a requirement to pay up, for every man, woman, and child, to buy some health insurance policy or other: the details of what one is to receive for that purchase acquisition are seemingly clear to no one).[31]

As Sloterdijk analyses this and other circumstances like it:

> When someone tries to 'agitate' me in an enlightened direction, my first reaction is a cynical one: The person concerned should get his or her own shit together. That is the nature of things. Admittedly, one should not injure good will without reason: but good will could easily be a little more clever and save me the embarrassment of saying: 'I already know that.' For I do not like being asked, 'Then why don't you do something?' (CCR 89)

And here we find ourselves at the end, here now following the Rocky-Horror like farce of the 'pleural shock' quoting Thomas Mann, 'I know death . . . I can tell you it's almost nothing . . . We come out of the dark and go into the dark . . .' (CCR 529). Mann's reflection on life and death is also made by Nietzsche who speaks of the human being as a rope suspended over an abyss, between animal and *Übermensch* (KSA IV, 16). Thus the human is dispossessed not only in this world, as Sloterdjk rightly reads Heidegger, but is similarly not at home in the world to come: a nothingness on either side: ' – a hiatus between two nothingness [*zwei Nichtsen*] – '(KSA XII, 473).

At the end, it becomes earnest for Sloterdijk and one can almost anticipate his later Rilkean word with his allusion to the golden, Goethian 'present', not at all unlike Pierre Hadot's last reflections: In the present, awareness climbs all at once to the heights of being' (CCR 547). This feeling, which Nietzsche for his part called 'the happiness of a god, full of power and love',[32] is also a benediction. *To learn*, as Nietzsche would put it, *to see what is necessary as beauti-ful*. And this Nietzsche also called a 'future "humaneness"'. This is Sloterdijk's 'presence of spirit' in which 'the spell of re-enactments is broken. Every conscious second eradicates what is hopelessly past and becomes the first second of an Other History.'

3

From Psychopolitics to Cosmopolitics: The Problem of Ressentiment

Sjoerd van Tuinen

As its subtitle makes clear, *Rage and Time. A Psychopolitical Investigation* continues a line of research that begins with the *Critique of Cynical Reason*, which already abounded with references to psychopolitics. Far from psychologizing political powers, psychopolitics deals with the ecology and economy of energies or affects that are articulated only on a collective level. In this sense Sloterdijk is indebted to crowd psychologists such as Hermann Broch and Elias Canetti, to the mimetic anthropology of Gabriel Tarde and René Girard, as well as to media theorists such as Marshall McLuhan or Jean Baudrillard. But his primary inspiration is Nietzschean, insofar as psychopolitics is inseparable from 'a self-aware anti-political therapeutics' which seeks 'not to depoliticize individuals, but to deneuroticize politics' (TS 90) with regard to the basic affect constellation of the West: *ressentiment*. The aim of this chapter is to demonstrate that, even if Sloterdijk's earlier and later strategies for overcoming *ressentiment* appear difficult to reconcile, they all contribute to the single project of a '*Scienza nuova* of cosmopolitics' (WF 376–81).

Ressentiment Criticism and Beyond

According to Nietzsche, *ressentiment* is a 'feeling of vengefulness (*Rachegefühl*)'. It occurs when, due to some impotence, a 'reaction ceases to be acted in order to become something felt (*senti*)'.[1] As interiorized reaction, it is the local and surreptitious illness that defines 'those who came off badly' in any healthy civilization, i.e. any culture based on a natural hierarchy between masters and slaves.

> While the noble man lives in trust and openness with himself (. . .), the man of *ressentiment* is neither upright nor naive nor honest and straightforward with himself. His soul *squints*; his spirit loves hiding places, secret paths and back doors, everything covert entices him as *his* world, *his* security, *his* refreshment; he understands how to keep silent, how not to forget, how to wait, how to be provisionally self-deprecating and humble. A race of such men of *ressentiment* is bound to become eventually cleverer than any noble race; it will also honor cleverness to a far greater degree: namely, as a condition of existence of the first importance. (KSA V, 272–3; GM I, §10)

It is this timeless portrait of the man of *ressentiment* which Sloterdijk polemically reproduces in his evaluation of our contemporary capacity for critique in the *Critique of Cynical Reason*.

The problem with critical theory as it has developed in the course of the twentieth century is that the discontents of civilization have grown to such an extent that reason is forced to dethrone itself, defeated by a new and indifferent 'realism' in which critique can no longer distinguish itself from the criticized. Already at the time of the first generation of the Frankfurt School, the only plausible standpoint of critique was a 'paralyzing *ressentiment*' to which Adorno referred as a sentimental 'concernedness (*Betroffenheit*)' and which Sloterdijk rephrases as 'a priori pain' (CCR xxxiii-v). The only thing that kept this '*ressentiment* criticism' (Max Scheler) from becoming cynical was its self-annulling aversion from practical life and power. This changes with second generation Critical Theory, in which the demoralizing self-interest in the rat-race of career critics prevails over the cultivation of a feeling of injustice (CCR xxxv-vi). The real object of Sloterdijk's diagnosis is therefore the pragmatic nihilism of a 'pseudo-critique' which has wilfully lost its innocence and compensates for its own bad conscience with an ever higher level of reflectivity or artfulness. Its point of view remains that of unhappy consciousness, but its *ressentiment* is now 'reflexively buffered' (CCR 5), such that, in the form of a cynical alliance of rationalism and *ressentiment* typical of 'Christian-bourgeois-capitalist schizophrenias' (CCR 107), it effectively perverts the imperative of *sapere aude*: 'Only in the form of derision and renunciation do references to the ideals of a humane culture still seem bearable. Cynicism, as *enlightened false consciousness*, has become a hard-boiled, shadowy cleverness that has split courage off from itself, holds anything positive to be fraud, and is intent only on somehow getting through life' (CCR 546).

Although Sloterdijk refers to neither, his diagnosis of critical conscience is very close both to Deleuze's diagnosis of Kantian critique as 'exhausted in compromise' in *Nietzsche and Philosophy* and to Deleuze and Guattari's diagnosis of split subjectivity under capitalism in *Anti-Oedipus: Capitalism and Schizophrenia*, in which the authors had already demonstrated that 'the age of bad conscience is also the age of pure cynicism'.[2] But instead of liberating desire by pushing the deterritorializing tendencies of capitalism ever further towards the schizorevolutionary pole, he seeks a therapeutic strategy that reintegrates on an existential and embodied level our lived being in the world (CCR 118–20). If consciousness is corrupted by a 'schizoid realism', then perhaps an 'anti-schizoid realism' (CCR 82) or 'kynicism' at the level of the animal body is still attainable. Hence the *Critique* pays tribute to the gay science of Diogenes of Sinope, the first avowed 'cosmopolitian', who did not contra*dict* idealism, but *lived* in defiance of it by publicly challenging moral bigotry and arrogance with intense sensuality and contemptuous sarcasm. For Sloterdijk, this sober but courageous and dignified life embodies the possibility of a reversal of values (VGN 46; TS 59) – tellingly, Diogenes was convicted for counterfeiting money, although he was never interested in power or wealth – at a moment when the long value constituting history of autonomous *ressentiment* had only just begun. For whereas *ressentiment* finds its legitimation in itself and thus has an interest in cutting itself off, only the offensive and spectacular exposition of the naked truth could break free from cynical discretion and relieve critical consciousness of its melancholic murkiness. The whole of the *Critique* must therefore be read as the genealogical quest 'in search of lost cheekiness (*Frechheit*)', which, as the opposite of a '*ressentiment* that appears as method' (ST 268; see SV 134), is the affect necessary for saying what one lives and living what one says. In a time when private cynicism has diffused into a mass phenomenon, it is not in the safe enclosure of academies but first of all in public parades of plebeian impudence that a reflectivity self-certain and self-sufficient enough for a total critique – a critique beyond *ressentiment* – can take place.

From Psychopolitics to Cosmopolitics

The crucial lesson of what Sloterdijk has called 'Nietzsche's materialism' is that enlightenment is always dramatic and performative. Reminiscent of Hannah Arendt's concept of public life as a place where participation (action) and communication (speech) coincide,[3] the public sphere for Sloterdijk is precisely this situation in which 'rational thought assimilates its own event-character in its reflections' (DB 9; TS xxv). The problem of public culture today, however, is that it is based on a double bind: it couldn't function without mass media, yet the latter have increasingly facilitated an intoxicating and self-deceptive proliferation *ressentiment*. Private resignation and public spectacle converge upon an 'event culture of *ressentiment*' (VGN 58) that alternates between sentimentality and cruelty and subjects its members to ruthless competition while imposing on them a taboo on revenge. 'Modernity has invented the loser' (RT 40). As Nietzsche already knew, *ressentiment* is not only in the way we breathe, it *is* the air we breathe. The silent majorities find and observe themselves exclusively in the *ressentiment* of 'victimological collectives' (WK 241) that restrict our relations to others to moral indignation, anti-elitarism, vandalism, scapegoating, and a constant call for more security (NHGS 155–6). With the explicitation of the project of a 'generalized immunology', the psychopolitical commitment of the *Sphären*-trilogy therefore lies in its proposal of a 'critical theory of air and a positive notion of the atmospheric *res publica*' (S II 353). The possibility of critique now depends, Sloterdijk argues, on a very classical mission of the philosopher in society, namely 'to prove that a subject can be an interrupter and not just a simple canal for the passage of thematic epidemies and waves of stress' (ST 85, 123, 262–3, 287; see CCR 310).

What unites both Sloterdijk's early and later engagements with the psychopolitical conditions of public life is an unreserved defence of what Kant called the *Weltbegriff* (*conceptus cosmicus*) of philosophy against its *Schulbegriff*. Since reason is never a private property, it is the extra-academic role of the philosopher to make himself at home in the world and to share his belief in global citizenship with others. Being born or being in the world, writes Sloterdijk, means 'belonging together in a well-understood Whole', a *theatrum mundi*, or in the sense of Arendt's principle of natality, being embedded in an *Offenheit* of shared engagements without which we would be powerless. (SB 27–39) Yet humans are not born into the world by themselves and accede into publicity without 'miscarriages', but must be helped to 'affiliate with the communal' (WF 344–5). As Nietzsche knew, to heal (*genesen*) always also means to bring something into the world, such that self-confidence implies world-confidence and vice versa. His systematic distinction between good and bad doctors reappears in Sloterdijk's work as the distinction between the 'happy positivism' (WF 281) or *megalopathia* (SB 28–32; WF 380–1; S II 303; WK 13) of the cosmopolitan philosopher and the 'negative psychology'[4] and 'unworldliness' (*Weltfremdheit*) of the priest and the gnostic.[5] Whereas the latter seduce us to flee into some 'sleep of the world', by merging with the herd or by withdrawing into the desert, the therapeutic task of the former is nothing less than to provide 'a second education, that not only transfers the human being from the nursery to the metropolis, but rather positions him at the heart of the process of global consolidation' (WF 380; see ET 234–60; GE 34–5). Standing on the brink of the public sphere, the 'thinker on stage' is therefore the 'psychohygienical' (GE 212–18), 'biopolitical' (GE 34–5; MLA 65) and 'biosophic' (S III 25) pedagogue and physician of civilization, 'from whom intelligence learns how

its passions arrive at the level of concepts' (S I 82) and thus how
to immunize itself against the 'affective epidemies' and 'viral infec-
tions' (RT 205) of *ressentiment*.[6]

Thymotic Economy I: Contempt and Pride

But isn't this cosmopolitan assignment of the philosopher merely
a nostalgic dream of nobility amidst the radical 'indifference'
and literal 'mediocrity' of 'last man' (VM 69–95; RT 183–226)?
Sloterdijk is more than aware that any attempt to 'make a difference' and 'defy the mass in ourselves' (VM 95) automatically takes
the form of a cultural struggle or *Kulturkampf* over the legitimacy
and genealogy of differences in general (VM 84). On the one
hand, he interprets 'the open wounds of modernity' in the clinical terms of an 'algodicy' – how to give meaning to pain – that
replaces that of the theodicy (CCR 460–8; TS 76–7). He diagnoses a typically modern *ressentiment* (VM 56) whose 'egalitarian
effect' is the principle of 'differentiated indifference' due to which
the striving for the ideal of universal dignity blocks itself and
terminates in contempt (no culture of authenticity can disguise
that, in practice, equal respect is not high-respect) (VM 87–8; SB
39–43; NHGS 163). But on the other hand, as a true Nietzschean
he prefers an alternative, more aristocratic kind of contempt, one
that is not the reactive disdain for the strong by the weak, but an
active affect capable of inducing new, more worthy possibilities of
life, 'a corrective, empowering (*potenzierend*) contempt' (VM 56).
This *Kulturkampf* is precisely what is at stake in *Rage and Time* and
God's Zeal, of which the genealogical project again implies the
question whether a different site of valuation than *ressentiment* can
be developed.

The major premise of Sloterdijk's *Kulturkampf* is provided by an
understanding of psychopolitics 'beyond eroticism' (RT 13) and
based on a 'noble anthropology' (WF 25–47) as opposed to 'black
anthropologies' (NHGS 149). As Sloterdijk suggests, the 'theistic
dressages in humility' of Christian anthropology and anthropotechnics persist almost unbowedly in dismal human sciences such

as economics and psychoanalysis (S III 762, 770). Whether the constitutive discrepancy lies between the finity of resources and the infinity of needs or between the pleasure principle and the reality principle, in each case the human condition as a whole is understood on the basis of the dynamic of the libido (the *homo oeconomicus*, Oedipus), and thus through an original and irreducible lack that must somehow be compensated and sublimated, if not repressed (the state, the death drive). It is this morally legitimating *idée fixe* of humankind as a defective being [*Mängelwesen*], which for Sloterdijk summarizes the whole morose analytics of finitude typical of modern anthropocentric discourse: 'Whenever lack is in power, the 'ethics of indignity' has the word' (RT 19; see NHGS 40–50).

By contrast, *Rage and Time* seeks to supplement libidinal economy with thymotic economy. Following Leo Strauss and Fukuyama's reading of Plato's *Statesman*, *thymos*, as opposed to *eros*, is the receptive sense that makes the soul the bearer of self-affirmative affects. If the blind rage or wrath (*menis*) of the Homerian heroes seems so incomprehensible to us, this is because for us everything that stems from pride or dignity, such as generosity, revenge, or readiness to die in battle, most often is 'only an empty entry in the dictionary of the neurotic' (RT 14). The Ancient Greeks, on the other hand, saw the world as a public stage on which to exteriorize their pride in 'an appreciation of war without limitations' (RT 3) that is inherently worth more than all the private suffering that may follow from it: 'In the case of pure rage there is no complex inner life, no hidden psychic world, no private secret through which the hero would become understandable to other human beings. Rather, the basic principle is that the inner life of the actor should become wholly manifest and wholly public. It should become wholly deed and, if possible, wholly song' (RT 9). In other words, because the subject merges without leftover with the event (RT 8), being merely a 'receptacle' or 'meeting point of affects or partial energies' (RT 11) that take it 'beside itself', there is no innate principle that suffices for the development of *ressentiment*.

As a consequence, thymotic economies, at least in their pure form, are not based on lack and calculation, but rather on affluence and extravagant dissipation, even on selfishly ambitious generosity. Moreover, egoism, self-esteem, vanity, *amour-propre* and ambition cannot be reduced to a narcissistic neurosis of the libido, because before they become egocentric they are always already socio-political affects par excellence (RT 19–20). In fact, if life in the Greek *polis* is unthinkable without the proper management and domestication of thymotic energies (RT 12, 23–5), it couldn't do without them. Whereas capitalist exploitation and hyperconsumerism have since long annexed the existing institutions of civil society, Sloterdijk therefore prophecies that the future of urban citizenship is feasible only as a 'pride-ensemble' (RT 19; NHGS 158–61) that 'requests every individual to step out onto the external stages of existence and expose his powers to prove himself before his peers (RT 16).

Thus it is no longer through the affect of cheekiness, but through *thymos* or 'stout-heartedness' (*Beherztheit*, RT 12) that Sloterdijk explores modes of non-ressentimental valuation: 'While eroticism points to ways leading to those "objects" that we lack and whose presence or possession makes us feel complete, thymotics discloses ways for human beings to redeem what they possess, to learn what they are able to do, and to see what they want' (RT 15–16). This does not imply, however, that *ressentiment* grows from the erotic part of the soul. *Ressentiment* is neither the same as nor implies jealousy. On the contrary, *thymos* holds both the source of *ressentiment* and the possibility of its overcoming, while *eros*, and the eroticization of *thymos* in today's 'dynamic systems of greed' (RT 196–203), merely amplifies its development (RT 40). Initially, it is therefore not lack that generates *ressentiment*, but *ressentiment* that generates lack. What makes the notion of *ressentiment* politically relevant is precisely that, as a fixation of thymotic affects, it denotes an 'exoneurosis' (ST 84) and not just some private shortcoming (NHGS 139).

Thymotic Economy II: Anger and Time

The basic therapeutical distinction of *Rage and Time* therefore revolves around an 'ill thymotics' and a 'healthy' or 'just' thymotics and it is here that Sloterdijk draws the genealogical caesura, as Nietzsche did before him, between Ancient Greek civilization on the one hand and Judaic-Christian-modern civilization on the other. In the former, the immediate exercise of rage is the privilege of masters while slaves are burdened with *ressentiment*. In the latter, the slaves develop a new type of rage based on a postponed and imaginary revenge that seduces the masters to internalize their rage and become slaves as well. Although Sloterdijk refers to Bataille's distinction between the general economy of dissipation and sacrifice and a restricted economy of accumulation, conservation and reinvestment, this distinction builds on an economical theory that was already implicitly present in Nietzsche's *Genealogy*. It concerns two radically opposed ways of managing the economy of pride, or more precisely, 'anger' as the pre-eminent affect capable of constituting political subjectivity. Whereas the Homeric hero expresses anger in immediate release and glorious sacrifice (RT 55–9), later Europeans tend to subject it to a process of 'sublimation, internalization, transference, and distortion' (RT 86). This latter economy of latent and accumulative anger is the soil on which *ressentiment* grows and on which the strong and intimate connection between rage and time is established (RT 59–62). Nietzsche had already defined the man of *ressentiment* by his incapacity to forget (KSA V, 291–2; GM II, §1), as a consequence of which he interiorizes his traumatic past in the form of a postponed revenge. Sloterdijk interprets the history of the West in the same sense, insofar as it springs from 'the psychic and moral wound that does not heal and which creates its own corrupt temporality, the bad infinity of an unanswered complaint' (RT 49).

However, the originality of *Rage and Time*, at least when compared to its precursor, is that it discovers a qualitative change in the restricted economy of anger during the past two centuries: 'Just like the monetary economy, the rage economy passed a critical marker once rage had advanced from local accumulation and selective explosion to the level of a systematic investment and cyclic increase' (RT 64, 62–8). Once *ressentiment* becomes disconnected from the context of its origination and acquires an independent, even entrepreneurial dynamic, we go from the 'project form of anger' also known as 'revenge' to the 'bank form of revenge' better known as 'revolution'. A revolutionary movement or traditional leftist party functions as monopolistic 'collection point and agency of recycling and exploitation for investments' and thus, Sloterdijk perversely argues, partakes of an essentially capitalistic economy of anger that contradicts and undermines the very political economy it seeks to promote. Thus if Deleuze and Guattari had already demonstrated how today the cunning and inventiveness of capitalism is many times greater still than that of the priest when it comes to the cultivation of *ressentiment*, Sloterdijk adds that there also exists a capitalism of *ressentiment* itself. 'Your *ressentiment* is safe with us', the Party says, which professionally reinvests and grows of its capital, for it believes that by growing it is made better and that its time, or the time of a final and total mobilization in the name of a global revolution (*Weltrevolution*), will eventually come. Moreover, the phrase 'God is dead' for Sloterdijk means that history and politics have taken over the wrath of God.

From a perspective situated after the twentieth century, the pre-modern economies of inhibitive anger turn out to be preparations for the modern disinhibitions of the 'terrifying force of the negative' (RT 25–8). This also explains Sloterdijk's shift from *ressentiment* to militant anger as basic affect: 'The vast majority of the many millions standing in line at the entrance to the final tunnel do not show any symptoms of pre-suicidal morbidity, however, but rather those of a faux-religiously channelled build-up of anger' (GZ 158). This new 'economy of *ressentiment*' forms the starting point of an attempt 'to continue the work that Nietzsche started and to put on the agenda a more fundamental reflection on the causes and effects of rage in modernity' (RT 289).

Yet if Sloterdijk seeks to go 'beyond' Nietzsche, this doesn't lead him to a counter-ressentimental rehabilitation of Christianity. On the contrary, the 'genealogy of militantism' and 'primary history of *ressentiment*' begins with the 'original accumulation' of post-Babylonian hatred and revenge (RT 81, 86) as it is projected on the wrathful God of the Old Testament. The God of the New Testament is only nominally based on its opposite and internalizes hatred and revenge in the form of bad conscience. Just as for Nietzsche, all great religions partake in 'a universal economy of cruelty', Sloterdijk is particularly interested in the derivation of the wrath of God from his universal love, as 'it is here that the dynamics of *ressentiment* responsible for the entire domain becomes especially evident' (RT 103, 105). The two greatest contributors to the neurotization and confusion of civilization according to Sloterdijk are Saint Augustine and Saint Paul. To the first we owe the 'sexual-pathological distortions' hidden beneath an ideological 'miserabilism' and a metaphysics of predestination which, under the guise of divine love, establishes a 'devious and systematic combination of a rational universalism of damnation and an unfathomable elitism of salvation' (GZ 61; NG 64–72, 88–100). But the heritage of the second is even worse. Nietzsche already distinguished Christ as the only true evangelist from Paul the dysangelist, when he held the former for a passive nihilist whose gentle nobility lay in teaching the reactive life how to die serenely, while the latter is a downright spiteful character, whose 'cynicism' led him to turn hatred into an instrument of universal love. For Nietzsche, in fact, Paul singularly impersonates the figure of the tyrannous priest, 'the instinct of ressentiment here become genius' (KSA VI., 192; AC, 24), who reigns through sin (the transformation of the death of Christ from an individual gift into an initial collective debt/guilt) combined with the undying hatred of a reactive life (the resurrection as interest and reinvestment that makes debt infinite, cf. Deleuze 2006, 153), initiating a long and terrible revenge that had to pass through all the stages of nihilism.

In a similar vein, Sloterdijk retrospectively reads Paul as the archetype of the 'messianic-expansionist' zealot, whose blind love of God and belief in universal salvation is positively correlated to the devastating hatred and terrorism of God's non-inflationary, 'eternal punishments' for those who have not yet been converted. Moreover, Paul stands out as proto-militant revolutionary, insofar as his 'furious eschatology' (RT 98) fundamentally changed the concept of time into an 'in-between time' or 'time that remains', a worldly time that already falls under the shadow of 'the time that comes': 'Paul is probably the first who lived a hurried life out of principle' (ET 282; see GE 85–6, 53; RT 98–105). It is merely the irony of a dechristianized modernity that it has its own zealots of universal truth in the guise of communism: 'the human-churchly fanaticism of the Jacobins', 'the militantism of Lenin's professional revolutionaries', 'the fury of the Red Guards in Mao Zedong's China' each of which Sloterdijk sees as 'feral imitations of the apostolic *modus vivendi*'. (GZ 66, 30) They all show the same apocalyptic cheerfulness – *Elendsübermut* (RT 48) or 'connection between forced exhilaration and *ressentiment*' (RT 117) – that is symptomatic of the manic drives of zealots and which can be summarized as 'going on the offensive by fleeing from the world' (GZ 60, 32; WF 104–17) or 'self-preservation unto death' (SV 16).

Thymotic Economy III: Generosity and Dignity

It is true that these reductive arguments on politics as a substitute for religion have been made many times, especially in the recent, post-communist and post-historical decennia. Are we therefore dealing with just another retrospective that confronts us with a world without alternatives? In order to appreciate Sloterdijk's (and Nietzsche's) originality, it is important to contrast his enquiry into the Pauline inspiration of militant universalists with another recent reading of Paul that couldn't be more politically and methodologically at odds with it. Whereas Badiou, in *Saint Paul: The Foundation of Universalism*, aims at 'resurrecting' some of the driving spirit both of Paul and twentieth century revolutionaries such as Lenin and Mao in post-political times, Sloterdijk interprets the function of the 'manic-apocalyptic affective states' as instruments used by priests to stabilize the soul and the social integration of believers. Following Nietzsche, he holds Paul to be the bad doctor par excellence, whose immunological mistake has repercussions for the understanding of truth: 'Whereas the pragmatic mentality contents itself with the belief that whatever helps is true, zealous behaviour insists on the axiom that truth is only to be found in a belief system which is entitled to demand universal subordination' (GZ 12).

It is true that, as Badiou writes, '[i]f Nietzsche is so violent toward Paul, this is because he is his rival far more than his opponent', insofar as the former makes use of the same formally universalist themes as the latter: the self-declaration of character, the breaking of History in two, and the new man as the end of slavery.[7] But the crucial point Sloterdijk makes is that the thymotic economies on which the aforementioned themes are based couldn't be more different. When Nietzsche dismisses Paul for being 'a rebel . . . against everything privileged' and disseminating 'the poison of the doctrine "equal rights" for all',[8] this is not because he is defending the privileges of historical aristocracy that, as Sloterdijk puts it in *Über die Verbesserung der guten Nachricht*, 'guarantee that *ressentiment* will always find its ideal speech situation' (VGN 53), but on the contrary because, from a clinical point of view, true aristocracy is exclusively a 'position directed towards the future' (VGN 49).

Whereas Paul gives us 'a narcotic, by means of which the present were living at the expense of the future' (KSA V, 253; GM Preface §6), Nietzsche seeks to escape from the restricted economy of gifts and poisons by making a 'noble present' (VGN 48, 30), i.e. a present – both in the temporal and economical sense – that cannot be reciprocated in terms of revenge or debt. His 'bestowing virtue' initiates a generous way of being, in which the taker on his part is activated by the gift to participate in the capacity of further opening up richer futures, thus raising the gift to the nth power. Nietzsche is thus 'the first true sponsor' (VGN 48), standing 'at the beginning of a new moral chain of causality' and a new concept of time: 'the future of humanity is a test as to whether it is possible to redeem ressentiment as the first power of history . . . History divides into the time of debt-economy and that of generosity' (VGN 50). In other words, whereas Paul teaches . . . charity [*Nächstenliebe*, literally 'love of the neighbour'] by *demanding* universal subjugation, Nietzsche '*pro-vokes*' a proud competition of glad tidings by teaching *Fernstenliebe*, literally 'love of the farthest' (RT 31) – a 'minor gospel' (VGN 33) for everyone and nobody that signals a 'grand politics' or a politics for a people to come. For it belongs to the nature of thymotic generosity that, instead of wanting to be alone, it aims at nothing less than a potlatch pluralism of gospels that is principally opposed to the monopoly of the Good or the True (ST 35–7; VGN 52–3; NHGS 118).

If Sloterdijk positions his own writing 'after Nietzsche' and thus against Paul (or contemporary leftist radicalism), this means that what is at stake is the 'de-radicalization of alternatives' (GZ 112), which might well appear as trivial and counterrevolutionary, but simultaneously points towards the cosmopolitical project of a 'civilizing learning towards an existence of all human beings characterized by the universally imposed necessity of sharing a single planet' (GZ 145–6; see ET 294–327).[9] This single planet is not the external object of struggle between competing but monomaniac visionaries of general interest, since these can only spring from a 'ressentiment against human freedom' (GZ 96), but the basis of our embeddednes in a world woven of a plurality of interests without common measure. In other words, dignity and freedom are understood in ecological terms. They do not depend on timeless universal values presiding over life, but solely on the creation of new particular ways of living together. This explains Sloterdijk's rephrasing of his earlier Arendtian principle of natality in terms of generosity. This generosity is not the false generosity of emission rights that function as indulgence for the slavery to self-preservation in our daily energy waste, but the true generosity of artistic production (the avant-garde, VGN 49, 56; ST 37) or technological innovation ('homeotechnics', NG 227). Both are fields in which, under the right thymotic conditions, 'to waste is a gesture that generates dignity or *mana*' (ST 334), and in which true self-respect and self-affirmation cannot be abstracted from an active responsibility – *noblesse oblige* – for what one has created, i.e. a responsibility that is based on abundance and embedded in 'ecologies of freedom' (KMPA 102).

This ecological embedment of generosity signals the repugnancy of today's 'dissimulation of lack' (*Mangelheuchelei*) in the West – economically a lack of money, juridically a lack of justice, energetically a lack of organic fuel, politically a lack of recognition, culturally a lack of tradition, etcetera. According to Sloterdijk, we even have a lack of lack, given the constant 'import of grievances from the other side of the world' (S III 805). We have already seen how everything happens as if the modern emancipatory movements collapse under their own success, because citizens continue to experience themselves as handicapped subjects. This happens as soon as recognition becomes the object of an 'imitative desire' (Sloterdijk implicitly quotes Girard, RT 201) oriented upon already established values in relation to which we, as subjects in the process of emancipation, perceive an envious lack. Here we face a veritable metaphysics of poverty, in which lack as empirical condition has become a transcendental norm – Deleuze would speak of a transcendental stupidity (*bêtise transcendentale*) – for its abolition.[10] For even if on a material level, there is not poverty but abundance, 'it suffices to subjectivize the notion of poverty in order to let its dimension grow to infinity' (S III 690; NHGS 90–1).

The eroticization – meaning both obfuscation and modernization – of thymotic economy under capitalism into a subjective 'need for recognition' cannot but lead to vulgarization and depoliticization. The price of today's post-historical and post-political 'dispersion of rage' is therefore an unlimited intensification of *ressentiment*. There has taken place a veritable perversion of recognition, in which pride is experienced only passively, as something that depends *on others*, while economy and morality converge in reflexes *against others* of naming, shaming, blaming and claiming. Politically this has resulted in populist claims to the carefree consumption of acquired rights and a new common sense based on typical right-wing issues of law and order, terrorism and migration. (NHGS 160) We have become mature (*mündig*), but not emancipated. Today we merely consume our own *ressentiment*, taking ever more care of ourselves through private insurance arrangements as if they were a compensation for life itself (ZWK 131), while ever more passively taking our responsibility towards the outside world.

Thymotic sovereignty, by contrast, is measured by the degree to which it resists religious, political and economic routines of compensation. Both natality and generosity are principles of an unconditional and asymmetric gift by means of which life breaks with the reactionary chain of retribution and escalation, from the biblical *lex talionis* to contemporary terrorist exchange, and substitutes it with a 'looser chain' (VGN 51) or a transversal 'chain of unchaining' (ZWK 171). Nietzsche's glad tidings function as a medium in which such a healing can take place. What he called the 'innocence of becoming' is essentially 'the innocence of dissipation' and thus also 'the innocence of enrichment' necessary for the possibility of further dissipations. (VGN 51) The Christian '*ressentiment* of the self' (RT 16) continues in the 'smouldering *ressentiment* against property' (RT 33), insofar as '[t]he Left's economic mistakes were always at the same time its psychopolitical confessions'

(RT 34). Only enrichment, Sloterdijk suggests, allows for a turn of capitalism against itself in which wealth is freed from feverish and secretive value accumulation and capable of a radical expenditure. This is how he seeks a return to the 'hetero-narcissistic' (VGN 68, 9, 43) expressionism of pride as it could be found with Ancient Greek heroes, whose expenditures were '"expressions" that were forces used for display' and promoted the 'self-communication and self-impartation (*Selbstmitteilung*) of the successful' (VGN 47–8, 66–9) as a surplus value.

Similarly, Nietzsche's unrestrained egoism and self-praise in *Ecce Homo* (Why I write such good books) is therefore not the indiscrete expression of some tormented libido, but an existential relation of speech to its own suffering in its tendency towards self-cancellation and to its own pleasure in its tendency towards self-prolongation (WF 207–9). As an immunitary act against the 'order of lies' and the 'metaphysically coded *ressentiment*' (VGN 28–31) that governs over all 'indirect eulogics' (VGN 9, 44), it constitutes an event that marks the beginning of an epoch in which 'the confession to one's own modus vivendi is the noblest speech act' (VGN 10). Of course, this characterization of a psychosomatically emanci-pated language simultaneously offers an adequate description of Sloterdijk's own style, to the extent that when Sloterdijk speaks of Nietzsche, he speaks of himself and thus participates in, or 'reso-nates' (VGN 8) with, this new jubilatory and hyperbolic energy of speech (NG 272–4).[11]

Since we cannot come into the world without coming into language, what is needed is a relief (*Freispruch*) of language that is at the same time a promise (*Versprechen*) of further capacities for speech (ZWK 165–6). This 'linguistics of enthusiasm' (WF 29) was already noticeable in his appropriations of the evangeli-cal *modus parlandi* for the purpose of 'ethnic investments' (SG 46) in *Versprechen auf Deutsch, Falls Europa Erwacht* or *Der starke Grund zusammen zu sein*. It becomes more manifest still in his recent works, where he c/kynically (VGN 47, 68; S III 681) explores wealth as 'source of ethos' (S III 685) against the 'miserabilistic International' (S III 680) that is founded on a discursive suppres-sion of the truth of its own prosperity. Not only critical theorists, but all of us are burdened with a schizophrenic embarrassment of riches, helplessly submerging in 'constant changes of mood of comfort and discomfort in our own well-being' (S III 684–5; ZWK 131). Against the essential 'conservatism' (S III 671) of our intellectual auto-immune reflexes, we should therefore ask whether 'it isn't typical for life in luxury that one is able to avoid the embarrassment of inquiring after one's origin?' (S III 690). Posing such a question isn't just a matter of rhetoric or parody, let alone of arrogance, but an attempt to speak without *ressentiment*, or what comes down to the same, to speak without squinting and regain our belief in the world.

Asceticism and Philosophical Life

Let us now return to the cosmopolitan assignment of the philosopher, which indeed stands or falls with the possibility of a noble way of life. Dignity or nobility concerns the truthfulness of a person's relations to his or her values. To detect baseness or *ressentiment* at the root of valuations, by contrast, is to detect valuations motivated by the very desires they condemn. As is well-known, for Nietzsche, the values that are typically infected by the *ressentiment* of their carriers are ascetic values. Yet it is a common misunderstanding that he rejected all forms of asceticism as ressentimental and nihilistic. The alternative of contemplative life (*vita contemplativa*) and active life (*vita activa*) is in fact neither exclusive nor exhaustive, but merely obscures their genealogical evaluation. For everything depends on the affective economy according to which these ascetic ideals are interpreted. From the erotic perspective, they cannot but be interpreted as the hypocritical defence mechanisms of a deprived life. But from the thymotic perspective, might they not turn out to be the means of a proud self-affirmation and self-intensification? It is this alternative precisely that is at stake in the contrast Nietzsche draws between the significance of humility, poverty and chastity for the priest and for the philosopher. Whereas the former needs them as renunciatory and other-worldly imperatives, the latter uses them as a mask for hiding an especially active and superabundant life, in which the instinct of a spiritual

life is sufficiently powerful to have conquered thought and subor-
dinated every other instinct to itself. In this second sense, *askēsis*
is not the form of a life-denying alliance between transcendence
and reaction, but rather an exercise for attaining the optimum of
natural conditions for a worthy *and* worldly life: a life which may
trigger *ressentiment* among others but which itself takes care not to
be infected by it (KSA V, 351–6; GM III §8) and is affirmative,
not of existence in general (a *contradictio in terminis*), but of its own
existence in relation to that of others.

Ascetism in the latter sense forms the basic intuition of
Foucault's later investigations into post-Socratic practices of the
self, in particular his etho-poetic definition of philosophical activity as 'an exercise of oneself in the activity of thought', always
aiming 'to know how and to what extent it might be possible to
think differently, instead of legitimating what is already known'.[12]
It also forms the basic intuition of Sloterdijk's *Du mußt dein Leben
ändern*, which, under the wealth of its material, contains the easily
decipherable confession of the author to an athletism or acrobatism
of spirit working against the 'spirit of gravity'. Perhaps this book is
closer to the Stoics than to the Cynics, since although it still bears
the mark of his project of a 'general immunology', it reformulates
its basic insights into the language of a universal ascetology. Today
we do not witness a return of the religious, Sloterdijk argues, but
a renewed interest in the immunitary constitution of man, religion
itself being first of all an immune strategy and spiritual system
of exercise. What Nietzsche has called the morality of custom
(*Sittlichkeit der Sitte*), the disciplining and inscribing practices of
all culture in its immeasurable historical extension, is indeed the
'anthropotechnical praxis' by which *homo natura* engenders himself.
The human condition is modified and kept in shape by means of
'vertical tensions (*Vertikalspannungen*)', the attracting poles that
direct the biopolitical exercises through which we attain the form
or power by which we is constituted. As a consequence, subject
is he who is the bearer of the series of trainings by which he is
'empowered (*potenziert*)' (SD 17).[13]

The importance of Nietzsche's discovery of ascetic culture
lies not so much in the discovery of a general anthropotechnics,
however, as in the genealogical distinction between the asceses of

the healthy, who goes through painful and protracted trainings in order 'to possess the right to affirm oneself' (KSA V, 294–5; GM II §3), and the asceses of the ill, for whom they are the paradoxical means of survival. In fact, since the purpose of genealogy is to evaluate cultural traditions by distinguishing between high and low ancestry, for Nietzsche it belongs to the philosopher's or physician's ascesis to attain the pathos of distance necessary 'to ensure their tasks are kept separate for all eternity' (KSA V, 371; GM III §14). We have seen that Sloterdijk fully subscribes to this therapeutic understanding of philosophical practice, such that instead of the spiritual asceses of the philosopher being opposed to his cosmopolitical vocation, they are in fact its precondition (WF 27–8, 46–7). Yet he also observes that, due to his aim for a future return to a time before the slave revolt in morality, Nietzsche focused almost exclusively on pathological forms of asceticism in service of 'the protective instinct of a degenerating life' (KSA V, 361–72; GM III §11–14), whereas our 'ascetic star' is a planet cultivated by all kinds of cultural drillings, including the disciplining of philosophers and the exercises of warriors and athletes.

By shifting the emphasis Sloterdijk contests Nietzsche's famous genealogical thesis of a slave revolt in morality (MLA 204–7). Instead he stresses the ascetological continuity between pagan antiquity and the Judaic-Christian world and the transfer of athletic and philosophical asceticism to the monastic and ecclesial way of living. With the distinction between the two cultures there also disappears the natural hierarchy between masters and slaves, who are now indiscernibly intertwined (WK 242). The new 'anthropotechnical difference' between good and bad trainings lies in the double nature of repetition as active or repeating repetition, such as in art or sports, and passive or repeated repetition, such as in religion or mass media culture (MLA 308; NHGS 92–3). In more political terms, this means that, for Sloterdijk, the fundamental difference is meritocratic rather than aristocratic, and hence of a more contemporary, perhaps even liberalist and individualist nature than that found in Nietzsche: it lies in the 'spontaneous ranking' (SD 19) between those who make something or much of themselves and those who make nothing or little of themselves (MLA 66). But despite this meritocratic shift, the clinical task of the philosopher is still the same today: to provide a renewed 'drilling of aristocrats', an education (*paideia*) that 'supports city dwellers to come into the world under megalo-athletic conditions' (SB 32) and turns them into 'athletes of state' (SB 31, 39) who are capable of thinking and acting cosmopolitically (cf. MLA 691–714).

Conclusion

As a consequence of this meritocratic shift, however, doesn't Nietzsche's concept of *ressentiment* risk losing its critical relevance? One may well wonder what the point is of a genealogical investigation if its vital distinction is reduced to an empirical, i.e. 'genealogically neutral' description of how good and bad, the attractive and repulsive poles of *any* culture, are organized. Tellingly, in a recent essay on the 'epistemic apparent death' of the theoretical life (*bios theoretikós*) called *Scheintod im Denken. Von Philosophie und Wissenschaft als Übung* (SD), Sloterdijk blames both Nietzsche and Horkheimer and Adorno's *Dialectic of Englightement* for tracing the genealogy of '*epochē* capable man', i.e. someone capable of stepping back from existential embeddedness and abstaining from doxic judgement, to the reign of *ressentiment*. Instead he sums up four tendencies that, in their conjunction, have provided the basic conditions under which the emergence of theoretical life can be reconstructed. From a psychopolitical perspective, Nietzsche was correct in seeing the rise of theoretical man as a reaction to the demise of the social and political culture of Athens around 400 BC into a permanent doxic agitation. Psychologically speaking, secondly, this explains how individuals could derive their worthiness from a proud but ressentimental defeatism rather than from practical urgency.

In sociological terms, however, these psychopolitical and psychological explanations ignore the differentiation of the Greek educational system as an immense anthropotechnical dressage of the figure of the student. Worse still, they ignore the mediatheoretical insight that the mental habitus of the theoretician is inseparable from practices of collecting, knowing, proving, reading in the medium of writing (SD 67–94, cf. S III 765). Since the appearance of theoretical man is inextricably convoluted with the sociological and mediological fate of the culture in which he is embedded, Sloterdijk concludes, pathogenical explanations do not suffice. But, again, do we not risk a superficial, all too psychological understanding of the problematic of *ressentiment* here? Has Sloterdijk forgotten that Nietzsche strictly differentiates between the philosophical form of life on the one hand and later science, which is often albeit not necessarily (GM III §23) slave to an ascetic will to Truth prepared by Christian father-confessor mentality (GM III §27; VGN 29), on the other? And isn't it precisely the sharpness of this distinction, which Sloterdijk now judges a 'caricatural' and 'outrageous simplification' (MLA 59), that has previously inspired the difference between the kynical enlightenment of gay science and the '*ressentiment* that appears as method' or *esprit de sérieux* (ST 268; SV 134) ever since his early *Critique*?

Aside from this recent and perhaps somewhat circumstantial departure from the rest of his work, we have seen how Sloterdijk's work shows a remarkable continuity in dealing with the central psychopolitical illness of *ressentiment*. From the beginning, its therapeutic strategy is committed to an ethics of dignity. It is based on immune strategies that are consistently phrased in the terms of 'a new critique of temperaments' (CCR xxxvii), a 'critique of pure humour' (S III 671), or a 'Dionysian politology of passions' and 'ecology of pain and pleasure that precedes any of the usual politics' of 'combative and discursive interests along with their discourses, weapons, and institutions' (TS 76). In this sense, the aim of the *Critique* is already the same as that of *Rage and Time*, namely a philosophical relief or retuning (*Umstimmung*, ST 16; S III 850; NHGS 117, 151) of the sad passions that determine the *Zeitgeist* no less than critical intelligence: a Dionysian cosmopolitics.

4

A Letter on Überhumanismus: Beyond Posthumanism and Transhumanism

Eduardo Mendieta

The pictures of planet earth taken from space by the Gemini flights during the mid 1960s became for Hannah Arendt a point of departure for reflecting on a new type of consciousness, a global consciousness of humanity's interdependence and fragility. The atom bomb played a similar role for Karl Jaspers. The cloning of Dolly the sheep in 1996, and the parallel Human Genome Project, begun in 1990 and partly concluded in 2000, played a similar role for Peter Sloterdijk. The Human Genome Project attempted to 'map' the human genome, that is, it sought to provide an accurate and complete reading of every gene that makes up the human species. The implicit promise would be that once we had decoded the script of human life, we would be able to fix it when broken, and improve it when so desired. At the end of the twentieth century we became post-human at the very moment science provided us with the possibility to refashion our own biological makeup. Few contemporary philosophers have responded to this new human condition with such fervour, consistency and originality as Sloterdijk.

Sloterdijk has dealt with the 'question of technology' at least since 1987 when he published *Kopernikanische Mobilmachung und ptolmäische Abrüstung* (KMPA). Indeed, his work ought to be read as a major, yet untapped, source of reflection on technology. Don Ihde has convincingly argued that Martin Heidegger's philosophy of technology is hobbled by the fact that it was mostly formulated before the advent of modern technology, which Ihde identifies with the bio, nano and info, meaning that over the last half century technology has become biotechnological, nanotechnological and infotechnological.[1] Sloterdijk takes up, in new directions, with and against, Heidegger's philosophy of technology into this new (hyper)technological age. If Gadamer urbanized Heidegger, Sloterdijk has modernized him. Sloterdijk is without question one of the most original readers of Heidegger to come out not just from Germany, but also from Europe generally. Sloterdijk's *Spheres* trilogy is to be understood, as he himself instructs us to do, as an attempt to disclose Heidegger's own aborted early project of a *Sein und Raum* (Being and Space) (S I 345). *Spheres* is to be read as the fulfilment of a promissory note buried in *Sein und Zeit*. Or, as Sloterdijk claimed in his collection of essays on Heidegger, his thinking is to be understood as a thinking that comes after Heidegger, but that also follows him. His thinking is Heideggerian, but also post-Heideggerian (NG). 'Rules for the Human Zoo' from 1999 (RHZ), as well as the 'Domestication of Being. The Clarification of Clearing' from 2000 (NG 142–234) exemplifies his post-Heideggerian Heideggerianism that aims to translate two of Heidegger's key notions (the *Seinsfrage* and *Lichtung*) into a 'natural history' of the technologies by means of which humans have made themselves into an animal 'open to the world', and into a social history of 'domestication' through which humans gather in order to be able to attend to 'being' as such.[2] Humans, we may say, were not born into Dasein, nor did Dasein claim them; humans made themselves into Dasein through their anthropotechnology, in such a way that they could step forth into ex–istence.

Sloterdijk has also been one of the most provocative German readers of Friedrich Nietzsche. He has produced at least three texts that deal directly with Nietzsche. We have *Thinker on Stage: Nietzsche's Materialism* (TS), from 1986; *Über die Verbesserung der guten Nachricht. Nietzsches fünftes Evangelium* (VGN), from 2000, and another text that emerged from his work as a fellow in the 'Kollegs Friedrich Nietzsche' in the Weimar Institute for Classics,

Das Menschentreibhaus: Stichworte zur historischen und prophetischen Anthropologie (MT), from 2001. Sloterdijk's work, thus, is to be understood as crossed readings of Nietzsche with and against Heidegger in the age of biotechnology. It should not therefore come as a surprise that his work has been associated with the term 'post-human'. What exactly, however, is 'post-humanism'? And how should we understand Sloterdijk's contribution to this new 'post'? In *What is Posthumanism?* Cary Wolfe opens with a discussion of the different positions vis-à-vis those that he wants to differentiate from his own post-humanism.³ There, Wolfe talks about trans-humanism as well as post-humanism, and refers us back to Nick Bostrom, who has offered what is perhaps the most comprehensive history of 'trans-humanist' thought.⁴

Bostrom's essay was published in the *Journal of Evolution & Technology*. There one can also find essays by Stefan Lorenz Sorgner, who introduced the term 'Overhuman' as a counterpart to trans-humanism and post-humanism.⁵ Sorgner's term 'Overhuman' is a translation of Nietzsche's notion of the *Übermensch*. Thus, between Wolfe, Bostrom and Sorgner we have a whole new lexicon: anti-humanism, inhumanism, post-humanism, trans-humanism, neo-humanism, over-human and, I would add, hyper-humanism. I want to introduce this later term, hyper-humanism, as a way to translate '*Überhumanismus*', a neologism used by Sloterdijk in the title of his 2000 lecture on the centenary of Nietzsche's death, which read *Über die Verbesserung der frohen Botschaft. Nietzsches Überhumanismus* (On the Improvement of the Good News: Nietzsche's Over-humanism) (MT 2). The title became, as was already noted, *On the Improvement of the Good News: Nietzsche's Fifth Gospel* when it was published. The claim is that Sloterdijk's post-humanism would be more properly named hyper-humanism at best, or *Überhumanismus*, in a lesser desirable way because of all the negative associations that have been loaded onto the Nietzschean term. For the moment we can say that hyper-humanism is the intensification of humanism's basic insight that humans are products of a production, carried out by humans on humans, but that is not directed intentionally. The human is a product, not a finished one, but one that is open to further production (MT 25). Humans are 'advening [*adventische*] creatures – from which something is coming and which themselves are coming' (NG 275). By becoming, coming to themselves, they become different, but they also don't cease to be their essence: this coming to the world and producing worlds by producing themselves. I want to claim that this is not a form of either trans-humanism or post-humanism, but an intensification of Renaissance humanism. I will thus briefly discuss some key aspects of Renaissance humanism and how these are retrieved and reworked in Sloterdijk's work. Then I will discuss Sloterdijk's appropriation of Nietzsche and Heidegger, and I will conclude with an overview of some of Sloterdijk's works in which he develops what I have called his hyper-humanism.

Renaissance Humanism

Renaissance humanism broadly refers to a cultural, social and institutional movement that began in Italy and eventually spread to other parts of Europe. The interests of humanists covered the spectrum from rhetoric, to poetry, to history, to moral philosophy. These subjects were approached via the study of Greek and Roman authors through philological methods that sought to differentiate the different versions of texts now made available with the libraries made available by the Byzantine emigration. This type of study was called *Studia Humanitatis*, literally 'The study of Humanity', but which today is known as 'The Humanities'. From this term was coined the cognate 'humanist' – namely someone who engages in the study of humanity through the philological, historical and moral study of ancient authors. At the heart of the humanist's primary pedagogical goal was the ideal of the education of a noble human being. It could be said that the Greek ideal of *Paideia* education for moral excellence, was what the Renaissance humanists sought to emulate through their *Studia Humanitatis*.[6] Thus, Renaissance humanism aimed to create a new type of human being through the study of the Greek and Roman classics. Yet, this pedagogical ideal should not juxtaposed inimically to the Christian ethos or beliefs about the human being. Many humanists were devoted Christians, who in fact saw the study of the 'Humanities' as a way to give new meaning and efficacy to the Christian views about human nature. The pedagogical dimension of humanism was intricately woven with a reflection on the dignity of human beings. Many Renaissance humanists saw their work as elaborations on the fundamental Christian doctrine of *imago dei*, which argues that the human was created in or after the image of God.[7]

This doctrine has been a source of major debate since its enunciation in Genesis 1:27, and subsequent theological adoptions with the Councils of Nicea and Chalcedon in the fourth and fifth centuries after the death of Christ. The crux of the expression concerns humanity's, as well as Jesus', divinity. In what way can we take the expression that 'humans were created in *the image of God*'? Renaissance humanists gave this Christian doctrine a distinct answer: that human divinity had to do with his rationality and above all his ability to create freely, even to such a degree that humans could create on a par with God, precisely because humanity's supreme creation would be themselves. A key theme of Renaissance humanists was precisely this 'glorification' and one should say 'deification' of humans.[8] Two Renaissance thinkers that merit specific mention because of the way they articulated human dignity, that is human divinity, in terms of what has been called neoteny and quasi divine creativity are Marsilio Ficino and Giovanni Pico Della Mirandola.[9]

There is another aspect of Renaissance humanism which is relevant to my general thesis about Sloterdijk's own distinct brand of hyper-humanism, and which is not generally discussed in the literature. I am referring to humanism as a movement that was above all concerned with the analysis of language, above all of poetic language, and language as the expression of humanity's distinctness. Curiously, this particular line of analysis of Renaissance humanism was pioneered by a student of Heidegger in the late 1920s, who went on to produce several key texts on the Renaissance precisely in opposition to Heidegger's dismissal not simply of the Latin philosophical tradition but also of the Renaissance understanding of the human. Here I am referring to Ernesto Grassi, who went on to become a key figure in the formation of the Institute of Studia Humanitatis in Berlin. Grassi also edited the *Jahrbuch der geistigen* Überlieferung with Otto and Reinhard, the two foremost German classics experts of the time, in which Heidegger's 'Plato's Doctrine of Truth' was first published. Later, Grassi was instrumental in publishing Heidegger's 'Letter on "Humanism"' in his series *Überlieferung und Auftrag*.[10] Grassi in fact pioneered a line of research that was later followed by none other than Karl-Otto Apel, whose *Habilitationschrift, Die Idee der Sprache in der Tradition des Humanismus von Dante bis Vico* (1975), argues that part and parcel of the dignity of the human being is his poetic use of language. Grassi put it eloquently in the following way:

> One of the central problems of Humanism, however, is not man, but the question of the original context, the horizon or 'openness' in which man and his world appear. The amazing thing, usually overlooked, is that these problems are not dealt within humanism by means of logical speculative confrontation with traditional metaphysics, but rather in terms of the analysis and interpretation of language, especially of poetic language.[11]

For Grassi, this distinctive Renaissance humanistic preoccupation appears not with the philosophers, but with the poets, specifically Dante. Dante's *De vulgari eloquentia* and *Convivio*, are philosophical reflections on the world-disclosing and world-grounding characteristic of *vulgari*, or pedestrian, language. Pedestrian language, however, has a poetic, or inaugurating dimension, for it is the site of the disclosure of the new and as such, it also becomes the site for the inauguration of the polis. In Dante, thus, poetic language is directly linked to the founding of the political. Through this thesis, Dante also came to a subsequent and equally momentous thesis, namely that 'the experience of the poetic word is the origin of human historicity'.[12] For Dante, then, language is a stage, a theatre, for a new world, which has a history and is the ground of human historicity. According to Grassi, and one could add Karl-Otto Apel, this line of thinking is followed up by G. B. Vico, who now offers us not a theologically inflected reflection on language, but a secularized anthropology that is grounded in the invention, interpretation and overcoming of myths. For Grassi, in contradistinction and in direct refutation of Heidegger, Renaissance humanism was concerned above all with the central philosophemes of 'unhidden-ness, openness, and that in which historical "being-there" can first appear'.[13]

This brief, and too hurried, a detour through some key Renaissance themes was undertaken for the sake of identify-ing honorable and distinguished precursors as well as sources of some of Sloterdijk's own interpretations of humanism, in general, and of Heidegger's relationship to humanism, as it was bluntly articulated in his famous 'Letter on "Humanism"'. By going back to some Renaissance humanists we have identified a cluster of philosophemes that are neuralgic to Sloterdijk's brand of hyper-humanism: the neoteny of human beings, the use of reason turned into technoscience to accomplish their own creation, and the central role that poetic, or aletheological language plays in the project of homonization. Indeed, following Grassi, we could say that one of the key philosophemes of Renaissance humanism was the poetic homonization of human, and the pedagogical transfor-mation of humans through their being made into the good readers of the classics.

Between Trans-humanism and Anti-humanism: Nietzsche and Heidegger

If there were a prophet of post-humanism, many would agree that it was Nietzsche. To many, however, he is also the prophet of anti-humanism. The philosopheme of the *Übermensch* is one of Nietzsche's most provocative, most misunderstood and also most vilified concepts. It is viscerally and compulsively associated with the National Socialist concept of the superior race. In Nietzsche's work, of course, the *Übermensch* is related to the blond beast, the creature capable of living beyond 'good and evil', beyond both resentment and regret. How does this new creature come about, and how does it proceed to evolve beyond or towards this over-human condition? Is it a biological evolution? Or is it a cultural evolution? In other words, what is Nietzsche's relationship to Darwin? As Nietzsche put it in *Ecce Homo*, 'scholarly cattle' have

attributed to Nietzsche a sort of Darwinism because of his introduction of the concept of 'overman', which for Nietzsche is not at
all associated with the worship of heroes, or the supposedly, best
fit, the biologically superior. Yet, for Nietzsche, the 'overman' is
not primarily the one with the 'highest constitutional excellence',
but who is above all a destroyer of values (KSA VI, 300; EH,
'Books', 1). The overman refers thus not to a biological state or
condition, but to an ethical relation. The overman is a figure of a
turning of the subject to itself; it is an ethical orientation beyond
the given values. If we read *Beyond Good and Evil* and *On the
Genealogy of Morality* together in terms of the how humans became
the kind of animal that submit to the 'herd instinct', what we dis-
cover is that humans evolved through their own domestication,
through their own submission to practices of their own design.
We became moral through the torture of the flesh. Conscience
was imposed from without by the mnemonics of pain. We made
ourselves calculable and reliable by subjugating our will to life to
the will to be good. But at the same time, by inventing morality,
truth, goodness, we made ourselves survive. These 'inventions'
were necessary errors, errors that allowed us to survive. As against
Darwin, who taught the survival of the fittest and the selection of
the weak, and thus projected the notion of progress – necessary
and teleological – into nature, Nietzsche upholds the contingency
and non-teleological character of human survival. For Nietzsche,
Darwinism is the introduction of Hegelianism into science (KSA
III, 598; GS 357) and thus the expression of an obsession with
oneself, with self-knowledge, and self-conception. Paragraph
14 of the section titled 'Skirmishes of an Untimely Man', of the
Twilight of the Idols (KSA VI, 120–1), and similar ones in the
Gay Science, make evident Nietzsche's anti-Darwinism, which
is but a rejection of the Hegelian aspect of Darwin's theory of
the evolution of the species. Darwin forgot 'spirit' and that the
'*weak have more spirit*'. If human history shows anything, it is that
not the strongest but the weakest survive, by the power of their
cunning and the imposition of their invented 'morals', 'truths' and
principles.

Nietzsche, already in 1873, that is to say prior to the texts that
have been so far quoted, indicated his views on Darwinism. In

'On Truth and Lying in a Non-Moral Sense', a text that remained unpublished during his lifetime, he begins:

> In some remote corner of the universe, flickering in the light of the countless solar systems into which it had been poured, there was once a planet on which clever animals invented cognition. It was the most arrogant and most mendacious minute in the 'history of the world'; but a minute was all it was. After nature had drawn just a few more breaths the planet froze and the clever animals had to die.[14]

Using Sloterdijk's language, here is an outstanding example of 'Copernican mobilization' (KMPA), that is to say a metaphorical dislodging of humans rendering them fluid and homeless. In the face of the metaphysical vertigo experienced before such absolute insignificance and meaninglessness, transitoriness and insubstantiality, humans marshal forth Ptolemaic 'truths'. We arrest the fall into the abyss of cosmic insignificance by holding on to fictitious hooks in the fabric of being. According to Nietzsche, humans invented truth not to die of metaphysical despair, and we make ourselves forget that we invented it. What is then truth?

> A mobile army of metaphors, metonymies, anthropomorphisms, in short a sum of human relations which have been subjected to poetic and rhetorical intensification, translation, and decoration, and which, after they have been in use for a long time, strike people as firmly established, canonical, and binding; truths are illusions of which we have forgotten that they are illusions, metaphors which have become worn by frequent use and have lost all sensuous vigour, coins which, having lost their stamp, are now regarded as metal and no longer as coins.[15]

Evidently, we are creatures of nature. Our drive to survive, to live is grounded in our bodily, somatic, animal nature. In order to survive, we invented the intellect and all of its accoutrements. Given what we have said on Nietzsche's alleged Darwinism and his concept of the overman, can we conclude that Nietzsche was either anti-humanist or post-humanist? It is clear that Nietzsche attributes to humans an almost unnatural ability to invent, to bring forth from within themselves that which is neither in nature nor granted to them by nature. We are the animals that migrated out of nature into our own mental world, our own metaphorical and allegorical worlds. We survived through our inventions, which above all are metaphors, metonymies and allegories. In this sense, we can think of Nietzsche's anti-Darwinism as a form of *oration,* or encomium of humanity. For Nietzsche, our dignity lies not in what nature has made of us, but in what we have made of ourselves, even against nature. We are above all, our own creation. The overman, the *Übermensch,* may be the next step in an non-biological and non-teleological transformation, but the blond beast is nothing but the offspring of the same poetic and self-domesticating task that fashions the pre-*Übermensch.* In Nietzsche we find the lineaments of what I called hyper-humanism, or what Sloterdijk has called *Überhumanismus,* namely an intensification of the dignification of human creativity and exceptionality.

If Nietzsche has been regarded as the prophet of post-humanism, Heidegger has been considered the prophet of anti-humanism. Indeed, along with *Being and Time,* the 1947 'Letter on "Humanism"' may be one of Heidegger's most read and commented texts. For our purposes, we need only focus on how this text makes evident Heidegger's relationship to humanism *tout court,* and whether in fact, we can read his renunciation of humanism as the pronouncement of an anti-humanism. The ultimate aim of our reading here is to arrive at a better understanding of Sloterdijk's distinctive reading and critique of this text. A superficial reading of the text can reveal this much. First, that Heidegger rejects explicitly three forms of humanism: Christian, Marxist and existentialist. Each one is a form of humanism that subordinates the human to responding to the call of God, *humanitas* as *Deitas*; the overcoming of social alienation, insofar as *humanitas* is sociality; and the rendering *humanitas* as the priority of existence over essence. We also know that behind the rejection of these contemporary forms of humanism, is the more general rejection of the humanist deciphering of the essence of the human in terms of reason. For classical humanism sought to ground the *humanitas* of humans in terms of both reason and its education.

Second, Heidegger is at pains also to reject any attempts to render the humanity of humans in terms of their *animality.* The humanity of humans is betrayed when we decipher it in terms of biologism. Third, Heidegger provides us with a list of metaphysical conceptions he is writing against, but which does not mean that he is endorsing their opposite. If he is writing against 'humanism', this does not mean he is endorsing the inhuman and the celebration of 'barbaric brutality'. If he is writing against 'logic' –in the sense of *ratio* – , he is not writing for the alogical, or irrationalism. If he is writing against 'values', he is not arguing against everything being valueless. If he is writing against the de-worlding of the human by defining the Dasein in terms of 'being-in-the world', he is not reducing the human to a denigrated terrestrial creature and thus denial of 'transcendence'. And finally if he speaks affirmatively of Nietzsche's 'death of God', it does not mean that he is speaking for atheism (W 177).

It is precisely in these rejections, refusals, and negations that some may read Heidegger's anti-humanism. But Heidegger is also explicit in what he affirms: that all forms of humanism are 'either grounded in metaphysics or is itself made to be the ground of one' (W 153). What does it mean to say that all humanisms are grounded in metaphysics or made to become one? It means above all that we have confused the essence of Dasein for an entity. It means that we have collapsed, obliterated, forgotten, thrown into oblivion Dasein's fundamental ontological character. The 'Letter on "Humanism"' claims with customary Heideggerian hyper-bole that humanism itself has been one of the main culprits in the oblivion of being. By reducing the humanity of the human to a metaphysical principle, Dasein's own ontological priority has been concealed. In this way the oblivion of being has been exacerbated.

Heidegger's 'Letter' is not simply a destructive missive. It is also an announcement, an epistle with a message – a *guten Nachricht,* in the sense Sloterdijk used the word to refer to Nietzsche's gospel. We have forgotten our essence by reducing our humanity to some or other metaphysical principle, warns Hcidegger. Articulated affirmatively, Heidegger's good news is: 'The human being is the shepherd of being' (W 162). 'The human being is not the lord of beings. The human being is the shepherd of being' (W 172). 'The human being is the neighbour of being' (W 173). The human is the neighbour of being because she 'ek-sists by dwelling' in being's house, which is language (W 164). 'Language is the house of being. In its home human beings dwell' (W 145). In these affirmations we are able to discern that in fact Heidegger is not simply rejecting all humanism. He rejects metaphysical humanism, and affirms ontological humanism, a term that can only be taken in a propaedeutic or heuristic sense. That humans are not lords of being, and dwell not as masters or owners, but as renters, as guests in the house of being, is not a demotion, not a loss. This loss turns into a gain for humans, for it frees humans to be guardians of the truth of the advent of being. 'To think the truth of being at the same time means to think the humanity of *homo humanus*. What comes is *humanitas* in the service of the truth of being, but without humanism in the metaphysical sense'(W 183). Barely hidden in the brusque dismissals and rejections, is the affirmation of a different humanism, a post-metaphysical, or rather, non-metaphysical, humanism: a humanism of expectancy, a humanism of the human to come who is truly ek-sistent, who sets forth into the openness of being. This ontological humanism may be also called alethiological humanism.

From Onto-Anthropology to Anthropotechnology: Making Human Incubators

Already in his 1983 *Critique of Cynical Reason* Sloterdijk had announced the project of a Heideggerian Left (CCR 209). There left-Heideggerianism meant the transformation of the critique of instrumental reason into a critique of cynical reason, the Kynical critique of established, ontologically and metaphysically grounded principles. Sloterdijk called this Heidegger's 'moral amoralism' – 'the last possible word of existential ontology to ethics?' (CCR 207). With the trilogy *Sphären*, undertaken in the mid 1990s and finished in 2004, Sloterdijk gives a new sense to the term 'Heideggerian Left'. Now, the project is to think through those elements of Heidegger's early work that remained unfulfilled and yet profoundly generative. For Sloterdijk this has meant at least three things: First, it has meant asking: what is the true meaning of 'being-in-the-world'? Second, how is it that humans came to the 'clearing' and how was this 'lighting' created in such a way that through it the 'clearing' of the world as world could also take place? (MT 13–14; NG 142–301). Third, how is onto-anthropology to be translated into a history of homonization, and more properly how is this history to be understood as the history of auto-domestication through anthropotechnologies?

Yet, what unites these three questions is the philosopheme of anthropotechnology, namely the way in which humans have undertaken to produce themselves through the creation/invention/construction of conservatories and incubators. In other words anthropotechnology gathers under its semantic tent the cognates of anthropogenesis, and thus both historical and prophetic anthropology. The aim of this project, however, is not to announce the coming of something that is no longer human, or that we have ceased to be human, but rather to precisely elucidate how the new technologies, the new biotechnologies are but chapters in the long history of anthropotechnologies. In order to get a better sense of how Sloterdijk carries out this project, we will focus only on three texts that illustrate exemplarily his aims and strategy.[16]

The obvious point of departure would be the by now famous text *Rules for the Human Zoo: A response to Heidegger's Letter on Humanism*, a lecture that was delivered on two occasions before it became the centre of a polemic in Germany (1997 and 1999 respectively).[17] The text aimed to do three things at the same time: first, it sought to provide a contemporary definition of humanism; second, it sought to re-frame Heidegger in relationship to humanism, now thought under a different light; third, it sought to link contemporary anthropo-biotechnologies with the millennial tradition of domesticating, breeding humans, that found their most stark articulation already in Plato. Sloterdijk redefines humanism as that movement that has always had one clear and unequivocal goal: 'the commitment to save men from barbarism' (RHZ 15). And thus its 'latent message…is the taming of men' (RHZ 15). This saving from and taming of humans was primarily undertaken through the creation of a community of friends through the common reading of texts – books as letters to distant friends. Here Sloterdijk raises the issue that at least since 1945, we have entered a 'postliterary, postepistolary, and thus post-humanistic' age, one in which society 'can produce their political and cultural synthesis only marginally through literary, letter-writing, humanistic media' (RHZ 14). We can no longer calm and domesticate the 'inner beast' through books.

With respect to Heidegger's own relationship to humanism, Sloterdijk out-Heideggers Heidegger, that is, he does to him what Heidegger did to Nietzsche, namely to show how he is still mired and sunk in that which he thinks he has overcome. Sloterdijk points out, perspicaciously, that Heidegger's *Brief* (letter) is a missive to future friends. He is trying to create friends in a future to come. And in this sense, he is still within the humanistic genre of 'action at a distance'. Then, Sloterdijk proceeds to show how concealed in Heidegger's rejection of metaphysical humanism is not an incipient anti-humanism or 'inhumanism' but rather the opposite. By juxtaposing his 'onto-anthropology' to that of classical humanism, Heidegger 'nonetheless indirectly retains the most important function of classical humanism – namely the befriending of man through the word of the other – indeed, he radicalizes this drive to befriend, and transfers it from mere pedagogy to the centre of ontological consciousness' (RHZ 18). Indeed, by defining the *humanitas* of the *humanun* in terms of the shepherding and guarding of the truth of being in and through language, the human is radically defined as the ur-writer of truth. In this deciphering of the human as the guardian of being, Heidegger has 'imposed radical constraints' on what humans can and can't do. The 'Letter on "Humanism"' – putatively a text of anti- and post-humanism, is now revealed to be a radical humanist text insofar as it re-enacts the humanistic telos of domesticating man in order to save him from his incipient barbarism. The 'Letter on "Humanism"' turns out to be nothing else than a new domestication of man.

Sloterdijk's reading of Heidegger's alethiological humanism is neither naive nor apologetic. It needs to be underscored that at no point has Sloterdijk ever denied that Heidegger was a Nazi. If anything, he has been explicit in deriding the mystical, the nationalism, and the negative theology implicit in Heidegger's thinking, especially that of the post-Turn (see CCR 195–209). Sloterdijk in fact is explicit about rejecting such aspects. He writes, for instance:

. . . Heidegger elevated Being to the sole author of all important
letters, and placed himself as their current scribe. Whoever speaks
from such a position is allowed to call attention to stammers, and to
publicize in silence. Being thus sends the most important letters. More
precisely, it addresses them to spiritually advanced friends, to receptive
neighbors, to groups of silent herdsmen. But, so far as we can see, no
nation, not even alternative schools, can be derived from this circle of
fellow shepherds and friends of Being – not least because there can be
no public canon of manifestations of Being. So, until further notice,
Heidegger's collected work stands as the measure and voice of the
nameless Ur-author. (RHZ 19)

As against this form of radicalized humanism that conceals its own
telos of tethering humans to some task in order to save them from
themselves, Sloterdijk turns to an elucidating reading of Plato's
politics, and more specifically, what he calls playfully Plato's zoo.
By reading *The Statesman* and *The Republic*, Sloterdijk shows how
Plato's own political ontology is but an elucidation of the 'rules
for the maintenance of the human zoo' (RHZ 25). Plato, as read
by Sloterdijk, allows us to read Heidegger in a new way, namely
as yet another exemplar in the ways in which humans voluntar-
ily and deliberately put themselves in 'theme parks', 'human
zoos'. From Plato's zoo, with its *basileus* and hornless animals, to
Heidegger's 'house of being', we have been ingenious architects of
prosthetic parks (NG 360), anthropogenic islands (S III 357–500),
and anthropospheres (MT 46). Succinctly put: 'Humans are
self-fencing, self-shepherding creatures' (RHZ 25). Humans are
the supreme domestic animal. Their being-in-the-world means
making worlds. Hominization, the history of how we domesti-
cated ourselves, is thus also a history of the worlds we have made
to cultivate, to breed, to domesticate, to preserve ourselves.

In what must be taken as the sequel to 'Rules' *Das Menschentreibhaus*
(The Human Conservatory – or Greenhouse), Sloterdijk expands
on many ideas intimated but left unelaborated there. In the last
two chapters of this book Sloterdijk expands on what he means by
anthropotechnology and the domestication of humans by humans.
In the third chapter, titled tellingly 'To think the clearing or: The
production of the world is the promise', Sloterdijk sets out to think

deeper or more expansively Heidegger's notion of dwelling. There the aim is to 'formulate a theory of residing (*Hauses*) as the place of homonization (*Menschenwerdung*)'. Or better yet, to translate Heidegger's *in-der-Welt-sein* into a theory of the production of this place, called human 'residing'. This leads us then into the direction of what Sloterdijk calls a 'palaeo-ontology' – a theory of the primordial place (*Ur-Ortes*) (MT 29). This analytic of residing or of the primordial place requires a new theory of 'Sein und Raum'. What this new analytic of primordial place shows is that 'dwelling is older than house and that 'Re-sidence' (*Ge-Häuse*) is older than man'(MT 31). As animals, humans migrated out of nature by building dwellings, dwellings that took them from out of nature, into their own environments, their own residences. In this way, then Sloterdijk is able not simply to rethink Heidegger's being-in-the-world, but also his conception of 'enframing'. Thus, what Heidegger called 'Ge-stell' is nothing else than 'Ge-Häuse': 'Man lodges and through accommodating clearly produces' (TM 41). This simply means that humans are the creatures who proximally do not come to the world, but rather arrive to a conservatory, one that will become its world. Human dwelling is first and foremost this primordial lodging – building sites for human domestication. What this also reveals is that all technology is primordially 'space-originating-technology' (*Raumschöpfungstechnik*) (TM 46). Before language could be the house of being, humans had to set up their own conservatories and incubators, through which they could create themselves. Thus, language is the second house of being, while *Ge-Häuse*, is its first. There can be language as dwelling because humans are more primordially the creatures of lodging and dwelling in anthropospheres of their own making. To think *aletheia*, clearing, is thus to think the palaeo-ontology of dwelling, of primordial place/accommodating. Being in the world is revealed to be more primordially this housing, this setting up of envelopes, of containers, green houses and incubators of humans.

The last chapter of *The Human Conservatory* (MT) should be no less polemical than RHZ. It is perhaps scandalously titled 'The Operable Man: On the Introduction of the Concept of Homeotechnology'. For Sloterdijk, homeotechnology is implicit in the concept of conservatory and incubator. But in a more distinctly specific sense: the setting up of human dwelling also means the establishment of specific conditions under which humans can make their constitution available to themselves. Dwelling implies, literally, controlling the environment inside the dwelling. In the same way that dwelling, residing, means to regulate our interaction with an environment, a surrounding world, it also perforce means to regulate the environment inside the dwelling. Residing thus means homeostasis. Through homeostatic dwellings we make ourselves available to ourselves. Domestication means, then, operability. Operability means establishing the kind of homeotechnologies that allow us to regulate how we auto-breed and auto-condition our humanity.

In *The Human Conservatory*, the humanistic technology of taming humans through the *Humanities* is now transformed into the subsidiary technologies of homeotechnology, what he calls here now 'biotechnology and nootechnology', that is technologies of the life and of the mind (MT 75).

> These technologies bring forth a refined, cooperative, subject that plays with itself, one that forms itself with complex text and supercomplex contexts. The authoritarian tends to disappear totally because its brute character makes it impossible. In an interconnected, intelligently condensed world, the lords and violators no longer have a possibility of success in the long term, while those that co-operate, promote and enrich – at least in their respective contexts – find more numerous, adequate and viable connections. And what this foreshows in the twenty-first and twenty-second centuries is the abolition of authoritarian residues, although no one believes this will take place without violent conflicts. (TM 75)

Here we find part of the answer to the question raised in the *Rules for the Human Zoo* about what can we expect of a society that has become 'post-literary, post-epistolary, and thus post-humanistic'. And the answer is: the proliferation of more anthropogenetic anthropotechnologies that in aiming to create a homeostatic anthropospheres lodge and accommodate a playful, but serious, refined, hypermodern subject that has dispensed with having to master and having to be mastered – fully operable man is beyond lordship and submission.

Lest we think that Sloterdijk is a reductivist technophile, who believes that technology is the only way through which humans breed and domesticate themselves, he published in 2009 a 723–page tome that has as a subtitle 'On Anthropotechnology' – the title itself announces what it is about: *Du muß dein Leben ändern* (You must change your life). The volume continues in the line of speculation laid out in *Rules*, continued in *Nicht gerettet* (NG) and extended in *The Human Conservatory*. Here, however, the aim is to understand what Foucault called the 'Technologies of the Self', except that here Sloterdijk calls it the '*Übung*', a term that could be translated in a variety of ways: practice in the sense of training, exercise, cultivation of a skill, the means by which one becomes an expert. The massive, fascinating, encyclopedic, expansive volume offers a history of Western culture in terms of the development of one set of 'exercises' by other, one regime of technologies of the cultivation of the self by other technologies of cultivation of the self. Every page of this book operates under two fundamental premises: first, 'Humans do not inhabit territories, but habits (*Gewohnheiten*)' (MLA 643). And second, that 'morals' (*Tugend*) are but the possibility to cohabit with and under others. Morality has to do with cohabitation. Indeed, all moral philosophy remains 'superficial' if it has not differentiated among practices or habits. To quote Sloterdijk, 'The *Critique of Practical Reason* lives on fragile presuppositions if it has not first clarified a fundamental anthropological premise, namely whether humans can be released from bad "habits" and re-anchored in new habits' (MLA 649). Above all, among those practices that need to be differentiated are those that determine what is to be abandoned and what is to be retained, what threatens and what is beneficial. The history of *Übungen* is perforce also the history of immunological struggles (*Immunsystemkämpfen*). Thus, 'all history is identical with the history of protectionism and externalization' (MLA 712). In this way, then, the *Critique of Practical Reason* becomes the *Critique of Technologies of the Self*. The analytic of Dasein becomes the analytic of residency, which in turn becomes the analytic of *Übungen*. This marks for Sloterdijk what he calls the anthropotechnological turn. Its result is by no means a quietist passivity, or an indulgent aestheticism, or even a decisionistic aestheticism that reduces ethics to the aesthetics of self-fashioning through different practices. Anthropotechnology, qua study of the different practices that lead to the creation of different habitats with corresponding habits, the setting up of different residencies in which to lodge and accommodate so that we can inhabit under and with others, means that 'humanity' has once again become a thoroughly political category. The members of humanity, in Sloterdijk's view:

> . . . are no longer passengers of the fool's ship of abstract universalism, but co-workers on the consistently concrete and discrete project of a global immune design. Although communism was from the outset a conglomeration of few correct and many false ideas, its rational core was: the insight that general living interests of a higher level could only be actualized at a universal horizon of cooperative askeses, that sooner or later would make themselves valid. It pushed for a macro-structure of global immunization: co-immunology. (MLA 713)

The aim of immunization is survival, but as Sloterdijk makes clear, this survival is only possible through co-operative *askeses* – the Greek term for what he means by *Übungen*. If humanism is that philosophical attitude that relentlessly returns to the *humanitas* of the human so as to render that humanity more honorable, dignified, so that it can not be violated and denigrated, so that it may remain always the measure of all that is human, we can say that Sloterdijk has been and remains one of the staunchest humanists. In his case, like with Ficino and Della Mirandola, humanity is its own greatest creation. In *Nicht gerettet* he wrote that 'one must become cybernetic in order to be able to remain a humanist' (NG 365). Sloterdijk embraces all technology – including technologies of the self – because originally they are but so many ways of constructing human and humanizing dwellings. Sloterdijk's humanism is neither post, nor trans, but hyper-humanism, the radical dignification and intensification of what humans have made of themselves and what they may yet make of themselves. Hyper-humanism says that the *humanitas* of the human is still to come, but what is yet to come comes from humanity and thus is still part of her *humanitas*.

5

The Coming-to-the-World of the Human Animal

Marie-Eve Morin[1]

At the core of Peter Sloterdijk's recent work, we find an attempt to develop a legitimately spatial ontology of human existence. This ontology positions itself 'after' Heidegger in both senses of the word: it is influenced by him and especially by the existential analytic of *Being and Time*, but it also seeks both to displace the emphasis on temporality towards a more fundamental thinking of the spatiality of human existence and at the same time to overcome Heidegger's understanding of modernity and of modern technology as the completion of nihilism. Sloterdijk himself in the preface to *Nicht gerettet. Versuche nach Heidegger*, using a somewhat worn-out phrase, describes his project as an attempt to think 'with Heidegger against Heidegger' and characterizes his relationship to Heidegger as posture of distance-proximity [*fern-nah Haltung*] (NG 7).

In this chapter, I wish to delineate the central trajectories of Sloterdijk's creative reappropriation of certain Heideggerian motives. Towards that end, it will be necessary to bracket off questions concerning the legitimacy of Sloterdijk's reading as an interpretation of Heidegger. Essentially, what Sloterdijk proposes is not really a *reading* of Heidegger, that is, a thorough engagement with the Heideggerian text itself. Even though I will sometimes point out how Sloterdijk's understanding of Heidegger cannot be reconciled with the texts themselves, the guiding question of this essay is not, 'Does Sloterdijk get Heidegger right?' but rather 'Does Sloterdijk have something interesting to say about our times?' Essentially, Sloterdijk wagers that the Heideggerian climate that weighs on our contemporary thinking is not adequate for grasping the globalized, technological world. The importance of Sloterdijk's rewriting and challenging of the Heideggerian understanding of human existence, that is, of the human being in the world with others, lies therefore in the way in which it leads to a dismissal or overcoming of a certain understanding of globalization as the epoch of modern technology and of the appropriate response to it as meditative thinking. Because so many continental thinkers of globalization adopt a more or less Heideggerian construal of modernity as the epoch of modern technology, enframing and the will to will, the repercussions of Sloterdijk's change of framework should not be underestimated.

In order to show how Sloterdijk is led to abandon or overcome the understanding of globalization influenced by Heidegger, I will first present what could be called Sloterdijk's onto-anthropology, his story of the pro-duction or the coming-to-the-world, of the human animal. At this level, Sloterdijk attempts a 'fantastic' reconstruction of the ontic event that must have granted the ontological event, that is to say the ontic event of the human animal first stepping out into the clearing of being. The development of Sloterdijk's onto-anthropology will show how the 'radical openness' of the human is predicated upon an act of insulation, the building of protective spaces, called greenhouses, incubators or spheres. Understanding this interplay between distance and nearness – how the human can be concerned with what is spatially and temporally remote insofar as he is distantiated from his closest environment – is crucial to understanding the second point I want to develop: Sloterdijk's onto-kinetics or his description of the ontological movement of existence. While Heidegger is caught up in the vertical movements of existence, falling and gathering, Sloterdijk wants to emphasize lateral movement, an expansion on the same plane [*Ausbreitung in der Ebene*]. This discussion of the directionality of movement will ultimately allow us, in the last part of this chapter, to link Sloterdijk's insight into the lateral spatiality of human existence to his interpretation of the history of humankind as history of globalization, that is, the history of different ways in which humans have understood the 'space' or 'sphere' they inhabit.

Sloterdijk develops this spatial history of humankind in the *Sphären* triology. Starting from the insight that humans are not only space-creating beings but that these spaces of immunity are essential to the production and the reproduction of the human, Sloterdijk attempts to correct the atopological discourse of the Moderns, who take as their starting point the self-sufficient individual (and hence emphasize consciousness and time as the form of the inner sense). To do so, he shifts the discussion towards the site or locus, the bubble, where the human appears (both at the individual level: the uterus and, as we will see, at the anthological level: the primordial housing) and reinterprets the development of humanity, from the primitive hordes up to our virtual networks and modern apartment complexes, in terms of 'spheres of immunity'.

Sloterdijk identifies three phases in the process of globalization: the metaphysical globalization, which gives rise to the One-All or the metaphysical Sphere, the terrestrial globalization, which is the epoch of travels and explorations on the surface of the terrestrial globe, and finally the global age. In this last epoch, which we are now entering, society is comprised of foams, the fluid aggregations of a multiplicity of small, enclosed bubbles, which are both isolated from and dependent on one another. In this chapter, I will concentrate on the transition from the terrestrial phase of globalization to the era of global foams. This shift is important since the third phase, as it is analysed by Sloterdijk, consists in the densification of the worldly interior, leading to reciprocal obstruction and hindrance. It is this third phase which, if we follow Sloterdijk, will no longer be explicable in terms of Heideggerian enframing and the will to will. This inevitably leads us to ask whether Heideggerian meditative thinking and poetic dwelling can still provide an adequate response to the globalized world in which we live today and, if not, what other form(s) our inhabitation of the globalized world might take. As we will see, Sloterdijk finds this response in a new form of operativity, which he proposes to call homeotechnology.

Sloterdijk's Onto-Anthropology

If Sloterdijk agrees to forming 'an alliance with Heidegger as the thinker of the ek-stasis and the clearing', it is only to the extent that we put aside 'his hostile affect against all forms of empirical and philosophical anthropology' and 'put a new configuration of ontology and anthropology to the test' (NG 153). From a Heideggerian perspective, it would be easy to object to the project of marrying fundamental ontology and anthropology, on the grounds that it inverts the order of knowledge to use an ontic science of the being called human to determine something ontological. Empirical anthropology and palaeo-anthropology are ontic disciplines that operate on the basis of a received understanding of what it means to be human (the rational, speaking animal) and gather facts about the human (bones, fossils, artefacts). These sciences have the human as their object of study but can explain neither how it is possible for any being, human or otherwise to understand itself and other beings in the first place, nor how that being can encounter and produce scientific studies on something outside itself. What is missed and what is left unquestioned by anthropology is what it means to exist in general and what it means to exist as a human. Even philosophical anthropology, whose task it is to constitute a regional ontology of the human, is not in a position to grasp what is essential about the human, its ek-stasis, since it operates with traditional ontological categories (such as substance or life) that are taken from the domain of what is present-at-hand (subsistent things).[2]

Sloterdijk is aware of this objection (NG 159–60) and does not take up anthropology as a discipline uncritically. If we understand being-human with Heidegger as the standing in the clearing of being, Sloterdijk agrees that anthropology as a traditional discipline, and especially palaeo-anthropology, says nothing about the human and how it came to be. Yet, Sloterdijk still wants to ask whether we can look at palaeo-anthropology from this side of the Heideggerian analytic of Dasein and through 'philosophical fantasies' (NG 154) reconstruct the event of the event, the event of this stepping out into the clearing of being. The goal of this enquiry is to produce a 'history of hominization as a coherent story of the exodus out of the uncleared nature into the danger that is named clearing' (NG 154). By emphasizing the 'fantastic' character of his enterprise, Sloterdijk seems to agree with Heidegger that 'knowledge of a pre-history [*Ur-geschichte*] is not unearthing the primitive and collecting bones. It is not natural science in whole or in part; if it is anything at all, it is mythology.'[3]

Sloterdijk does not question the co-belonging of the human and the clearing, or the event that gives both the human and the world in their co-belonging, such that beings can appear as what they are (so that there is being – *es gibt Sein*). In fact, his onto-anthropological fantasy presupposes that we understand the Heideggerian clearing, that we start from our position within the clearing and that we then think *from below* the being-claimed of Dasein by being. Yet, even though one recognizes that 'the dignity of the clearing is inviolable' (NG 154), that is, that it is impossible to say anything intelligible about what is prior to or outside of the space of intelligibility, one can still ask about the anthropological pre-conditions of the event of being, of the opening of a space of intelligibility. Since the human is the only being to whom the world is opened or revealed – the only being that is world-forming, in the Heideggerian sense – the question becomes: what allowed the human, an animal among other animals to leave the domain of life and enter the domain of being? This question presupposes that the basic situation of Dasein, its 'standing out' in the 'clearing' of being, is not some sort of trans-historical structure but is rather the result of a very specific (pre-)historical process, namely primitive man coming to differentiate himself from nature through the demarcation of a space of dwelling within his natural environment.

Sloterdijk starts by using the well-known Heideggerian discussion of the difference between animals and humans in *The Fundamental Concepts of Metaphysics*: the animal is poor in world, Dasein is world-forming.[4] Instead of starting from this difference, Sloterdijk wants to show how this difference happens within the human animal, how the human animal itself goes from being world-poor to being world-forming. The animal lives in an ontological cage: the environment [*Umwelt*]. The *Um* of *Um-welt* designates the enclosing fence, within which biological systems

are interactively engaged with and opened to other beings that are
there with them (NG 162). The closing of this enclosure limits
and relativizes the world-opening. Becoming human means breaking out of this enclosure, stepping out into the 'cagelessness' or a
radical openness that we call 'world' (NG 168).

Through this radical openness, the human becomes aware that,
above and beyond the mere environing world, from the side of
the world, there is always more to come, more to be expected.
The world as the horizon of horizons is the unreachable enclosure around the whole that gives to everything that exists, appears
or happens a final aggregation, i.e. its connection and coherence
[*Zusammenhang*] (NG 184). The difference between an environment and a world is not merely its dimension. Environments vary
in size, that is, the number of entities that an organism is opened
to and lives with vary – for example, the environment of the tick,
to use Uexküll's famous example, is more limited than that of the
dog – but all environments are limited in that they remain closed
to what is not given here and now. What becomes apparent in the
opening of the world is that *not* everything appears, *not* everything
is given (NG 204).

What Sloterdijk's anthropological reflections show is that,
paradoxically, this break-through towards the horizon of horizons
is rendered possible by an insulation and distantiation from our
closest natural environment. It is this insulation and distantiation
from nature – a disconnection of the body [*Körperausschaltung*]
from its environment (NG 179) – that will grant the human its
ecstatic essence, its being able to stand out into the open, to be
in the world as a whole. The human is the result of distantiation
techniques, which produce both a leeway (or window of observation) in which something can come to appearance in a new way
(NG 182), as well as protective spaces against nature that eman-
cipate the human from the necessity of a direct adaptation to the
environment (NG 179). The most original of these distantiation
techniques is the throw of the stone.

> The pre-human produces the first holes and cracks into the environ-
> mental fence when he, by means of throws and blows, becomes the
> author of a distance technique, that has repercussions on himself. [. . .]

> [The lithotechnique] maintains the relation to the object and frees the
> way for its mastery. [. . .] The limits of my throws are the limits of
> my world. The sight that follows the thrown stone is the first form of
> theory. (NG 180–1)

In the Introduction to his *Lectures on Aesthetics*, Hegel also discusses
the throw of the stone as one of the child's first impulses to alter
external things. In this external alteration, the child is not only able
to observe the effect he has on the external world (Sloterdijk's first
form of theoretical consciousness) but also to recognize himself in
it and thereby 'strip the external world of its inflexible foreign-
ness'.[5] On the one hand, even though Sloterdijk does not explicitly
emphasize the moment of self-recognition in the transformed
external world, that is, the reflection back into self, he seems to be
describing how the throw of the stone as the first form of objective mastery leads to subjective self-awareness. On the other hand,
the moment Sloterdijk does emphasize, and which is absent from
Hegel's description of the child is that the stone is a weapon. In
throwing stones, the human animal drives every unwanted being
out of his 'living space' and produces a protected space. While
combat and flight are negative forms of evasion, the throw of the
stone is positive in that it keeps the contact with the object while
keeping it at a distance and thus mastering it (NG 180–1).

These protected spaces are opened by the lithotechniques
Sloterdijk calls greenhouses, incubators, or spheres. They correspond to the middle position between a being enclosed in an
environmental cage and the pure terror of being held out into the
indeterminate, indefinite open.

> If having-an-environing-world can be understood ontologically as
> being-surrounded by an enclosure encapsulating all relevant circum-
> stances and conditions for organic life [. . .] and being-in-the-world
> must be interpreted on the contrary as ecstatic projection into the
> open-clearing, then it is necessary to assume that there is a middle-
> world position or a between, which is neither the enclosure into the
> environmental cage nor the pure terror of being-held into the indefi-
> nite. The transition from the environment to the world shows itself in
> the spheres as between-worlds. (NG 173)

Spheres are these intermediary worlds or intermediary openness: they are membranes that protect against the outside but are not airtight and impervious like environmental enclosures. They separate the human from the pressure of the environment, allow him to develop in a non-adaptative way and prepare the world-opening of the human, that is, prepare his sensibility for what is either spatially or temporally remote.

The home, the dwelling place is therefore essential to the coming-to-the-world of the human animal. 'The pre-human must first be homely, must first be housed, before he can become ecstatic' (NG 199). 'Dwelling is older than the house and the housing [*Ge-Häuse*] is older than the human' (NG 174).[6] Furthermore, this primitive *Ge-Häuse* is the result of a positive *Ge-Stell*, a positive 'enframing' (NG 197).[7] This means that technique does not destroy our ability to dwell but makes it possible in the first place. While Heidegger sees both ancient *techne* and modern technique as ways of revealing, the latter in its challenging forth of what is as standing-reserve, destroys the human's ability to dwell on the earth. What Sloterdijk uncovers is a more primitive *techne*, one that opens the pre-human in the direction of humanity. It is this *techne*, as that which produces the human in the first place, that will inform Sloterdijk's relation to technology, and especially to technologies of the human.[8] Against Sartre for whom we are on a plane where there is only the human and Heidegger's answer that we are on a plane where there is only being, Sloterdijk affirms that we – and this does not only apply to modernity – are 'on a plane where there is essentially technique' (NG 225; see W 165). Why? Because the human animal's standing in the clearing of being so that beings can be encountered as what they are, is predicated upon a primitive and primordial technique. There are humans as those who understand being because there is technique (NG 225).

It is worth emphasizing the complex interplay of distance and proximity in Sloterdijk's story of the coming-to-the-world of the human animal. What has been described so far is a certain ontological opening of the human thanks to a distantiation from the environment through a form of insulation: a more profound enclosure allows for the breakthrough out of the environmental fence. It is a certain distantiation or de-coupling, a certain protective nearness that allows the pre-human to develop a sensibility for what is remote. Being-in-the-world means being-able-to-be-with what is not given here and now, yet this openness is mediated by a being-in-a-sphere. If openness to what is remote is essential to being human, so is the protected space that grants this openness. To exist means to be exposed to entities as a whole but this exposition cannot be withstood as such, hence the need for familiarity, nearness. The human as ek-static, as standing-out is therefore never directly exposed to the 'great outside'. It always turns this outside into something livable, understandable, domestic (NG 210).[9]

Sloterdijk's Onto-Kinetics

What is the movement of human existence? The question concerns not how humans concretely travel around the world or move their bodies but how their being is moved so that they feel compelled to move around and travel. Here again, Sloterdijk takes his cue from Heidegger who has developed a kinetic ontology over and against the traditional ontology of substance. As Sloterdijk somewhat paradoxically puts it: Movement is the foundation of Heidegger's ontology (NG 29). To be human is not to be a thing with this or that essential characteristic (logos, thinking) but to be opened and moved in a certain way. Yet, in between what he identifies as the two movements of the Heideggerian fundamental ontology – falling (or downward plunge) [*Absturz*] and turning (or turning to gather oneself) [*Kehre*][10] – Sloterdijk will insert a third, horizontal or lateral movement, which he thinks is neglected by Heidegger: experience [*Erfahrung*]. Indeed, for Heidegger, lateral movement is always interpreted as dispersion, as a form of downward plunge. This is clearest in the description of curiosity in *Being and Time*. Curiosity is wanting to see something purely for the sake of having-seen it. 'Dasein seeks what is far away simply in order to bring it close to itself in the way it looks' (SZ 172). In curiosity, Dasein does not tarry alongside what is near, but jumps from one thing to the next. Therefore, curiosity characterizes a certain restlessness at the heart of Dasein's existence, which disperses and uproots, and renders dwelling or inhabiting impossible. At the beginning of the essay 'The Thing', Heidegger will mourn the abolition of true distance by the radio and the plane.[11] Since today everything can be near at once, since there is not true remoteness, there is also no true nearness. There is only the movement of curiosity. This primo-dial movement of everyday – inauthentic – existence is a falling. Despite the essential projecting character of existence, inauthentic projecting according to what 'they' say and what 'they' do has no gathering power, it remains caught up or entangled in the falling. This is the downward plunge [*Absturz*] and the swirl [*Wirbel*] described by Heidegger in § 38 of *Being and Time*.

The taking-over of the fall by the falling Dasein happens in *Being and Time* thanks to an 'anticipation', a running-ahead [*Vorlaufen*], where Dasein lets itself fall right up until the unsurpassable limit of its own death. The gathering power of this 'anticipation' allows it to modify passive thrownness (being-thrown) into an active throw, a fore-throw [*Entwurf*]. Sloterdijk likens this gathering countermovement to the opening of a parachute in the primordial falling that would allow Dasein to become aware of its condition or position as falling and thereby give the rest of the fall another meaning, by taking over its own falling movement, by projecting itself resolutely where there previously were only trivial or acci-dental drifting (NG 37). As Sloterdijk recognizes, it is not clear in *Being and Time* whether Dasein can of its own accord gain an entirely new direction, or whether what is called projection and resolution is not just a kind of interiorization of the movement of falling. Be this as it may, the movement of existence, the falling, would only be able to be 'saved' by a countermovement, a *Kehre* or a *Gegenschwung*, or as Sloterdijk sometimes calls it, a conver-sion [*Bekehrung*]. Heidegger's onto-kinetics teaches us, according to Sloterdijk, that the human movedness [*Bewegtheit*] is a give and take that disperses and gathers, lights up and conceals.

According to Sloterdijk, Heidegger's onto-kinetics does only half of the work. What is missing is an understanding that the falling of existence does not happen predominantly in the vertical dimension. Coming-to-the-world must be understood, according to Sloterdijk, first and foremost as an expansion on the same plane [*Ausbreitung in der Ebene*]. Coming-to-the-world is always already a synthesis of a vertical fall and a horizontal entry (NG 44). Yet Heidegger, so Sloterdijk, has no understanding for the positive character of lateral movements such as researching, testing, elaborating, developing, travelling, making friends, translating, linking texts and traditions, forming of alliances, etc. (NG 54). These movements, which Sloterdijk gathers under the term experience [*Erfahrung*], are not merely manifestation of a falling but positive manifestation of the ecstatic character of human existence.[12]

Heidegger does indeed have a concept of experience, yet experience for him is always primordially the experience of being. Despite the fact that Heidegger emphasizes the pathlike character of this experience, his paths never 'lead anywhere else than where existence already is' (NG 55).[13] Sloterdijk explains,

> When [Heidegger] teaches the leap into the open, he means an open on the spot [*auf der Stelle*]. He behaves as if he must wander always deeper in the region [*Gegend*] where he was born. What he calls dwelling becomes an interminable exercise of thinking-oneself-as-belonging to a non-indifferent place. He meditates his own landscape as the hearth of a task and the region [*Bezirk*] of a bindingness. (NG 52)

Sloterdijk reminds us of the time where Heidegger wrote to an acquaintance of his who expressed the desire to travel abroad paraphrasing a saying by Lao-tzu: 'Without taking a step outdoors, You know the whole world.'[14] For Heidegger, the sensibility for what is remote is cultivated only thanks to a rootedness in a non-insignificant place of belonging.

On the contrary, for Sloterdijk, human existence primordially takes on the character of exodus, removal, and relocation, that is, of experience in Sloterdijk's sense. This movement of experience – and this will turn out to be important – is cumulative: one goes from one thing to the next and builds a context, a coherence, or a connection [*Zusammenhang*]. Hence, lateral movement is not mere dispersion, but displays its own gathering force by building series, networks, proximities, passages, routes.

In emphasizing experience as the lateral movement of existence, Sloterdijk pushes the discussion of the spatial character of Dasein's worldly existence, cursorily developed in §§ 22–24 of *Being and Time*, into the centre of the analysis of human existence. In these sections, Heidegger shows that to be in the world, to exist, to be 'there' is always to be uncovering entities by bringing them closer (*ent-fernen*, translated as de-severing) and therefore always to be possessed of a certain directionality. If it is true that 'in Dasein there lies an essential tendency towards closeness' (SZ 106), then this tendency is more one of re-moting, of bringing near; it is more a lateral movement than a vertical rootedness. It is this emphasis on the positive character of the spatiality of human existence and on the lateral and cumulative movement of de-severing, by opposition to the sheer dispersion of curiosity, that also leads Sloterdijk to a different reading of the history of globalization.

Globalization and Technology

As we have seen, in the terms of Sloterdijk's onto-anthropology world-opening is dependent on an insulation, on the building of a protective space. Put into Heideggerian terms, this means that the *ekstasis*, the being-outside of oneself constitutive of human existence, needs to be structured and protected: Being-in-the-world is only possible as being-in-a-sphere. Likewise, we have seen that in the terms of Sloterdijk's onto-kinetics, existing means experiencing and that experiencing has its own gathering power: the multiplications of interconnected spheres, which Sloterdijk will call foams. This onto-anthropo-kinetics has a direct bearing, as I now hope to make apparent, on Sloterdijk's understanding of the history of humankind as the history of globalization, as the history of the different spheres humans understand themselves as inhabiting. Understanding this historical development will allow us to see in what way Sloterdijk provides a counter to Heidegger's diagnosis of our contemporary epoch as that of modern technology and of the will to will.

In the *Sphären* trilogy, as already mentioned, Sloterdijk divides the history of globalization into three conceptually distinct, yet temporally overlapping, phases: the metaphysical or cosmological phase, the terrestrial phase, and the globalized age. If the human comes to the world (and hence becomes human) by being housed in a microsphere and succeeds in reproducing himself thanks to these microspheres, then the history of globalization must be construed as the history of the movement from these microspheres to an all-inclusive macrosphere and finally to the proliferation of plural spheres. I do not have the space here to discuss this complex historical narrative or assess its validity.[15] I merely wish to outline the basic movement of that history, in order to show how and to what degree the 'turn' sought by Heidegger through 'meditative thinking' might be brought about by globalization itself.

On Sloterdijk's account, the first phase of globalization is called 'metaphysical' since humans, though still inhabiting fairly limited protective spheres, nevertheless understand their world as an all-encompassing sphere with no outside, whose centre they occupy. At this stage of the globalization process, the human sensitivity for the remote takes on what might be called a 'theoretical' sense. Humans project themselves into a cosmos, which they seek to understand. Humans occupy a very specific place in this cosmos, the centre, and even though humans observe the stars and study the universe from their vantage point, they do not explore it, they do not venture out of their assigned place. The second phase of globalization, terrestrial globalization, starts with the realization that humans do not inhabit a metaphysical Sphere, a One-All, but a terrestrial globe standing open for travel and exploration. In these terms then, what Sloterdijk calls terrestrial globalization is the epoch of the lateral movement *par excellence*. It is the age of exploration, discovery, relocation, connection.

Even though Sloterdijk, to my knowledge, does not himself make this connection explicitly, we can see how his analysis of terrestrial globalization aligns with Heidegger's discussion of the essence of modern technology as the completion of Western metaphysics as nihilism – his discussion of machination, enframing, standing reserve, and challenging. The history of Western metaphysics from Plato to Nietzsche is interpreted by Heidegger as the history of nihilism, of the slow abandonment of beings by being.[16] The modern epoch represents the fulfilment of nihilism, the obliviating of being to such a degree that even this oblivion itself is

forgotten. At this point, the falling movement of curiosity, discussed
in *Being and Time* as a transcendental structure of existence, comes
to dominate human life. This epoch is also that of modern technology, where everything that exists is encountered as available for
wilful manipulation or transformation – even paradoxically humans
themselves, who view themselves as objects available for infinite
transformation and mastery. By understanding everything as available, modern technology opens the way for the mere dispersion of
human existence among the beings of the worldly environment.
Yet, it also harbours in itself 'the growth of the saving power'.[17]

Heidegger's approach to global technology, according to
Sloterdijk, results from his misunderstanding of the positive character of lateral movement, which becomes apparent in the latter's
onto-kinetic analysis. Because Heidegger sees the urge of human
existence to relocate and expand as nothing more than a radical
dispersion, Heidegger cannot avoid interpreting terrestrial globalization as a falling movement. (For example, in 'The Thing', the
radio or the plane that connects and makes everything available represents a loss or a falling away from true nearness.) Yet, Heidegger
cannot advocate any wilful transformation of this epoch of technology; such a response would only confirm nihilism. What is needed
instead is a certain retreat from terrestrial globalization and the nihilism that Heidegger sees in it, towards a more primordial form of
dwelling, towards a meditative or mindful thinking [*das besinnliche
Denken*], an implicit dwelling in a place unaffected by explication.
Through mindfulness, according to Heidegger, 'we actually arrive
at the place where, without experiencing it or seeing penetrat-
ingly into it, we have long been sojourning'.[18] Mindful thinking
is nothing mystical but rather a step away from everyday dealings
with beings back into the essence of metaphysics (and of modern
technology) and towards the essential realm of being.[19] When this
thinking is described as being on the way, this movement describes
no wandering, but rather a deepening of the reflection that pushes
roots into the essential sojourning place of the human, the clearing
of being. Ultimately then, Heidegger advocates a stationary dwelling and a static contemplation, which refuses both to explore the
world and to seek to transform it. In this context, lateral movements
amount to simple nihilism, simple dispersion.

Sloterdijk shows however the lateral movement of existence is a positive force, since lateral movements have the power to gather. As a consequence, one need not see terrestrial globalization in purely negative terms. Instead, by paying attention to the inherent dynamics of terrestrial globalization, the internal necessity of completion and overcoming becomes apparent, and the mutation into a new era thus acquires a much more positive sheen. Terrestrial globalization is, to be sure, destructive. Untrammelled spaces are conquered. Social and geographical boundaries are disfigured and remapped. Yet this obliterating force does not provoke the outright annihilation of the world, neither in the normal sense nor in the Heideggerian one. The movement of terrestrial globalization is not primarily a falling/dispersion that would need to be gathered in by a counter-movement, such as that of a more primordial dwelling (on earth under the sky in the face of the immortals and in a closeness to things). Rather, the expansive movement of terrestrial globalization creates its own connections, connections that disperse and gather at the same time. Since the globe on which the lateral movement of the expansion of terrestrial globalization takes place is finite, this expansion creates a sort of densified 'globalized interior' in which populations, things, and pieces of information interact like air pockets compressed by the multiplicity of neighbouring bubbles: foams. (In this sense, space exploration is an attempt at curbing this completion, it is the dream of the infinite perpetuation of an unhindered lateral movement into the unknown.)

In the globalized world of foams, lateral movement becomes more and more difficult. It is at this point of densification and inhibition – at the point where there is no 'unknown, unconnected outside' into which human existence can move, expand, and relocate – that terrestrial globalization gives way to the epoch of global foams. What happens, and what Sloterdijk describes, is the necessary mutation of lateral movement from the wilful dis-inhibition [*Ent-hemmung*] of terrestrial globalization into the co-operation of the age of global foams, a mutation that can be understood as a post-Heideggerian transformation of the will. In the epoch of global foams, the traditional figure of technology as the challenging and domination of matter and persons no longer describes what is actually taking place. The dense contexts of the globalized world – foams – do not passively receive wilful actions or masterful dis-inhibition in a favourable way (NG 231). Every action reverberates through the foams and comes back to the actor, forcing him to take on responsibility for countless unpredictable repercussions. (There are many examples of this, from the financial and economic crisis of 2008, to the ecological crisis, the impossibility of escaping atmospheric pollution or the growing problem of space waste.) The force of inhibition that results from this re-coupling of consequences becomes a stronger force than the nihilistic technological will. For Sloterdijk, we are now condemned, not to freedom and commitment, but to trust and co-operation. [20]

It would of course be naive to suppose that this situation of trusting, peaceful dwelling has already been achieved. In *Im Weltinnenraum des Kapitals*, Sloterdijk brings up two forms of active dis-inhibition, two forms of stubbornly voluntaristic lateral movement that cut through the dense world of foams: liberalism and terrorism. The error of both the liberal and the terrorist seems to be to believe that unilateral movement is still possible in an unhindered way. Both of these lateral actors behave as one-way projectiles that bore a linear trajectory through the dense and opaque worldly context [*Zusammenhang*] as if traversing an empty space. The liberal and the terrorist do not realize that they are essentially connected with what they are trying to destroy. In this context then, Sloterdijk welcomes the transition to the age of global foams since it promotes the stabilization of the 'worldly interior' (IWK 299). We should not retreat from technological globalization into a non-technological dwelling, but on the contrary seek to create more connection, more densification, since it is precisely this *trop-plein* of things, connections, and information, that pushes us towards trust and responsibility, towards peace and co-habitation.

Ironically, the image Sloterdijk proposes to describe this transmutation into the era of global foams shows interesting parallels with Heidegger's notion of releasement [*Gelassenheit*] or non-wilful dwelling. Sloterdijk uses the first Atlantic seafaring by Portuguese explorers to describe the mutation of lateral movement into co-operation. Of course, at some level, the exploration of the 'New World' represents the figure of terrestrial globalization

par excellence: the penetration into the unknown, into the alleg-
edly uninhabited 'outdoors' by European explorers, the building
of liveable spheres abroad, and the connection of these external
spheres to the domestic ones. Yet, Sloterdijk does not use seafaring
as a model for colonial expansion. What interests him is the way
in which these explorations, which embody the lateral movement
of existence, could be transformed into safe returns. The explorers went beyond the limit from which they could rationally hope
to return. They let themselves be carried away by the trade winds
into the open. By surrendering themselves to the unknown, by
testing out where the wind would take them, the explorers let
themselves be taken up by the counter-movements of the winds in
the North Atlantic, the *volta do mar* or the turn of the sea. In doing
so, they transformed the adventure of setting off into the open sea
into a secure journey and routine maritime passage, back and forth
across the Atlantic. The explorers could not wilfully return to the
homeland; this could only be accomplished by letting themselves
be taken in by the sea, by entrusting themselves to its own turning
movement.

The *volta do mar* embodies the mutation characteristic of moved
Dasein in the epoch of global foams. Its movement is neither
passive, nor active, neither a passive falling nor an active turning
and gathering, but rather a letting oneself be carried, a moving-
with instead of a moving-through. The *volta do mar* does not
describe the kind of co-operation that exists among subjects who
dominate objects. Rather it invokes the co-operation between
subjects and objects, co-operation as being-in-the-world. If this
co-operative, trusting being-in-the-world still gives rise to technical production, it also transforms our understanding of modern
technology as mere domination. Sloterdijk calls the post-modern
form of technology, homeotechnology. Homeotechnology is a
form of technique where what is worked upon, what is appropriated by technique, is not seen as a mere standing reserve for the
imposition of a will, but rather as an 'active' participant in the
processes of technological production. The outcome of a homeo-
technological production can never be completely different from
its starting point, and the production process can never be totally
indifferent to the materials it employs. Homeotechnology then

cannot but remind us of Heidegger's description of the craftsman in 'What Calls for Thinking?' who is in a responsive relation to the wood 'as it enters into man's dwelling with all the hidden riches of its essence'.[21]

This excursus into Sloterdijk's creative, and to be sure controversial, reappropriation of Heidegger has shown us how human existence is an interplay between both a relative enclosure into a protective space and a expansive movement of re-motion, that is, between being-in-a-sphere and ek-stasis. It is when we apply this insight at the level of world-history that we see the importance of Sloterdijk's transformations of the Heideggerian paradigm. If according to Sloterdijk we are not saved by the Heideggerian meditative thinking and its step away from dealing with entities into the mystery of being, it seems that we might be saved by the world itself. The densification of the world and the proliferation of connections will force us to transform our way of moving laterally. The globalized age will be, Sloterdijk thinks, an age of trust and prudence, or it will not be. Of course, there are whole regions of our world that do not seem to be connected to the 'worldly interior', not only human populations in remote and destitute places, but entire ecosystems (for example, seabed ecosystems).

Sloterdijk's wager is double: that the movement of terrestrial globalization will not leave these regions unconnected for very long, and more controversially, that these regions will benefit from their entry in the globalized world. This last point will undoubtedly seem overly optimistic to many, especially since it seems to render political intervention, for example, in the form of government policies irrelevant. Sloterdijk's point might become more plausible if one considers, for example, the effect that atmospheric pollution has had on the 'worldly interior' (in the form of global warming) and the ways in which this effect forces agents to take responsibility. We can also think of oil spills or nuclear accidents in the same vein. What Sloterdijk's analysis implies is that responsibilization is an effect of increased connection and the disappearance of an unconnected exterior (e.g. the atmosphere, the 'Third-World', etc.) where we can literally 'dump' the undesired effects of our unilateral actions. It is forced upon us by 'the world' itself and not by any policies of our own making. Yet, the question remains:

will this responsibility be forced upon us soon enough? Will absolute interconnection, which would force everybody to become
prudent and responsible, come about before we, by our unilateral
actions, end up provoking the destruction of our earth itself?

6

A Public Intellectual

Jean-Pierre Couture[1]

> There are only plausible and implausible arguments, creative and stagnant thoughts, courageous and cowardly reflections, plentiful and limited opinions, interesting and dull ways of writing.
>
> Peter Sloterdijk, *Frankfurter Allgemeine Zeitung*,
> 27 September 2009

Jean-Paul Sartre once posited that intellectuals are *personae non gratae* in democratic regimes. The one 'who interferes in what does not concern him'[2] has always been considered unwelcome, says Sartre, whether from the standpoint of the political man who relies on general apathy, the scientist who seeks only to accomplish his task quietly, or the silent majority which hates to be harpooned by embarrassing questions on the trip between work and home.

After the end of Sartrian heroism and its corollary model, the total intellectual, it appears that the required conditions for the performance of this *habitus* have significantly shrunk, since the irreversible professionalization of intellectual production has compacted the space for the so-called generalists who stand outside narrow, purely academic networks. But this compressed space hasn't been totally annihilated. After the *intellectuel* à-la-Sartre, there is a still a persisting niche for public intellectuals, ones who – in addition to their roles as focused specialists – distinguish themselves by their ability to communicate ideas to people outside their own field and with whom they still wish to share a common language. The critical study proposed by Richard A. Posner on American public intellectuals clearly defines the key motivations of those particular actors of the democratic scene: 'a public intellectual expresses himself in a way that is accessible to the public, and the focus of his expression is on matters of general public concerns of (or inflected by) a political or ideological cast'.[3] This pedagogical role of the classical *homme de lettres* who lends his mighty pen for the sake of political and civil causes is closely bound to the shaping of the bourgeois public sphere in the eighteenth century, when the philosopher-gentleman, being economically independent or supported by enlightened sponsors, dared to attack ruling powers without any fear for his own professional position. This insolent autonomy has not only permitted some legitimately critical thoughts, but also designates the mental and material core conditions of this golden age that has been followed, from Voltaire's novels to Kantian systems, by the new era of professional thought.

Posner's study recognizes this cultural shift: 'The independent intellectual occupies a distinctive niche as a gadfly and counterpuncher. [But] [t]his niche is likely to go unfilled as more and more public intellectuals opt for the safe and secure life of a university professor.'[4] One can therefore understand that this tendency is related to the development of distinct and mutually exclusive intellectual markets: 'The expansion and improvement of universities, and the decline of the nonacademic public intellectual, have moved in lockstep.'[5] For the purpose of this chapter, these structural consequences can explain to some extent the strong competition between specific cultural capitals, rewarded performances, and advantageous strategies in each of these contending markets.

Indeed, Peter Sloterdijk's major role as a public intellectual in contemporary Germany seems to exacerbate the strength of this rivalry between two modes of intellectual production, and probably even more so because he stands at the exact border of both universes.[6] Quite aware of the opposition between academic and media worlds, Sloterdijk tries to avoid this rigidity by asserting that there are only, in the last instance, interesting and uninteresting thoughts. Though this assumption legitimately invites readers to judge texts on the basis of their content and audacity rather than their authors' institutional affiliations, it has to be admitted that the contempt expressed both by scholars and public intellectuals for their counterpart – contempt that is not unrequited by Sloterdijk – strengthens the hold of the aforementioned tendencies over intellectual life and inhibits all true debates that may have to occur between these positions. As a matter of fact, Sloterdijk often attacks those philosophers who have no interest in descending the cloud-enshrouded steps of the Ivory Tower, though this gap between the 'celestial' inhabitants of pure academia and the 'earthy', 'mundane' generalists of the public sphere ensures that genuine interaction between these positions remains impossible. In contradiction with this 'from-professors, to-professors' philosophy, the Nietzschean posture advocated by Sloterdijk is not the only one that has diagnosed some discontents in the culture of the German academic world, which traditionally 'developed an inability to promote philosophy beyond university [and had] no genuinely philosophical interest in mediating and communicating'.[7] Struggling against this tendency, Sloterdijk wishes rather to embody an agonistic stance that dares to publicly raise controversial questions restricted by neither political sensitivity nor scientific prudence.

In this chapter, the role of Peter Sloterdijk as public intellectual will be positioned in a broader game structure that juxtaposes different intellectual ethoses. The specific focus is an examination of his 'debate' with Axel Honneth in summer 2009. This curse of polemical events has clearly shown that both authors respectively incarnate two antagonistic poles of philosophical lineages and political ideologies: the chains of Adorno–Horkheimer–Habermas–Honneth against Nietzsche–Heidegger–Sloterdijk were here engaged in a struggle for the monopoly on the legitimate discourse about the fate of the welfare state, public finance and progressive taxation. After a closer look at Sloterdijk's shocking position against compulsory taxes and the criticisms it had to face, this chapter will show that this vision is partially anchored in his broader writings, where he depicts Rhine capitalism as a 'luxury society' that is based on a resolute denial of comfort that unfortunately hinders the birth of a truer philanthropic culture. For Sloterdijk, contemporary social theorists like Honneth should take this (although ironic and certainly naive) portrait of post-necessity society as a radical anthropological novelty that commands nothing less than a cultural and political mutation.

A Foreseeable Collision in the German Intellectual Sky

A close disciple of Jürgen Habermas, Axel Honneth has been director of the Institute for Social Research in Frankfurt since 2001. In line with the famous school's multiple post-Marxist turns, he works on 'the paradoxes of capitalist modernization', with particular emphases on liberal issues such as justice, recognition, and exclusion in democratic regimes. In the shadow of his prestigious elders Honneth seeks to preserve the moral heritage of critical theory, its intellectual vigilance, and its duty to defend the underprivileged, and these features distinctively marked his interventions during the summer 2009 controversy. Retrospectively, however, it appears as though the Honneth–Sloterdijk polemic was already forecast, if not predetermined, by the Habermas–Sloterdijk scandal of 1999. At this point, the voice of 'discourse ethics' attempted in vain to manipulate some journalists into discrediting the moral and political integrity of Sloterdijk.[8] But in less than a decade after this months-long public struggle, Sloterdijk nevertheless achieved the rank of an international philosopher, and this newfound position differed strikingly from his weaker status in 1999 when he struggled against the Frankfurt School's former figurehead. In the new sky over *Berliner Republik*, most of the post-Second-World-War generation were pushing for a change of guard in all spheres of society, even if this would break with the moral interdictions of their elders. In the acrimonious eyes of Honneth, this 'milieu' represented by Sloterdijk should be seen 'as an elite which has read Michel Foucault and which, with the help of a free, elastic, and acrobatic mental attitude, has been able to rapidly seize every power position'.[9] Though the good old days of the Frankfurt

School's preeminence really seem to be gone, Sloterdijk's (public) ascension to a position of prominence represents more than just the outcome of an intergenerational conflict. Rather, it is as a result of an unusual and ambitious path that Sloterdijk has been able to put forward an intellectual ethos that has put into question the usual prestige granted to the milieu of scholars.

For the sake of a sound illustration of this rivalry, I would like to recall the fact that, by early 1999, Sloterdijk gained access to the highest functions of German intellectual publishing. Siegfried Unseld, president of Suhrkamp (which is notable for being the publisher of critical theory and its followers), wanted to get closer to an author he then considered as one of the most significant contemporary philosophers. Consequently the publisher brought forward, alongside his well-established collaboration with prestigious names like Ulrich Beck or Jürgen Habermas, the fresh ideas of Peter Sloterdijk. This move was far from beneficial for the defenders of the austere tradition of *Sachbücher*, who feared the potential fallout of this sudden change in Suhrkamp's publishing policy. From then on, it was established that 'essays will be the main form of contemporary culture theory'[10] and this truly sounded like a turning point that bore the mark of Sloterdijk.

Some asserted with irony that Unseld 'can have lunch Mondays with Habermas, Tuesdays with Sloterdijk, and Wednesdays with [Peter] Handke'.[11] This intellectual libertinage was perceived nevertheless as a real danger to the publisher's scientific reputation. Faced with the sudden influence of Sloterdijk on their long-time patron, some journalists feared the imminent marginalization of the scientific voice of Habermas and a confirmation of a tendency whereby 'rigorous social sciences are about to be diluted in cultural studies' and confounded with frivolous literature only interested in 'life's problems, portraits of present time, and other life-style sociologies'.[12] In the eyes of the old guard, this presumed shift from knowledge to triviality is intertwined with another academic travesty: the unfair position of Sloterdijk in Unseld's immediate circle. In other words, the fact that a 'pop-philosopher' gained access to these hot spots of production and reproduction of the intellectual field only served to fuel the aforementioned vitriolic tensions and concerns about what is to be called 'legitimate philosophy' and properly considered as being part of the publisher's scientific vocation. Certainly, this promotion (and its expected consequences) framed and poisoned the terms of the 1999 scandal. But far from blocking Sloterdijk's intellectual ascension, this episode served as a new launch pad for his own works, a gift for which he is very thankful. Having passed away in 2002, Unseld will never know if his move was a good one, but his protégé did not forget to dedicate to him *Im Weltinnenraum des Kapitals*, his essay on contemporary capitalism: 'In memoriam Siegfried Unseld'.

To return to Honneth's above remark: these otherwise polemical and pejorative analyses are symptomatic of a broader feeling of resentment towards Sloterdijk on the part of the 'scientific', scholarly community. From the perspective of the self-appointed scientific voices of academia, Sloterdijk's success is the result of a fraudulent *coup de force* by an author who has delivered merely 'minor' cultural capital (as bestseller and media personality), and yet has nevertheless managed to reach a privileged position for the definition of the intellectual field and its discursive conventions. In this light, it is possible to sustain the idea that those who oppose him are trying to reverse (1) the growing influence of an actor who has until recently been maintained in a subaltern position, (2) the threatening change in the hierarchy of legitimate cultural capital within instances of consecration, (3) the actualization and reinterpretation of authors and philosophical lineages (from Nietzsche to Heidegger) that have been banned by dominant central positions (Frankfurt). These are namely the typical core issues of an intellectual game which has been well defined by Pierre Bourdieu in terms of struggle in the field:

> [The] field as a structure of objective relations between positions of force undergirds and guides the strategies whereby the occupants of these positions seek, individually or collectively, to safeguard or improve their position and to impose the principle of hierarchization most favourable to their own products. The strategies of agents depend on their position in the field, that is, in the distribution of the specific capital, and on the perception that they have of the field depending on the point of view they take *on* the field as a view taken from a point *in* the field.[13]

But a foreseeable collision between intellectuals born of different milieus is not only due to their distinct positions in the field. It is also due to the heritage to which they wish to be faithful and through which former disputes in the history of the field reoccur. Randall Collins emphasizes that masters of past generations excelled at the transmission of their creativity to younger authors, who would then carry on their ideas and occupy, in turn, the intellectual co-ordinates (alliances and rivalries) that come along with these. Thus, the Honneth–Sloterdijk quarrel, as seen through the lens of intellectual network sociology, is by no means an accident but an event programmed by the intrinsic logic of a game structure, which only needs a little spark to manifest itself. Intellectual creativity, says Collins, 'is not a one-shot event, but a process stretching around the persons in whom it manifests itself, backwards, sideways, and forwards from the individuals whose names are the totemic emblems thrown up by their networks.'[14]

With regard to the case that is relevant for our purposes, this structure can be traced back to the early twentieth century when the Marxist orthodoxy of Lukács, an influential figure for the upcoming Frankfurt School, condemned without appeal Nietzsche's irrationalism. In line with this heritage, the young Adorno would remain true to this Manichaean condemnation of German irrationalism, represented in his eyes by Martin Heidegger's 'jargon'. As this accusation resurfaces in Honneth's discourse against Sloterdijk, this polemical game and its intergenerational transmissibility can thus be represented in a simple network of collisions as shown in figure 1.

By using Collins' model of intellectual network design, I capture here the very structure of inherited polemics in the last decades. Dates refer to significant texts that have shaped this antagonistic structure. In 1931, Adorno's first public lecture ('Die Aktualität der Philosophie') accused Heidegger of being responsible for the decline of reason. In 1953, Habermas ritually repeated the same attack on the same author ('Mit Heidegger gegen Heidegger denken') and so philosophically situated himself as a scion of the Adorno lineage. In this intergenerational set up, the young Sloterdijk polemically defined himself as a 'left Heideggerian', a move that condemned him therefore as a 'person of interest'

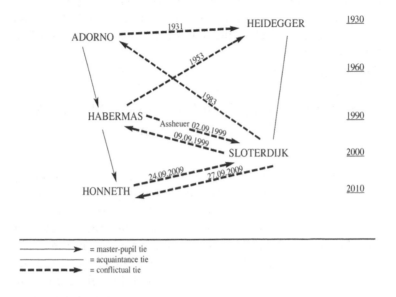

Figure 1. Network of Collisions in the German Intellectual Sky

by Frankfurt figureheads. The suspicion was particularly heightened once he wrote, in his first book in 1983, that Adorno's critical theory was depressive because the 'masochistic element has outdone the creative element' (CCR: xxxv).

In the light of Collins' analysis, this scheme not only shows that '[it] is intergenerational networks dividing up attention space that make intellectual history in every sense',[15] it also draws the trajectory along which Honneth and Sloterdijk had to, sooner or later, get into frontal collision. As contemporary monads in a network continuum, each of these disciples embodies distinct philosophical lineages even as they developed thoughts and idiosyncrasies that have granted them the status of original author. In an ideal-typical manner, I propose to label their intellectual interventions in two ways. On the one hand, Sloterdijk proposes a *Gedankenexperiment*, a set of provocative propositions which freely speculate and do not seek to be applied in reality, but which nevertheless seek to encourage a radical change in mentality. On the other hand,

Honneth is bound to a *Verantwortungsphilosophie*, a public debate ethics that has to serve as the linchpin of the agora and defend analytical prudence as well as the political and scientific responsibility of the intellectual.

From Grabbing Hands to Giving Hands: A Rendez-vous Manqué

'Today, we are not living "in capitalism" – as thoughtless and hysterical rhetoric suggests it over and over again – but in an order of things that should be defined *cum grano salis* as a mass media-driven, tax-grabbing semi-socialism. [. . .] Thus, the direct and selfish exploitation of the feudal era has been transformed, in the modern age, into a juridically constrained, and almost disinterested, state kleptocracy.'[16] This is the outrageous bombshell Sloterdijk threw against the consensus on the principles of the German welfare state. When questioned by the *Frankfurter Allgemeine Zeitung* about the 'future of capitalism', he decided to answer with this dark portrait of a state that strips down its most productive citizens (*Leistungsträger*) not for the sake of its social responsibilities (the public treasury can no longer afford it), but to accomplish the Proudho-Marxist programme that is born out of a deep resentment against property and wealth. 'Expropriate the expropriator' has become, writes Sloterdijk, 'expropriation for expropriation's sake' and this ensures that nobody owns anything because 'property is theft'. Starting with a critical examination of these hateful theses against comfortable life, Sloterdijk rather speaks under the banner of a sort of Nietzschean prodigality and suggests nothing less than an alternate taxation system that would rely on the noble ethics of giving hands: 'This courageous turn would have to show that, in the eternal struggle between greed and magnanimity, the latter can sometimes win.'[17]

This curious proposition is certainly naive, but it is far from being innocent – its sender purposely provokes the German *doxa* by playing all the notes of its scale. That is why the progressive weekly *Die Zeit* consequently published, a few months later, a strong response from Honneth against the unacceptable prescriptions of Sloterdijk. In his letter, Honneth crudely denounced 'the irresponsible thesis that has been thrown at the world's face with such nonchalance',[18] and he immediately reiterated the convention by which the welfare state (in Germany, France, Great Britain and elsewhere) has to be seen as 'the result of the fierce struggle of the workers' movement', whose actors simply 'claimed the equality in treatment that has been promised by the liberal constitution in democratic countries'. No need here to refer to 'greed, envy, or resentment' to be able to understand the legitimate battle of these oppressed people 'that only seek to actualize the moral principles of modern law'. These factual and moral clarifications are delivered alongside a series of recriminations against the '*écriture automatique*' à-la-Sloterdijk, a star who not only became the darling of the media but who dangerously seeks to serve now as political advisor.

But Honneth's text is cautious enough not to take any position on the issue of public debt, nor does he comment on the numbers Sloterdijk refers to when he depicts 'hyper progressive' taxation as a system where 'the top 20 percent of taxpayers produce over 70 percent of the State's income'[19] (a fact he treats as a potential precursor to a 'civil war over taxation'). There is not even a single serious word on the 'ethics of giving hands', which stands as Sloterdijk's core proposition: it seems that it is out of the question, from Honneth's standpoint, to let anyone be seduced by the tricks of this 'soothsayer'. Yet in spite of this scepticism, if one truly lends oneself to the *Gedankenexperiment* that is here proposed, it might appear that the concept of 'donation' is far more provocative than what Honneth dared to see in it; 'giving' is certainly the great denial of the liberal vulgate and its egoistic subject (whose twin became the social-democrat subject who *still* defines himself by lack and dissatisfaction even if he enjoys an opulent, privileged position). If socialist hatred towards property has been transformed into state kleptocracy, says Sloterdijk, one should see first in this movement the tragic incapacity to envision humans as creatures capable of magnanimity. From the stance of forgotten aristocratic virtues (honour, pride and prodigality), Sloterdijk argues that it is about time that prosperous people truly *give* instead of being *forced to give* in the name of a negative anthropology that multiplies the 'envious' on the one hand and, on the other, the 'greedy'. Why are we not able to give? Why does the state transform this presumed incapacity into a general principle? In an affirmative manner that would let down the mask, the cultural turn promoted by Sloterdijk would have the Prodigious say: *I am wealthy, therefore I give*. This would then uncover the hypocritical shame of comfortable life (a material status that is enjoyed nowadays by an unprecedentedly large number of people in Western countries) and help the Prodigious to acknowledge their *objective* plenitude, one which needs to be broadly shared.

But this was not exactly the bucolic field on which this new 'philosophy of money' has been received by the all-too-responsible position of Honneth and a dozen other left- or right-wing intellectuals who also rejected Sloterdijk's proposition. Among these critics, Honneth is by far the most eager to fight an 'objective enemy', in a spirit of vengeance against the illegitimate ascension of this 'intellectual decorated with the highest academic distinctions'.[20] As if everything were predetermined, *Die Zeit* immediately opened its pages to Sloterdijk in order to set up a kind of second-rate repetition of the 1999 scandal (see figure 1), but this desired collision would not happen. While refusing the fight in a letter published in the *FAZ*, Sloterdijk denigrated the terms of this fake controversy and mocked the accusation of his challenger: 'If our nervous philosophy professor is incapable and unwilling to fairly apprehend a twelve-page essay, without rough distortions and without turning the thesis on its head, then it makes no sense in advance to speak with him about the difference between our respective "modes of philosophizing".'[21] Sloterdijk also complained about the fact that Honneth only sewed a sheer fabric of 'last-minute quotations' that betrayed not only his 'eight thousand pages delay' but also his capacity to comment on the works with some competence.

This exchange of *ad hominem* salvoes undoubtedly undermined the birth of the 'debate'. Ten years after his prolonged yet at least modestly successful skirmish with Habermas, Sloterdijk showed that there was no need to put himself in dialogue with Frankfurt in order to consolidate his position. Furthermore, he dared to establish here an asymmetrical relationship between himself and the declining school. But even though the Sloterdijk–Honneth affair didn't take place as planned, the German press begged nevertheless for some additional comments and analyses from both sides. For his part, Honneth confessed that he still favoured 'the real protection of equality of chances' even if he recognized nonetheless that this mission 'can no longer be placed in the charge of the old welfare-state programme, which has lost its basis through demographic and economic changes in the last decades'.[22] Sloterdijk, on the other hand, proposed a manifesto against the spirit of 'lack and need' that paralyses Germany, where he exhorted his fellow citizens to face the unprecedented state of luxury that now characterizes Western standards: 'The truth indeed is that we can no longer be understood, and have not been in a position to be understood for some time, by most other cultures on Earth.'[23] Acting both as counselor of the prince and naive speculative philosopher, Sloterdijk also wants to anchor his political proposition in his broader diagnoses, found in the works that Honneth & Co did not dare to take into account: 'I start from an anthropological stance where humans are seen as being more than greedy grabbers. They have to be considered as giving-beings as well as taking-beings.'[24] But the question still arises as to how this thesis may shed some light on a generally misunderstood (if not misleading) proposition.

Did Pop-Phenomenology Really Fall Down the Well?

From a North American standpoint, these attacks on progressive taxation and the illegitimate (if not invasive) public expenses of the welfare state are far from new. The great success of the neoliberal trick by which working people are told to complain about public taxes without putting into question the usurious interest rates they pay everyday for the benefit of private banks' profits is proof of this. Similarly, one need only look to the fashionable 'philanthropic' discourses of charitable families and fortunate CEOs: the media overwhelmingly present them as saviours that have to fight tearfully for their right to contribute to welfare issues through their private foundations. Among recent and risible manifestations of this contemporary patronage is Guy Laliberté's trip to outer space: the hedonist creator of *Cirque du Soleil* wanted to raise awareness of drinking water rights around the world while enjoying the status of being 'the first clown in orbit'.[25] This enterprise took shape through an 'exploit' that surely has been inspired by the latest managerial tendencies and other teenager stunts à-la-Sir-Richard-Branson of the very cool firm *Virgin*. Is this the *clownesque* side of the new noble philanthropy Sloterdijk has in mind? More seriously, if America is far from enjoying the degree of protection which characterizes the countries of the Rhine capitalist zone (Canada finds itself on a very precarious fault line between these social tendencies), one has thus to recognize that the grandiloquence of the general principles that Sloterdijk has put forward sounds more like hollow universalism: indeed, what is revealed is the particular context of a 'deluxe debate' which exclusively concerns the West European space where neoliberalism has, in fact, neither grip nor roots.

This context of exceptional luxury is precisely the one on which Sloterdijk has intensively reflected in the last decade, even if this has provoked much anger on the side of the social-democrats who, out of blunt realism or political strategy, do not want to confront themselves with the wealthy condition of the nation. This phenomenology (of the denial) of luxury in late modernity is at the centre of two main works: *Sphären III. Schäume* (which sees in 'foam-cells' a convincing metaphor to understand the contemporary social architecture) and *Im Weltinnenraum des Kapitals* (which revolves around a macroscopic history of modern capitalism that ends up in post-history and post-necessity). Under the scope of 'climatology', Sloterdijk proposes a study of the composition of the atmosphere that goes along with these newly highlighted processes of volatilization. Lightness, frivolity, antigravity, discharge and levitation are seen here as the heavy patterns of the dominant mentality in this new foam-like structure of society. This climatology of luxury interests itself also in the anthropological and political consequences of the monstrous display of unprecedented wealth:

> If we attribute to climatology such an important existential signification, it is because we need, for philosophical reasons, to bring

the question beyond technical climatic installations and optional modifications of the composition of the air we breathe: what is really thought-provoking is the task of tempering the being-in-the-world, but at the existential level in general; that is, the ambience of there-being between the poles of heaviness and lightness. (S III 723–4)

As life in foam-cells means that lightness overthrows heaviness, this climate certainly bears some dismaying consequences for members of the old heavy party (whether they be the proponents of miserableness in the age of democratic indulgence or the ones that still value a 'being-grave' attitude in an age of great exoneration).

In foam, the precedence of gaseousness over solidness (the soil of the ancient fatherland) and liquidness (the conquering modern navigation) designates metaphorically the mutation of material and mental states that are no longer consistent with the traditional discourse of political economy (need) and the sacrificial discourse of political engagement (suffering). And yet the eruption of great luxury is not an unexpected development; quite to the contrary, says Sloterdijk, since the motivating forces of this luxury process are as old as the human species itself. The long history of the onto-anthropological propensity towards luxury is first and foremost anchored in the development of human habitat. Starting with the tribal circle, the first hominids clearly sought to free each tribe member from the weight of nature through the creation of a comfortable and habitable human-made world. The history of luxury has therefore become a history of discharge and exoneration, concepts on which Sloterdijk meditated long before his 'spherological' project:

> Luxury makes humankind possible and it is also through luxury that our world is born. Humans are, and have been since the very beginning, animals that mutually indulge and exonerate themselves by taking care of each other and by treating themselves with more security than any other living creature could ever dream of enjoying. Humankind arises through its secession with Mother Nature. We can then relate the birth of humankind with the spirit of *taking-care-of*. (WF 334)

The anthropological theme of discharge and exoneration (*Entlastung*) necessitates, Sloterdijk asserts, that any enquiry into the ontological

roots of humankind and the development of capitalism be pursued
by using a 'theory of constitutive luxury' (S III 676) as a means of
conceptualizing both the origin and endpoint of mankind. In this
light, Sloterdijk proposes the word 'indulgence' (*Verwöhnung*), a
term that that has its etymological roots in the German word for
'habitation' (*Wohnung*): 'Indulgences and pleasures, seen as terms of
historical anthropology, designate the psychophysical and semantic
reflexes of the exoneration process that is inherent to civilization,
but that could only have become fully developed and truly visible
as soon as the goods ceased to be rare' (WK 332). Nevertheless, the
use of this kind of assertion to describe the economic order of the
contemporary capitalist archipelago has not gone without provoking some discontent among those who would rather insist on the
persisting existence of poverty and scarcity within the great sphere
of comfort. For Sloterdijk, there certainly are some 'residues of
misery that stubbornly maintain themselves in the greater zone of
prosperity' (S III 680), but this tragedy is both falsely used to mask
the wealth of the very large majority and maliciously recuperated by
a discourse that hypocritically denies comfort and that has become
unaware of the power of its own caprices.[26]

While purposely provoking some patterns of thought that have
sedimented into a noble lie, Sloterdijk has decided to embrace a
counter-analytical position to unmask – in the general context of
the rising power of luxury in the airy society of foam – the denial
of comfort, the negation of indulgences and pleasures, and the
corollary imaginary shortfalls of large middle classes, which operate
through a highly ritualized 'structure of fine-tuned grievances'
and which borrow words from 'the tradition of the wretched' to
sustain the illusion of their misery. This culminates, says Sloterdijk,
with the result that all social demands of the Indulged 'are submit-
ted to the law by which luxury in power has to be retranslated
in the jargon of misery' (S III 682). He also sees in this harmful
cleavage between real prosperity and imaginary discomfort something that conveys the worst consequences not only for Europe's
enlargement (a process Sloterdijk strongly advocates) but also for
the sake of a genuine awareness of the finitude of Earth's resources.

As he explores the darker sides of this denial of indulgence,
Sloterdijk makes use of his uncommon sense of irony to cast light

on the discontent in the society of comfort. In order to do so, he proposes to put exoneration and discharge at the very centre of the symbolic air-conditioning system in foam. In contradiction with the mythology of lack and need, he thus sets the tone for a new historiography that would consider the process of endless growth of surpluses by revisiting metaphorically the five levels of the discharge system that is part of the over-affluent 'Crystal Palace':

> In the postmodern Crystal Palace, an elevator of indulgence has been installed to bring its inhabitants to the five vast levels of the discharge system. [. . .] On the first floor, we find people that have achieved, in full or in part, the dream of enjoying incomes without providing any services; the second floor is frequented by relaxed citizens that benefit from political security while being unable to fight for it; on the third we find those who enjoy general immunization, but without being capable of relating themselves to their own history of suffering; the fourth floor is pervaded by consumers of a knowledge, the acquisition of which does not require any experience; and, on the fifth floor, we find those who have been able to become famous by having neither performed anything nor published a work, but rather through the simple public appearance of their person. (WK: 334–5)

This ironic portrait of a post-necessity, post-materialistic, and post-political society is seen as a historical novelty that has to be seized in full. For instance, Sloterdijk's prognostics on the fate of the Euro-American Crystal Palace are always presented in the double dimension of horror and hope: the destructive exclusivity of this autistic egosphere of comfort (the dark face of the alienation of one humanity at the service of another) goes along with the new virtues of a light and frivolous mentality that may lead humanity to enjoy a state of culture that would move beyond 'lack and need' resentment (the bright face of the common emancipation of humans who frugally live on a round Earth).

Far from being cynical or indifferent about the real human misery that is kept out of the Crystal Palace, the subtleties of Sloterdijk's analyses have simply not caught the attention of his scholarly interlocutors who, as mentioned above, had strategic interests in protecting themselves from the sudden ascension of this reckless intellectual. Even if it appears truly fraternal, his philosophical look at 'luxury that has seized power' becomes nevertheless a bit confusing when it is transplanted in the field of the political. While trying to convert his philosophy into effective politics and to move from the sky of ideas to the solid ground of human affairs, Sloterdijk might repeat the tragicomedy of Plato's expedition to Sicily. As the old philosophers' proverb tells it, this move from heaven to earth is the archetypal peril which, in the case of the ancient astronomer Thales of Miletus (and how many philosophers after him?), led him to fall into a well.

As a matter of fact, all the conclusions of Sloterdijk's manifesto for the defense of the *Leistungsträgern* transform his philosophical insights into fireworks of ideological advice that are addressed to the main German political parties. While being tired of the 'red-green' and 'red-black' coalitions, Sloterdijk delights himself with the rise of the 'yellows' (the color of the liberal party) who, by reaching their highest historical summit of 93 seats in the Bundestag in September 2009, now participate in the new 'yellow-black' coalition. As if he was preparing his own expedition to Syracuse, Sloterdijk took advantage of this new parliamentary context by throwing in a long series of recommendations and prognostics. The victory of the blacks and yellows (conservatives and liberals) is seen here not only as the new political expression of the most productive citizens of the nation, but also as a huge challenge for the reds (social-democrats). In order to continue winning battles for the cause of the unprivileged and oppressed, the German Left would have to now make its appeals 'first and foremost to the hard core of the *Leistungsträgern* of society, and only secondarily to the unemployed they seek to help in the first place'.[27]

As further advice unfolds, it seems that the initially idealist waves of this *Gedankenexperiment* are finally meant to crash upon the reef of reality. This turn is not only due to summer 2009 polemics: rather, it is symptomatic of the latest works of Sloterdijk who, since the publication of *Zorn und Zeit*, has presented himself as a prescriptive thinker who has broken with the tone of his previous works. As Robert Pfaller wisely points out: 'A distinctive mark of Peter Sloterdijk's philosophy, especially within the context of German tradition, seems to be its striking serenity. [. . .] This detached attitude appears to save psychic energy and to subsequently allow for a pleasurable release in beautiful and witty poetic verbalizations.' But this love of the object has been rather metamorphosed today into a disappointed language of forgetfulness and decline as the author, writes Pfaller, 'describes our contemporary period as marked by a specific oblivion: *forgetfulness of pride.* [. . .] Here again a certain shift in Sloterdijk's methodical approach becomes visible.'[28]

This shift from description to prescription is a temptation that has been the burden of many political thinkers: as long as they are held apart from dominant structures they criticize hegemonies, yet the moment they are heard, they flatter them. This certainly summarizes the relationship between Plato and Dion in Syracuse or between Diderot, Voltaire and Catherine II of Russia (and countless other alliances with 'enlightened despots'). These were opportunistic marriages that always wound up with striking divorces which have seen these unsuccessful attempts banished to the wells of history. In his youth, Sloterdijk described this move from criticism to politics as a move from kynicism to cynicism, that is, as 'cheekiness that has changed sides'. This statement may well apply today to his own path: 'The cynical master lifts the mask, smiles at his weak adversary, and suppresses him. *C'est la vie. Noblesse oblige.* Order must prevail' (CCR: 111).

To render justice to the authentic commitment of Sloterdijk to German public debates, the latter remark certainly deserves some further qualifying. As an uncommon public intellectual, the reflexivity of Sloterdijk towards his own works makes it difficult to easily categorize his claims. It has been said that his equivocal style is simultaneously provocative and ambiguous, bombastic and coded, scandalous and polysemous. Despite the fact that the *franc tireur* of the 1980s wants to become the counsellor of the prince of the opening 2010s, it thus remains that Sloterdijk still has high expectations for democracy and its Eros of public discourses. By avoiding lukewarm statements, this iconoclastic theorist truly stands in the middle of recurring scandals that seek to reconcile his fellow citizens with the necessity of *dissensual* discourses, and to embody an agonistic position that overshadows any contending proponents of zero-sum enunciations at zero personal cost.

7

The Language of Give and Take: Sloterdijk's Stylistic Methods

Wieland Hoban

It should transpire that luxuriant
self-reflection provides good training
for confrontation with the problem
structures of advanced civilizations. (KMPA 51)

'Truth. Not Style' – thus the title of a short piece published by
Christoph Menke in *Die Zeit* (15.10.09)[1] in the course of the
controversy set off by Sloterdijk with his anti-taxation reflections
in 'Die Revolution der gebenden Hand' [The revolution of the
giving hand] (*Frankfurter Allgemeine Zeitung*, 13.6.09). While the
commentaries and statements by a number of authors in various
newspapers following the original article largely degenerated into
increasingly diluted polemics with less connection to the subject
itself than to the other contributions that had appeared in the
meantime, Menke's text, responding not only to Sloterdijk himself
but also to the comments by the literary scholar Hans Ulrich
Gumbrecht (*Die Zeit*, 1.10.09) on the respective styles of Sloterdijk
and his chief critic Axel Honneth, is notable both for its intellectual
coherence and for the fundamental nature of the questions raised.
Menke dismisses Gumbrecht's claim that the different philosophical styles of Honneth and Sloterdijk have to be taken into account

(as reflected in Gumbrecht's title 'Der Spieler und der Baumeister' [The player and the master builder]) and asserts:

> The belief that the dispute between Axel Honneth and Peter Sloterdijk is primarily a matter of two different philosophical 'styles', as Hans Ulrich Gumbrecht believes, misses both the content and the severity of the conflict. The contrast between 'risky' and 'safe' with which Gumbrecht wishes to describe that between Sloterdijk and Honneth may be suitable for describing the different driving styles of men and women; in the field of thought, however, it is meaningless. Here the concern is the truth of the idea, and no idea becomes true simply by questioning a widespread consensus (and thus touting itself as 'dangerous') [. . .]

Though the question of style is taken up here by Menke only after being brought into play by Gumbrecht, it is in fact central to Sloterdijk's work as a whole. One does not have to agree with Gumbrecht's partial trivialization of intellectual differences to acknowledge that a text by Sloterdijk should be read in a different way from one by Honneth or Habermas (to name his previous Frankfurt School sparring partner), that it is not simply a treatment of ideas but also of thinking and formulation itself. In this sense, style – the mere fact that style is present in a substantial sense – is central to Sloterdijk's philosophy. This is one of the reasons for some philosophers' dismissal of Sloterdijk as a 'mere' essayist or quasi-literary writer. Even those who see him as more than that, however, should be aware that his emphasis on style and the ways he sometimes relies on it to assert his arguments are not unproblematic, and that any thorough engagement with his thought needs to look critically at his stylistic approach and, where called for, circumvent it in order to penetrate to the true substance of his ideas.

One figure that represents both the style and the argumentation of Sloterdijk's recent writings in particular, and of all his work to some extent, is that of giving and taking. Though, as I will argue below, his journalistic efforts do not show the same degree of rigour and coherence as many of his lectures and books, the *FAZ* article does play a key role in characterizing Sloterdijk's current position. His detractors would say that the more accessible form led him to unmask himself all the more blatantly; others, while not dismissing his arguments, might state that they present aspects found throughout his work in a cruder form, and with the added problem of spending too much time in a field that is not his own, namely economics.

As far as concrete practical content goes, 'Die Revolution der gebenden Hand' is of secondary importance here; a discussion of this can be found in the preceding chapter. Because of its impracticability, among other things, his idea of replacing the current 'kleptocracy' with voluntary generosity and showing the unproductive that nothing will come of nothing – as well as re-associating financial success with traditional aristocratic virtues, rather than greed and ruthlessness – is of less interest to us than the philosophical and authorial behaviour Sloterdijk displays in his exposition. The first sections of the essay show a remarkable empathy for the views he is subsequently to reject, invoking Rousseau and Proudhon to present the view that property is theft, and our modern society based on that theft: 'The first to take is the first to undertake – the first citizen and the first thief.' Subsequent section headings speak of 'Righting an Initial Wrong', 'Thieves in Power' and 'Business as Kleptocracy'. Anyone reading the article for the first time after hearing about the controversy it triggered may well be surprised to see how much time Sloterdijk appears to have for socialist and anarchist positions. It is only in the seventh segment, under the heading 'The Money-Sucking Monster', that he makes his own stance unambiguously clear. Having summarized the view of the wealthy as achieving prosperity only by taking from those lower down in the economic food chain, he shifts the balance: 'In fact, one should look at the present-day state if one wishes to see the activities of the taking hand in their most cutting-edge form.' After that he presents the arguments that provoked such vehement disapproval from various quarters.

To appreciate the significance of style in this context, and the significance of giving and taking for that style, we must first look at these two terms not simply in the immediate material sense they have in the tax/property debate, but in their full associations and resonance. It is clear that Sloterdijk's allegiance lies with the giving side, and that one of his aims in this essay is to re-associate prosperity with generosity; here giving is for those with something to contribute and the magnanimity to do so, while taking is for those who have no gifts of their own and can only grasp for the earnings of others, motivated by petty selfishness and *ressentiment*. In short, greatness of spirit versus poverty of spirit. The etymology of the word 'generous' reveals a most apposite connection: its earliest ancestor is the Latin *generosus*, meaning 'of noble birth'. In its origins, at least, it refers not so much to that generosity evident in the hospitality of people who have little themselves, but are happy to share, so much as the generosity of the aristocratic patron who donates to cultural institutions. To give, one must have; and in order truly to have, one must be motivated not by greedy resentment but by pride:

> I want to advance a society based on competition between proud givers, not a dull-minded confiscation of owed goods. [. . .] If we were to shift the emphasis back to the proud, giving virtues, we would in time move towards a different civilization. That wouldn't necessarily be a post-capitalist society, but it would leave behind the current greed-focused system.[2]

Pride is a central category in Sloterdijk's recent work, and this is mirrored in the adoption of the adjective *thymotic* (based on the Greek *thymos*) – though this is not a particularly quirky example, customized terminology is an integral part of his style, and a Greek term such as this is especially suited to reframing a concept that has certain base associations in more noble terms. The field of thymotic affects and effects is explored most comprehensively in *Rage and Time*, where he bemoans the loss of pride as a virtue since antiquity through various factors, including the Christian emphasis on humility and the psychoanalytical view of humans as the playthings of subconscious urges and archetypes. Referring to the circumstance that such figures as Narcissus and Oedipus came to be considered representative of human nature, he writes:

> The choice of these mythical models reveals more about the person who made the choice than about the nature of the object. How should it be the case that a young man with a moronic character, someone

incapable of differentiating between his mirror image and himself, is
supposed to make up for the weaknesses of a man who only gets to
know his own father in the moment when he kills him and then, just
by accident, bears offspring with his own mother? Both are lovers
travelling obscure paths. Both get lost in erotic dependencies to such a
degree that it would be difficult to decide which one of them is supposed to be the more miserable creature. One could convincingly start
a gallery of prototypes of human misery with Oedipus and Narcissus.
One would feel sorry for these creatures but not admire them. Their
fates, if we trust the teachings of the psychoanalytical school, are
supposed to reveal the most powerful patterns for the dramas of everyone's life. It is not difficult to see which tendency is the basis of these
'promotions'. Who would make human beings into patients – as
people without pride are thus called – can do no better than to elevate
such figures as these into emblems of the human condition. (ZZ 29;
RT 15)[3]

The connection between the thymotic, the giving hand and the
generous style becomes clear. So far, however, we have considered
the category of generosity more in its (im)practical applications
than as a stylistic quality, which it very much is in Sloterdijk's case.
In fact, I would suggest that his work is at its most problematic
where it indulges most in the 'generous style'.

Style, by becoming self-sufficient, overrides the truth of the
substance, relying on 'generously' imprecise statements that serve
to develop the stylistic gesture; generosity degenerates into generalization. Once again, we can find this both in Sloterdijk's
journalistic efforts and his larger-scale works; an overriding emphasis on the thymotic and psychological side of discourse allows a
circumvention of more specific issues. Sloterdijk's responses to
Honneth's vehement criticism of his article – which, one should
add, takes that particular example as a point of departure for an
attack on his work as a whole –, as well as Menke's comments,
give an illustration of his evasion of specific criticism through a
thymotically oriented personalization, and offers an interesting
opportunity to examine the stylistic methods that reinforce this.

In the reply published in the *FAZ* on 27 September 2009 to
Honneth's article 'Fataler Tiefsinn aus Karlsruhe' [Fatal profundity

from Karlsruhe] (*Die Zeit* 40/2009), Sloterdijk's first mention of Honneth is as the 'Frankfurt philosophy professor'; this, it turns out, will be his titulation throughout the article. While factually correct, it is clearly intended to belittle Honneth as a 'mere' academic, rather than a thinker of more generous dimensions; this is reinforced when Sloterdijk refers to Honneth's article as the philosophy professor's *Referat* – a term commonly used for seminar papers or student presentations. And, in this case, it would presumably be a somewhat inferior student, having ventured an opinion on Sloterdijk's work when 'the truth is that concerning my work, our professor has a backlog of, at a charitable estimate, between six and eight thousand pages on which to catch up'. This reminder of Sloterdijk's great productivity, as well as serving to discredit Honneth as a critic from the start, also displays the intention to dwarf him and his work alongside the far more generous scale of Sloterdijk's œuvre. The question of whether Honneth's precise criticisms have any validity as such – regardless of how well he knows Sloterdijk's work – is thus essentially bypassed. Sloterdijk portrays Honneth, 'our unfortunate Frankfurt professor', as one of those 'left behind' who can only display his 'stagnation and frustration'. So, just as society's unemployed non-achievers resent and envy the prosperous for their well-earned affluence, the petty and unsuccessful academic is motivated purely by his bitterness at failing to achieve what the more generous, intellectually wealthy thinker has.

While Honneth's article displays an undeniably combative tone suggesting – in keeping with his decision to speak about Sloterdijk's work beyond the *FAZ* article – a long-mounting aversion on which he has finally decided to act, Sloterdijk's decision to ignore any distinctions between Honneth's arguments and those of Menke indicates a fundamental reduction and dismissal of their position as such. In the *Spiegel* interview, he remarks:

> To me, what the statements of the Frankfurt professors reveal most of all is a very great disappointment in themselves. If there is actually any anger in them [the interviewer had referred to Honneth's 'anger'], it is drowned out by a lament posing as an indictment – a lament about the fact that they have not succeeded in attaining the publicistic hegemony

they would like to possess, and feel that they should, on account of their intellectual pretensions.

Though the more aggressive tone of Honneth's text may make it more amenable to such a reduction, this characterization hardly applies to the substance of Menke's argumentation. On the contrary: in his concise one-page article, Menke wastes little time in getting to the heart of the matter:

> Here Sloterdijk introduces his fundamental social distinction, which is intended to bring about the downfall of the idea of equality as such. This is *not* the distinction of how far one progresses along the path to perfection. It is rather the distinction between those who are prepared to tread the path of perfection, to subject themselves to the demanding trials that tear them from their previous lives and lead them towards diligence, achievement and excellence, and those who simply remain within the commonplace as lazy, stupid, inept people. These *cannot receive any recognition*; the bond of equality with them has been broken. For it is only through practice and effort that one makes oneself – that one makes oneself a self. Thus whoever does not practise and make an effort, whoever does not hear or disregards the imperative of excellence, does not simply fail to realize what it means to be a self; rather, he *is* no longer a self. So how could he still be recognized as an equal? Whoever does not practise and make an effort, whoever is lazy, stupid and inept, has rendered himself a non-self – someone whom we, those who practise, can no longer recognize. Sloterdijk's conclusion, then, is that taking the idea of excellence seriously means summoning the courage and the strength to exclude those 'left behind'.

This is not the place to examine the quality of Menke's case and the degree to which it accurately refutes Sloterdijk's hypotheses; it should be clear, however, that these are specific socio-ethical arguments based on defined criteria, not simply the ad hominem broadsides of an embittered rival. Just as Sloterdijk complains that many readers of Honneth's article will form an opinion of Sloterdijk without having read it, he sweeps Menke's entire argumentation under the carpet and leaves his readers, insofar as they believe him, with the impression of a substanceless diatribe written purely out of resentment. This seems more indicative of disin-genuousness than negligence.

In *Rage and Time*, Sloterdijk applies the thymotic generosity of his philosophical style to matters of somewhat broader import, for example the problem of militant Islam and the societies that feed it. Though our concern here is less the veracity of Sloterdijk's claims than the way in which he makes them, an awareness of certain facts can sometimes make it easier to identify his strategy by highlight-ing what he has obscured or disregarded. His reflections on Islamic terrorism show, in addition to an uncritical adoption of conserva-tive clichés, a greater interest in developing stylistic figures than keeping to the facts. This is very much in line with the un-petty generosity of the aristocratic giver, and he even applies this idea to a subject such as this:

> Rage that manifests itself in punishment or acts of injury is connected to the belief that there is too little suffering in the world on a local or global level. This belief results from the judgment that suffering could be 'deserved' in certain situations. The rage bearer sees in those people who are unjustly without suffering his most plausible enemies. He will never be content with the fact that pain is distributed unevenly to the point of intolerability. He wants to return a fair share of the *excess* of pain that has been stored up inside him to the person who caused it but has not yet been punished. He is infused with the knowledge that those without pain exist in a state of acute deficiency, and what they are missing is suffering. Seeing the deserving go unpunished leads the vengeful individual to the conviction that he owns what others are lacking. He wants to become a donor, a profligate spender, even if he must force his gifts onto their recipients. Their habit of refusing to accept only provides rage and hatred with an additional motive to turn against its addressees. (ZZ 90f.; RT 56)

This portrayal of the terrorist as a sort of altruistic sadist draws the reader's attention first of all to the author's stylized, quasi-literary description. Yet after peeling this layer away, one is left with a simple realization: like many right-wing political commenta-tors, Sloterdijk reduces the motivation behind Islamic terrorism – especially the suicidal variety – to religious ideology and social frustration, not to mention a certain remoteness from reality. An empirical study such as Robert Pape's *Dying to Win: The Strategic Logic of Suicide Terrorism*, however, based on data relating to 315 incidents – every such attack around the globe between 1980 and 2003 – presents rather different findings. Before launching into a thorough historical, ideological and demographic examination of the phenomenon, Pape already gives a foretaste of his conclusions in the first chapter:

> The data show that there is little connection between suicide terrorism and Islamic fundamentalism, or any one of the world's religions. In fact, the leading instigators of suicide attacks are the Tamil Tigers in Sri Lanka, a Marxist-Leninist group whose members are from Hindu families but who are adamantly opposed to religion. This group committed 76 of the 315 incidents, more suicide attacks than Hamas.
>
> Rather, what nearly all suicide terrorists have in common is a specific secular and strategic goal: to compel modern democracies to withdraw military forces from territory that the terrorists consider to be their homeland. Religion is rarely the root cause, although it is often used as a tool by terrorist organizations in recruiting and in other efforts in service of the broader strategic objective.[4]

It is worth dwelling on this particular issue, as the utter refutation of Sloterdijk's stereotypical claims through the abundant facts gathered by Pape shows how far stylistic self-absorption can lead an author away from more objective analysis. Pausing in his application of the giver/taker paradigm for a moment, Sloterdijk draws on unsubstantiated generalizations quite commonplace in the right-wing media:

> The third and politically most important reason for the inevitably growing dramatics of political Islam (even if at this hour, after a series of defeats, it seems to have lost quite a bit of its initial attraction) results from the demographic dynamic of its field of recruitment. Just like the totalitarian movements of the twentieth century, it is essentially a youth movement or, more specifically, a movement of young men. Its verve to a large degree results from the excess of vitality of an unstoppable giant wave of unemployed and, socially speaking, hopeless male

adolescents between the ages of fifteen and thirty – in their majority second, third, and fourth sons, who can enact their futile rage only by participating in the next best aggression programs. (ZZ 344; RT 221)

Naturally Sloterdijk is speaking about terrorism in general, not simply the suicidal variety; as he fails to acknowledge such distinctions in any case, however, his remarks can be taken as indicative of a general attitude. As far as age goes, his bracket is confirmed by Pape; what it fails to reflect, however, is the differences of average age between the different groups of suicide attackers. Lebanese terrorists were the youngest, averaging 21.1 years, while Chechen rebels averaged 29.8 years. As for gender, while the clear majority overall is male, there are major differences: al-Qaeda used no women, Palestinian groups used 5 per cent, the Lebanese 16 per cent, the Tamil Tigers 20 per cent, the Chechens 60 per cent, and the Kurdish PKK 71 per cent.[5] The graver inaccuracy lies in Sloterdijk's demographic summary; the stereotype of the aggressive young man with no future is thoroughly taken apart in Pape's study:

Suicide terrorism is commonly ascribed to poverty; the underlying logic is usually that suicide attackers come from among society's losers, individuals who are so poor now and so unlikely to prosper in the future that they have little to live for and so are more likely to sacrifice a pathetic existence for some illusory blessing. If this explanation were correct, one would expect suicide terrorists to score low on the main indicators of socio-economic status – education and income level – both in absolute terms and by comparison with their society. However, the socio-economic facts for an important pool of suicide terrorists – Arab suicide attackers – present a different picture.[6]

Overall, Arab suicide attackers are much better educated than the conventional profile would lead one to expect.[7]

Arab suicide attackers are typically from the working and middle classes and seldom unemployed or poor. [. . .] Seventy-six percent had working-class or middle-class jobs – technicians, mechanics, waiters, policemen, and teachers, for example – compared to lower levels for these groups in their societies as a whole.[8]

In a case study focusing on the mastermind of the attacks on the World Trade Centre in 2001, Pape writes:

> Mohammed Atta in no way matches the stereotype of the pathetic creature who seeks death and chooses suicide attack as a convenient means of escape. He did not come from a poor family; he was the son of a lawyer. His family lives, to this day, in a Cairo apartment filled with ornate furniture, and has a vacation home on the Mediterranean coast. His two sisters are university professors. Atta himself earned a bachelor's degree in Cairo in 1990 and went to Germany for graduate work in urban studies at Hamburg Technical University, where his professors describe him as a good student.[9]

From a strategic perspective, attempting to kill as many people as possible follows conventional military logic; the greater a country's losses, the greater the pressure on the – perceived or actual – occupier to retreat. Sloterdijk, however, in keeping with his wilful portrayal, interprets this circumstance rather differently:

> As a rule, the donation of pain is sent to a precise address; however, the gift usually extends beyond the immediate recipient to affect those near her as well. Often the donator of pain agrees to this excess: if the individual designated as object of rage led a pain-free life, then most likely the people in close proximity also led lives without suffering, defective lives. In this sense it never appears to be completely false for the donator of pain to involve these people. The more desperately the rage bearer's unconditional wish to give expresses itself, the less it is limited by a certain determinate addressee. (ZZ 91f; RT 57)

Pointing out all the holes in Sloterdijk's arguments on Islam and terrorism – which form a notable contrast to the more sophisticated doctrinal and historical discussions in *God's Zeal* – would supply material for an entire essay; what is most significant here is the way in which he presents unsubstantiated claims on world politics and demographics in conjunction with the development of his own stylistic tropes, performing an act of self-seduction into complete non-objectivity. Furthermore, his contemptuous characterization of Islamic terrorists as 'an agitated subproletariat or, even worse, a desperate movement of economically superfluous and socially useless people' (ZZ 347; RT 223) uncannily echoes the criticisms recently levelled by Menke.

An important factor in the power of arguments is the authority their advocates purport to have. Sometimes, as in Pape's book, this authority is derived from facts rather than rhetoric, while elsewhere, as in *Rage and Time*, it comes from the author's air of confidence and the manifest breadth of knowledge he demonstrates elsewhere. Beyond questions of mere factual accuracy, the promotion of a certain authorial *image* is an important part of this, and is substantially determined by personal style. While some authors – adherents of Critical Theory, for example – often invoke the authority of an intellectual tradition to which they demonstrate varying degrees of allegiance, others – such as Sloterdijk – derive pathos from presenting themselves as mavericks who cannot be confined to any one school of thought. Interestingly, Honneth begins his indictment of Sloterdijk by addressing precisely this aspect:

> Whatever Peter Sloterdijk has written in the last two decades seemed reconcilable neither with the dominant zeitgeist nor the views of its opponents. What distinguished him from the bold advocates of a further economization of our society was the gesture of a fundamental questioning of all the achievements of social modernity, while his proud rejection of any bias towards the weak and disadvantaged set him apart from the hesitant objections of capitalism's critics. Nonetheless, his combative tone of non-conformism provoked reverent admiration from many quarters: finally, as already seemed clear with the *Critique of Cynical Reason* (1983), a new freethinker had entered the philosophical stage who, with the solitary determination and radicality of a Nietzsche, was confronting all those habits of thought that had long imposed an almost unbearable blandness upon our time.

One can perhaps criticize Honneth for the later aggression of his argumentation,[10] but the content of this opening paragraph is certainly borne out by a wide reading of Sloterdijk's works and public statements. It is not insignificant here that many of the shorter texts published under his name were originally lectures, as the rhetorical style and attempts – some more subtle, some less so – to manipulate the reader/listener are clearly at home in the realm of public speaking. One such text is *Die Verachtung der Massen*, which begins with a consideration of Elias Canetti's *Crowds and Power*. Arguing the work's importance, Sloterdijk writes:

> It is he [Canetti] who gave us the harshest and most inventive socio- and humanological book of the twentieth century: *Crowds and Power*, a work that most sociologists and social philosophers have viewed with suspicion and disdain and passed over since its publication in 1960, because it rests on the refusal to indulge in what sociologists do *ex officio* and almost without exception: to flatter the current society, which is their object and simultaneously their client, via forms of critique. (VM 10f.)

Naturally it makes sense for one non-conformist thinker to invoke the work of another; Sloterdijk's strategy in presenting Canetti's work in these terms – as something maligned or ignored because it did not conform to conventional expectations in its critique – clearly relates to his own desire to be perceived in a similar way. As many of Sloterdijk's readers/listeners may not be familiar with it, few are likely to object to his portrayal of its reception. But is it accurate? In her book *'Masse und Macht' in der Geschichte* [*Crowds and Power in History*], Petra Kuhnau writes:

> That a positioning in the context of these disciplines [ethnology, sociology, philosophy] has only occurred to a very limited extent can also be attributed to the circumstance that *Crowds and Power* is a work which lacks any clear location between literature and social science.[11]

As Kuhnau's study examines the question of the work's reception in considerable detail, and Sloterdijk provides nothing – not even anecdotal evidence – to support his own claim, it is difficult to believe that his view is entirely genuine, as opposed to a way of bolstering the desired image of himself and his philosophy via Canetti. This is particularly significant in the specific context, relating to the necessity of contempt – which Sloterdijk defines in specific terms – as a mobilizing force. Interestingly enough, he presents a formulation that already contains what Menke would condemn him for ten years later:

> The concept of the masses includes characteristics that inherently incline one towards a withholding of acknowledgement. Denied acknowledgement constitutes contempt – just as denied and rejected physical contact constitutes disgust. (VM 31)

A 'withholding of acknowledgement' – this somewhat euphemistic formulation typifies Sloterdijk's way of addressing potentially incendiary questions. For all the rhetorical character of *Die Verachtung der Massen* and other published lectures, he normally saves more barbed phrases for newspaper articles.[12] Speaking of the history and logic of the 'drama of contempt' that has shaped the dynamics of societal evolution, Sloterdijk once again emphasizes that he is pursuing a largely untrodden path: 'Academically organized philosophy has evaded the issue'. (VM 32) Reading this statement in the light of the recent controversy, one is reminded of his condescending titulation of Honneth as the 'philosophy professor'; the theme of the independent versus the institutionalized thinker is no new one. In an earlier lecture, *Kopernikanische Mobilmachung und ptolemäische Abrüstung* [Copernican Mobilization and Ptolemaic Disarmament], we find similar views: 'It is the seriousness of life's great questions that inspires the author and spurs him on to say more than the expert is entitled to' (KMPA 87). Though Sloterdijk has been an institutional academic for the last two decades, he was not when he wrote those words, and clearly this attitude, posturing aside, has remained central for him. While Honneth dismisses it as mere vanity, it should also be understood as a challenge to one's own thought: 'Philosophers have only flattered societies in different ways; it is a matter of provoking them' (VM 63).

Such provocation can have mixed results, admittedly, and the debates that arise form the background against which subsequent provocations will be viewed. For example: how does one react to criticism, even condemnation? Does one involve oneself in the debate or remain aloof, leaving such disputes to colleagues and journalists? Perhaps it is wisest to decide this on a case-to-case basis, as the issues and intellectual content of each debate will differ. What seems strange in Sloterdijk's case, and surely does the reception of his work no favours, is what one might term a consistent inconsistency. He emphasizes the need for provocation, yet withdraws or resorts to generalized dismissal when confronted with its consequences. Admittedly, the quality of criticism in such cases varies, and there are indeed situations in which the following applies:

> The infiltration of the features section by the gutter press – staged by the usual non-suspects – is a crisis phenomenon that betrays an overpowering trend of medial reorientation from information to the production of uproar. Instead of encouraging distinctions, this faction of the press sees its chance in triggering mass psychoses of simplification through journalism based on stimulus words. (RMP 57f.)

This passage from the postscript to *Rules for the Human Zoo* brings up an interesting problem. Sloterdijk is quite right to speak of 'stimulus words' [*Reizworte*]; more than six decades after the end of the Second World War, the public awareness in Germany is still highly sensitive to anything that recalls aspects of Nazi ideology – even indirectly, for example in discussions about social inequality and immigration. Sloterdijk is, of course, fully aware of this, and rails against such attitudes on a regular basis. The question, then, is how far the provocation is desired – and how genuine his response to the attacks it provokes. It would be in keeping with his positions, and his emphasis on thymotic rather than neurotic or weak-willed behaviour, either to remain aloof or to demonstrate his superiority through a systematic demolition of his opponents' arguments. Instead, he laments the stifling intellectual climate without responding precisely to it:

> Whoever so much as points out that problems of respect and contempt exist in the space of contemporary society is, if everything goes as usual, shouted down in the mass media – as if the mention of a problem were already the violation of a general agreement to silence, and as if the mere reminder of a quandary were already an insult demanding to be avenged. (VM 62)

This quotation and the previous one both relate to the controversy over Sloterdijk's brief reference to eugenics in *Rules for the Human Zoo*. Whatever may have been said in the ensuing debate, the initial outrage was in fact triggered by a minimum of provocation; reflecting on Plato's vision of the statesman as the constructor of communal life, he states:

> The task of this über-humanist would be no less than arranging that an elite is reared with certain characteristics, each of which must be present for the good of the whole. (RHZ 26)

This is a natural extrapolation of Plato's ideas, and comes directly after Sloterdijk has acknowledged that such notions are highly explosive against the background of fascist eugenics. It is rare for Sloterdijk to make concrete suggestions for direct action, and here too – whatever suspicions readers might entertain about sentiments lurking between the lines – he *mentions* rather than postulating. He is quite right, then, when he remarks in his postscript: 'Certain publicists turned these questions into prescriptions' (RMP 60). This does reflect the automatism found among *some* centre-left critics – but not the arguments of thinkers such as Habermas or Menke. And here lies the problem: by invoking a self-fulfilling prophecy, Sloterdijk essentially creates a vicious circle of non-dialogue in which it is difficult to assess how far and in what way he does ultimately wish to provoke. Instead of taking critics on their own terms, he presents himself and his ideas as victims of a 'campaign against the extraordinary' and 'hatred of the exception' (VM 94), phenomena he sees as a threat to excellence in general. If Honneth, by daring to speak about his œuvre in general, gives Sloterdijk the chance to disqualify him as an expert on his thought because he has supposedly not read enough, all the better. The greatest irony of the entire debate surely lies in the fact that ultimately, in real terms, Sloterdijk was not actually calling for anything. Asked in the *Spiegel* interview what he suggests for an alleviation of the statist burden, he replies:

> A thought experiment. Let's imagine what it would be like if the sums that are currently raised through enforced taxation came from spontaneous donations made by citizens.

That, essentially, is it: a thought experiment. Sloterdijk circles a particular terrain and makes his opinions clear – but there is no practical conclusion. The final paragraph of the infamous *FAZ* article features six conditional verbs in six and a half lines:

> The only force that *could* resist the plundering of the future *would* be based on a socio-psychological reinvention of 'society'. It *would* be no less than a revolution of the giving hand. It *would* lead to the abolition of enforced taxes and their conversion into gifts to the general public – while the public domain *would* not have to go bankrupt in the process. This thymotic transformation *would* have to show that in the eternal battle between greed and pride, the latter can gain the upper hand from time to time. [My emphases]

The reader might well wonder how exactly taxes can be converted into donations; the article reaches its surreal anti-climax in this fantastic suggestion. This is surely the point at which style itself becomes provocation; the giving hand reveals itself to be empty, and the non-conformist's weapon of uncompromising thought turns out to be firing blanks. It is hard not to see an irony in earlier comments such as these:

> Hence today's philosophy is only truly professional when it is allowed to demonstrate how it would say something if it were actually saying anything. (KMPA 89)

> By saying almost nothing and wisely avoiding any statements that go too far – and what statements do not go too far –, modern philosophy achieves incredible things. (KMPA 90)

When Sloterdijk made these two statements, his philosophy had an element of idealism that appears to have dissipated in recent years. In *Kopernikanische Mobilmachung und ptolemäische Abrüstung*, as later in *Weltfremdheit*, he attempts something relatively uncommon: to speak about contemporary classical music as a non-musician. Rather than entering the discussion as the 'generous' giver to share his wisdom, he demonstrates both an unusual degree of insight and a humility and willingness to learn that few would expect of him today. The polarity manifest in recent years as that of giving and taking is present, but its flavour is different: here we find post-modern openness and levity versus the grim discipline of modernist self-denial. Instead of material greed and *ressentiment*, he considers the rejection of tonality and traditional forms in post-war classical music. While he sees – following on from the irreverent figure of Diogenes in *Critique of Cynical Reason* – a more productive future in a certain provocative levity, a re-emphasis on playful freedom rather than entrapment by aesthetic regulations (with a reference to 'radicality as a promise of morality, intransigence as a criterion of authenticity and unyielding dissonance as a guarantee of truth' [KMPA 40]), he acknowledges the latter's importance: 'Without the forces of taboo – in the case of our topic, one can also speak of a nervous veto or incarnated exclusivity – modernism would never have been able to gain its penetrative power' (KMPA 71).[13] Setting himself apart from advocates of a musical post-modernism that draws on found material, collage and irony in the absence of any faith in genuine newness, he even states: 'We do not want to explore the world as it is, but to invent it as it is not' (KMPA 115). If we compare this very modernist gesture to the quasi-feudal 'revolution' evoked in the taxation debate, the latter seems characterized by a certain dissociation of the revolutionary idea from its appropriate surroundings of renewal. In contrast to many thinkers and artists, we do not find a change of style combined with a consistency of content so much as a consistency of style with a modification of content. This suggests that at times, style plays a more defining role in Sloterdijk's work than the particular topic to which it is applied.

What conclusions, then, do we draw from all this? Readers of the present essay may have the impression of an attack on Sloterdijk's work per se; that is not, however, what it is intended to be. He is a thinker of rare breadth, and the matters he writes about straddle many disciplines and categories of thought, as well as subjecting many historical periods and occasionally different cultures to scrutiny. His output is vast. This critique of his style – understood in a more fundamental sense than is often associated with the word – operates on the assumption that there is substantial intellectual profit to be gained from an engagement with his work. It also, however, acts on the observation that like many thinkers who do not restrict themselves to one narrow field of expertise, Sloterdijk's philosophical precision and depth are not equally pronounced in all areas. As is to be expected with the breadth of his perspectives, he is most convincing where – as in *Sphären* – his canvas is the most expansive and he has space to develop his thoughts circumspectly and in many layers, without having to resort to reductions. Indeed, it is indicative of the difference in approach that one cannot speak there of stylistic methods or 'moves' in the same sense; where the project is the creation, layer by layer, of a three-dimensional transhistorical panorama, style is not instrumentalized as it is in polemics. Certainly his style – in the usual sense of the word – is recognizably the same, drawing on the same wealth of neologism, augmented by Heideggerian word permutations and cross-cultural juxtapositions. The entire impulse driving the work, however, is one of exploration, a gradual uncovering of contexts, connections and processes – establishing links, for example, between Homer's Sirens and the sound-oriented prenatal research of Alfred Tomatis, or the constellations of shared space between the placenta and the foetus on the one hand and the members of the Holy Trinity on the other.

In his more insightful works, such as *Sphären*, Sloterdijk provokes thought rather than provoking the reader. But his excursions into economics cannot match his analyses of aesthetic history, and his newspaper articles do not show the acumen of his books, even if one takes the difference of medium into account. As Gumbrecht suggests, one must learn to treat him as a player and sometimes an actor, someone who draws on different methods to convince the reader, and that some of these methods are more cynical and transparent than others. It is in the interests of a fruitful and differentiated reception of his work that I maintain the importance of drawing attention to its weaknesses, and emphasizing which elements need to be seen through in order to concentrate on what is more substantial. Without such differentiation, I see uncritical acceptance or wholesale dismissal as the only alternatives, and these are surely both unproductive in the field of philosophical thought.

8

Peter Sloterdijk and the Philosopher's Stone

Nigel Thrift

There is an urge, consubstantial to the philosophical tradition, [that] whenever you are told to limit yourself to the philosophical tradition, whenever you are told to limit yourself inside a well-defined specialty, to jump on [to] the other side of the fence in order to embrace the Whole.[1]

The fifth figure is Laplace, who has his street just opposite. His main claim to fame is his hypothesis on the formation of planets, which he explained to Napoleon. But he was also a physicist, and we owe to him the law defining the relationship between the tension of the walls of a sphere, the pressure within it, and the radius.[2]

Pierre-Simon Laplace is one of the few characters missing from the voluminous cast list of Peter Sloterdijk's meisterwerk, *Sphären*. It is a surprising omission, one might think: after all, as Hazan points out, Laplace was responsible for the discovery of the spherical harmonics (or Laplace coefficients), the eccentricities and inclinations of planetary orbits and even aspects of surface tension. But it also illustrates the difficulties of works of synthesis which try to integrate all of historical and philosophical anthropology into one shining – or even burnished – arc of knowledge. Evidence. Even

the most abstract of philosophers needs to call on empirical corre-
lates every now and then for inspiration while for a social scientist
the danger is equal but opposite: too much evidence can dampen
any inspiration at all.

In this chapter, I will want to consider the use of evidence in
works of philosophy like *Sphären* in order to question the sharpness of the divide between philosophy and social science. That is
neither an easy nor a pliable prospect. For a social scientist like
myself, it is a scary moment when you start to address the question
'what is philosophy?' Many, many philosophers have already done
a far better job of addressing this question than I ever can. That is
equally true of the question 'what is social science?' Many, many
social scientists have done a far better job than I ever could have.
But there comes a point where the two domains of knowledge
begin to bleed into one another in non-trivial and even eloquent
ways and that point is interestingly reached in the work of Peter
Sloterdijk. In this chapter, in other words, I want to look at what
happens when continental philosophy and social science intersect,
most especially through the medium of a medium – space – which
continually interferes with their premises about how and why evidence quite literally matters.

It is an interesting point to ponder in more ways than one.
Social scientists and others have often been so intimately involved
in the domain of continental philosophy that Judith Butler has
argued that as much continental philosophy takes place outside the
formal domain of continental philosophy as within it: continental philosophy has, as she puts it, 'doubled' with what, for some
continental philosophers, are troubling consequences.[3] And continental philosophy has routinely impinged on the domain of social
science. Indeed, in the extreme case, some social scientists seem to
not so much draw on continental philosophy for inspiration as to
regard it as revealing manifest truths about the world which social
science is there to illustrate.

Be that as it may, there are still dividing lines which are deeply
felt. For example, there is a moment where Žižek highlights
an 'unphilosophical' section in Derrida's *Spectres of Marx* where
Derrida breaches the rule of only concerning himself with that
which is inherent to philosophy. So he

lists the disasters in this world in ten points. Unbelievable! I didn't believe my eyes as I read that; but there they were, ten points; and they attested to an extreme lack of thought: unemployment and dropouts without money in our cities; drug cartels; the domination of the media monopolies and so forth. As if he wanted to give the impression of being not merely a great philosopher but also a warm-hearted person. Excuse me, but here I can think of only a relatively fatal comparison: at the end of works of popular literature there is usually a short description of the author – and in order to valorize their curriculum a little, one adds something like: 'she currently lives in the South of France surrounded by many cats and dedicated to painting ...' That is more or less the level we're dealing with.[4]

Take away Žižek's routine outburst of exasperation, which has its own rhetorical brand, and still the paragraph illustrates where a boundary has been crossed.

Or does it? Just look at Žižek's own books and articles, which often seem to be suspiciously full of jousts with and judgements upon topics which wander precisely into this apparently forbidden and flimsy empirical domain, or indeed consider the pages of journals like *Radical Philosophy*, replete with commentaries on the fallen world, and it is clear that many philosophers do routinely intervene in issues such as the ones that Derrida raises. One might, I suppose, argue that they are simply intervening in the guise of concerned citizens, though it is interesting how often they seem to think that they have, in some way or the other, privileged access to what is going on. Again, one might argue that philosophers can be counted as general-purpose sages, an argument that is more convincing in countries like France than in Anglo-Saxon countries where a more practical bent often holds sway.[5] Finally, it might be argued that philosophy, concerned with the nature of the world as much as how we can know it, can hardly avoid such issues.

Whatever the case, I want to argue that Peter Sloterdijk offers a different way of proceeding. Right at the outset, I should say that Sloterdijk is the very model of a worldly philosopher. But his appearances on television and his waspish articles in the general media are not what I am concerned with here. Rather, in his philosophical work, I want to argue that Sloterdijk offers the beginnings of a different way of engaging with the world.

Peter Sloterdijk writes a lot about a lot of things. But one of the things that strikes me is his closeness to worldly matters. Of course, philosophers in general have ranged far and wide across the universe, commenting on topics as different and diverse as neuroscience and astrophysics, psychology and music. Equally, there have been other philosophers who have stuck close to worldly matters: the examples of Walter Benjamin's engagement with the grain of everyday life or John Dewey's commitment to an empirical philosophy come most obviously to mind. Be that as it may, most philosophers still draw a strong dividing line between what they do and the formal study of the world using all the methodological apparatuses of the humanities and social sciences. But because Sloterdijk styles himself as a hyperbolic thinker, he gives himself carte blanche to address almost any issue that he finds interesting, including those that are bound to stir up controversy, such as his provocations around the human zoo and, latterly, the welfare state.

In some senses, it is possible to argue that Peter Sloterdijk's work has become so quickly noted outside Germany because he struck lucky in the timing of the reception of his work. His work became popular at the same time as and in concert with an upsurge of interest in some of the topics he was most interested in – affect, space, geopolitics. But that would be quite unfair. These topics were only ever a small subset of his interests. Anyone who has ever read Sloterdijk or heard him speak knows that he is a voracious reader who can be interested in most things. This promiscuous relationship with the world is what makes him so interesting since it leads him to make unexpected connections which are rarely able to be easily sheeted home to just one domain of knowledge. They lead to his distinctive style of hyperbolic reasoning which might as easily be termed hyper-connected and hyper-ambitious. But they do also produce frustrations which infuriate some commentators.[6] Sometimes Sloterdijk's work seems more like notes towards comments (e.g. GZ). At other times it plays so fast and so loose with history and anthropology that it runs the risk of tripping over itself in a rush to judge judgement. And, at other times again, it produces merely a grandiose restatement of familiar plaints (as in many of Sloterdijk's comments on capitalism or Europe) or is clearly calculated mainly to cause as much enjoyable offence as possible (as in his recent comments on the welfare state).

But if we zero in on Sloterdijk's finest work, *Sphären*, it produces an entirely different sense of intellectual presence – as a complex and variegated account of the externalization of the will. After all, *Sphären* is populated, in a very unphilosophical way, with a host of empirical examples drawn from the full range of the arts and humanities and the social sciences and, indeed, the natural sciences, while its text is interspersed with numerous photographs and diagrams. It is a work of philosophy certainly but it is also a diverting intellectual history, and a thoroughly engaging civilizational history in the manner, most recently, of Morris (2010).[7] It includes all manner of excursions which cover the whole gamut of topics, from anthropology to architecture and from zen to zoology.

So what distinguishes Sloterdijk's work in *Sphären* and why? I will answer my own question in three parts. In the first part of the chapter, I will suggest, in an accounting of *Sphären*, that Sloterdijk comes from a tradition which values engagement with the world, but of a sort which is intense rather than fleeting, which battles against what is often seen as the superficiality of modern life. Though, as a committed Nietzschean, Sloterdijk often disavows the *pharmakon* of religion, his work has his mentor's sacred sense of what is effusive and enigmatic and ecstatic in the world (see GZ). In the second part of the chapter, I will argue that Sloterdijk fell across a way of articulating that disappointed and yet still transcendent willedness, namely space, understood as a process of the birth and rebirth of what might be called, although it is an impoverished description, environments. Then, in the third part of the chapter, I will argue that his commitment to space produced an excess which could not be contained, a way of both promoting belief in the world and allowing new worlds to come into existence as a series of 'spheres', worlds which are gradually explicitated, and thus moving from the sacred in to the empirical domain. In making this move, Sloterdijk, in company with a number of other thinkers, is not just providing a description of coming-into-existence but is forging a new kind of philosophy which is also a new kind of social science, or, alternatively, a new kind of social science which is also a new kind of philosophy, by producing what I will call a methodological shift towards a philosophically informed technics of coming-into-existence. This shift will have consequences in the world to come, since it is both a vehicle for reframing questions and a means of building worlds in which those questions can be put more insistently – and explicitly. And, so I will argue, it is precisely in keeping with a philosophy understood as a vehicle to alert minds and to aid the evolution of humanity.

I will leave some issues in abeyance, however. In particular, though I necessarily touch upon it, I am not interested in the question of what exactly constitutes continental philosophy. I am well aware of how fraught a question this can be. That said, I would hazard a guess that part of continental philosophy's charm comes from its extreme malleability. Because it is ill-defined, it can mean a lot of different things to a lot of different people. It occupies the same spot in philosophy as human geography is often seen as occupying in the social sciences, as an eclectic and ill-defended mix with all the accompanying advantages and difficulties that brings with it.

The Surrounding World

Life – even the most contemplative of lives – cannot be lived at a remove from the world. What seems clear is that at some point Sloterdijk transited from a thinker interested in general philosophical issues to a thinker who strove to engage with the world. For many of those involved with philosophy the question of the surrounding world, understood in various ways – as place, as context, even as the pursuit of a quality like *eudaimonia* which necessarily varies according to situation – is very often one of the keys to philosophical position. And it is not an incidental one. Think, in the extreme admittedly, of Heidegger, whose 'surrounding world' was, at least for a period, closely connected to the National Socialist doctrine of a community of people rooted in the land.[8] Or, to cite a less extreme case, think of *eudaimonia* which in its original etymology referred to a sense of wellness (*eu*) but also to being protected and looked after by a benevolent spirit who was often of place (*daemon*). In each case, what we see is a generalization of philosophical position becoming consequent upon what surrounds that position.

Sloterdijk had evinced an interest in space for many years, chiefly through the study of Heideggerian but also Nietzschean thematics. But his involvement with space in the *Sphären* project is on a quite different level. Unlike time, a favourite contemplation of philosophers, space brings with it an emphasis on difference, on distribution, and on the mechanics of variation which is not just variation around the mean of a principle of some kind but a kind of constant drifting which has its own dynamic and texture. Perhaps that is why, until the late twentieth century, philosophers often tended to keep away from the subject of space, notwithstanding some notable exceptions. Space required a kind of confidence in facing up to constant variation that they did not have, a confidence that all of the world could not be placed in one conceptual tent – and that no philosophy could possibly encompass it all.

At the same time, post-Bergson, notions of time were themselves changing. As time began to be decomposed by the discoveries of science, becoming both larger and smaller, so it became possible to go back to notions of time which had been prevalent but had subsequently been largely discarded in Western accounts. Time was allowed to show up as spirals,[9] as rings,[10] as helices,[11] but not so much, in this new iteration, as a cosmological move, rather as a part of a simple practical relationship with the everyday. Spaces were increasingly able to be defined not as enormous set-pieces meant to both simulate and punctuate the linear time of modernity but as nonlinear space-times which resembled the frames produced en masse by the media and which obtained their power from accumulation and from the aggregated and necessarily complex effects produced by sheer number and scale.[12]

Thus, space and time were no longer marked out as separate but became merged as a set of disturbances and vortices which were only able to be stabilized by grands projects of 'landscapization', to use a phrase from Deleuze and Guattari, which acted both to enshrine will and to drive will forward. Space-time therefore comes to resemble both a civilizational norm and an analyst's couch combined, a work of engineering intended to allow the landscape itself to become a reservoir of collective memory and will, a means of understanding what is to be done next, with all that entails.[13]

In my understanding of *Sphären*, Sloterdijk provides a history of the evolution of this *'minded'* understanding of surrounding that works out from the earliest times to the present.[14] Space is understood 'gynaecologically' as a set of envelopes or surrounds or shelters, self-animated spaces that give their inhabitants the resources to produce worlds. His account of the explicitation of these atmospheres is relatively well-known and I will only give the barest of details here, therefore. For Sloterdijk all being is being-with; there can be no I without us to put it in a non-Heideggerian way. This extension of Heidegger which, incidentally, is common wisdom in much of modern psychology and neuroscience,[15] is made strange because Sloterdijk adds in a spatial dimension of being-with-in-a-world that is a sphere (whether the sphere is a womb, a home, a polis, a nation, an empire, or some other sheltering envelope), a move which allows him to picture pictures of what life might be when generated from within existence: 'Human beings are at bottom and exclusively creatures of their interiors and the results of their work on the form of immanence that is inseparable from them. They thrive only in the hothouse of their autogenic atmosphere' (S I 46). Without our worlds, in other words, we are nothing. We cannot live/think unless we can surround ourselves.

Moving out from this root account of environments as 'climatizations' formatted by their inhabitants, Sloterdijk offers a philosophical history of these hothouses, different forms of being there which exist because human beings 'have given them form, content, extension and relative duration when they inhabit them' (S I 47). He argues that Western history has taken place as three roundelays of different forms of surrounding: a Greek-inspired notion of an ordered cosmic sphere that encompasses all of human experience, a period of globalization in which the earth becomes an object of active survey, open to travel and exploration in a 'free outside' which itself becomes an interior, and a 'post-historical' period of bubbling foam in which there is no unknown outside, which produces a multiplicity of lifeworlds and all manner of microclimates which communicate frantically – but in autistic ways.

But this brief preamble itself requires interpretation. We can, I think, see where Sloterdijk is trying to go simply by pointing to his Nietzschean legacy (CCR). To begin with, in following Otto Rank's Nietzschean-inspired emphasis on willedness,[16] Sloterdijk was interested in studying how new worlds were born, in exploring spaces that are able to act as both creatures and creators, and in parachuting into milieux which can act as both exteriority and interiority in parallel with each other. Sloterdijk's mission, like Rank's, is to help neurotics become creative artists, but on a multi-civilizational scale. He wants to achieve separation from outworn emotions, thoughts and behaviours but this separation requires a continuous process which is somewhere between analysis and action and somewhere therefore between philosophy and the empirical. In other words, Sloterdijk might well be thought of as a kind of methodologist of what Rank calls the striving force. He is not so much concerned with theory building as what one might call world view, with the construction of varieties of creative experience – of the individual and the cosmos manifested in her, and of the cosmos and the individual manifested in it.[17] This is the view of the creative artist. As Rank might have it, pay not with the interpretative theoretical understanding of system building and scientific rationalization which is intended to insure against doubt, but with the immediate experiencing of a world view. Accordingly, much of Sloterdijk's critique of the 'undeclared counter-reformation' (GZ, 17) taking place in modern Western society concerns its lack of will, its attenuated and too comfortable world view, a state of passivity which is made possible by the construction of an atomized and isolated bubbling foam which relies on the creation of the meaningless difference of 'private skies'. He wants to achieve a new 'multicivilizational' balance in which we could continually ask, without guilt, not 'how can we be less excessive . . . but which of our excesses brings us the life we want? And, of course, how are we going to find this out?'[18]

Then, the Nietzschean legacy endures in another way in

Sloterdijk's work too. Nietzsche understood the Moderns as slaves to the pursuit of happiness and the moral denial of social life. He took Kant to be the main retailer of this view, a philosopher who produced a norm ethics which had taken over from the ethics of the Ancients, which was based on virtue and character, in an attempt to produce a science in which morals must be context-free and virtue and character become, like the passions, simply an auxiliary to norms and precepts, mere inclinations. Again, space allows virtue back in as a surround which is more than an inclination. Virtue and character, passion and emotion can again take their rightful place in the pantheon since they can no longer be reduced to mere context but rather again become a part of the ethical scaffold of the world. Indeed, they can become prime movers of the live/think of building surrounding (RT).

In other words, by adding in space, it is possible to add all manner of things into the world, to, quite literally, give them a rightful place. But this is not a case of back to the Ancients. Sloterdijk is well aware that Kant cannot simply be cast aside like some kind of nagging termagant. Rather, he wants to convert the world into a kind of filmic map in which both the big picture and the minute details can survive, both the experience of physical history and the flow of ideas, both ambience and demarcation, both survival and novelty, all played out as both succession and distribution. Some spaces are preternaturally Kantian moments of order, others are moments of Nietzschean passion. It all matters. These different aspects of space are brought together as landscaping organisms which both produce the world and hedge it in, forming within their orbit atmospheres that gradually take on a life of their own. They act as selective animations with their own dynamic momentum that resembles a climatic regime in that it both creates a new medium and makes it possible to breathe within it, whether the air be fresh or stale.[19] Hence, the Sloterdijkian emphasis on atmospheres and what might be called the pursuit of air quality and, alongside this emphasis, the instigation of regimes of detoxification.

Building Space

But what does a methodology of world building look like? It looks like both a technology of the spirit and an empirics. In other words, it flows easily into cosmological questions but, and this is crucial, it retains its links with all the minutiae of everyday life. The two cannot be separated out. So philosophy (of a certain processual stripe) and social science (of a certain processual stripe) come together as a socio-technical mixture, which is itself a part of what is being constructed. Indeed they can no longer be held apart since they are a part of a technology of world-building in which human beings can no longer be treated as the measure of all things in the classic correlationist manner in which there is no human without world and no world without human. The world is not an object for thinking subjects in the way espoused by so many philosophers but rather a continual snowfall of events which are held in place by what spaces it is possible to construct and breathe in, what interiors it is possible to make possible.

The world is immiscible then: it is worlds, always, and these worlds are not all human since all entities can make links. There is no 'universe as a whole'. In this pluraversalistic conception, space becomes pivotal since it is the medium of contact, the means through which dormancy is turned into psyche,[20] the stuff of worlds and world-building. It also explains why the thematic of birth and rebirth is so crucial to Sloterdijk. It provides room, both literally and metaphorically, for whole species of spaces to grow and bloom, spaces of empire, spaces of capital, spaces of signal and communication, spaces of eros, spaces of dreams.

Philosophically, *Sphären* is many things, therefore: as I have already pointed to, an updating of Nietzsche which in adding willedness as an actual project of spatial engineering concretizes and makes explicit the work of striving; as a supplement to Heidegger which adds in space but in doing so changes everything that Heidegger stood for; or even as an 'Egyptian' extension of Derrida in which space is a kind of decentred, even fractured latency. But it also has to be seen in its own terms as an attempt to move philosophy into new domains. What if philosophy allowed the world to speak back? What if it varied its methodology, moving into diagrammatic domains formerly regarded as 'unphilosophical'? What if it formed a new umbilical (or rather umbilicals) to the world (or rather worlds)?

A New Methodology, A New Prospect

To throw some light on these questions, three frames might be brought into alignment which can help us in pursuing such an ambition. One frame that begins to point us in the right direction might be thought of as a kind of anti-philosophy or, more accurately, a non-philosophy which argues that most modern continental philosophy is based on a common syntax which disables it from the start, so to speak. In other words, the start needs redefining.[21] Interestingly, such a non-philosophy exactly grapples with the issue of examples in this domain of knowledge. Thus Laruelle, surely correctly, calls for much greater emphasis on philosophers' use of examples, as symptomatic of a specific structure of thought which produces a relation of the universal to the singular, what Laruelle calls, somewhat clumsily, 'empirico-transcendental parallelism'. According to him what distinguishes one philosophical form from another is simply how this form is filled in for any particular case. Although Laruelle's critique ends up with a specific solution which seems to me to be unconvincing, effectively to jettison the need for such a correlation between the universal and the singular, still he provides a step on the way to another conception of how philosophy might proceed, which is also a social scientific entrée.

Another frame that begins to point us in the right direction is a diagrammatic turn which can lead thought in new directions.[22] In this turn, thinking in diagrams becomes a necessary outline of a process without fixed endpoints, a set of moving forms, a comprehensive showing of spatialization which creates both a world and a means for other worlds to react to it. Texts continue to be central to philosophy but they are off-sided by other means of representation of thought. 'I'm willing to bet that at this point in time, the

best philosophical way to prove the possibility and reality of movement is not to walk away, as Bergson recommended to Zeno, but
to take the line for a walk, as Paul Klee said.'[23] Yet another frame,
one which completes the reorientation, is what has come to be
called speculative realism, a form which seems to me to come
closest to what Sloterdijk is trying to achieve in that it provides
room for both the hyperbolic and the singular in one package.
Thought can be pushed in new directions with the emphasis being
on the push provided by igniting entities which either lie dormant
or conspire to have effects which we cannot see but can still apprehend in however an inchoate manner, as plasma or dark matter.[24]
In this way, new attachments to the world can be made.

The construction of the thought collectors which would
presage a new methodology of 'hyper-drawing'[25] would more
closely approximate the contours and confines of space as it moved
attachments around rather than seeing either space or attachments
as static lumps of influence. That methodology – *experimental rather
than illustrative* – would have the following characteristics. First,
it would not, could not, be narrowly text-based. It would move
beyond conventional orthography and take up other registers of
representing the world. Second, it would understand that thought
itself is a map. Ideas travel and often but not always mutate as they
do so. Sometimes they travel well, sometimes badly.[26] Third, it
would acknowledge the skills of world-building as being precisely
that – skills, to be learnt, digested, and worked upon. Thoughtful
gardening mixed periodic convulsions of landscaping, in other
words.[27] Fourth, it would no longer talk about the world as though
it were just one thing that can be critiqued in the grand and grandiose manner that we all learnt from eighteenth and nineteenth
century philosophers and which still continues to frame what an
intellectual is supposedly meant to do.[28] Fifth, it would be equally
at home with hyperbolic claims and the empirical detail that always
provides a corrective and the consequent proliferation of performative methodologies which allow thought to bring the world
into existence by inventing new co-ordinates and following new
paths.

All around, there are signs that such a methodological amalgam
of philosophy, the social sciences and the creative arts is coming

about, is making its way into the world, as explicit world-making practices[29] which are concerned with simultaneously producing new prospects and prospecting and which are busily redefining what we regard, to come back to the first paragraph of this chapter, as *evidence*. It can be seen in the growth of work which does not stop at the conventional academic boundaries but pushes on through into actual practices of building and experimenting, both at once. It can be seen in the effort to produce new political fora, in physical as well as ideational forms.[30] It can be seen in the elucidation of new forms of performance. It can be seen in the ways in which formerly separate disciplines are bleeding into each other as they perform each other's domains: human geography, performance, installation and site-specific art, architecture, design, the material culture elements of archaeology and anthropology, are all binding with philosophy, producing different ways of staging, lighting and understanding worlds and producing new atmospheres.

In turn, such a methodological vision is gradually changing the relationship between continental philosophy and social science. They will no longer be completely separate disciplines but something that describes both an arc and an ark of knowledge Here is a new fertile crescent of spatial experiment generating and generated by gradual mutation,[31] which is united in its search for landscapes of thought/mediums of growth by diagrams that are always more than.[32] And, in provoking this ambition, at least, Sloterdijk's work in *Sphären* surely and confidently lights the way. It becomes a kind of philosopher's stone, able to turn base metals into gold.

9

Literature in Sloterdijk's Philosophy

Efraín Kristal

Literary works offer Peter Sloterdijk important interpretative paradigms, not just examples to illustrate his insights, which the German thinker translates from an artistic into a philosophical register, resisting being exclusively located in either of them. His ideas with respect to literature resonate with some views expressed by the early R. G. Collingwood regarding the connections between art and life, if it were possible to decouple them from a Hegelian vocabulary (of mind and spirit), and engage them with the concerns of post-humanist thinkers who resist positivist or empirical attempts to naturalize cultural or artistic expression. For Collingwood 'art is practical: in art the mind is trying to bring itself into a certain state and at the same time to bring its world into a certain state'.[1] Collingwood also argued that 'from the historical point of view the work of art does not exist as such; all that exists is the imaginative act, and this imaginative act is a resultant or expression of activities which are not imaginative. Hence there is no history of art; there is only the history of humanity.'[2]

Literature matters to Sloterdijk because it is an art, and art, for him, is a privileged activity in the creation of the world in which we live, particularly in our post-metaphysical age:

The development of the concept of art and the discovery of philosophical aesthetics coincide with the demise of metaphysics. The whole of the area of so-called 'higher worlds' or 'highest values' entered a period of decline towards the end of the eighteenth century since it had become impossible to avoid the perception that the whole of any such area was something that we ourselves had created. Something that we ourselves have created can't be addressed with the same kind of belief that was appropriate to something created by a god. Ever since the end of the eighteenth century, this became a kind of twilight zone where it was also possible to see the danger of a growth of nihilism, and it was there that art began to assume an enormous importance, and precisely because art makes it clear that it has a non-nihilistic way of coming to terms with the fact that we ourselves are responsible for the creation of what we think of as the essential. Art defends the truth of life against flat empiricism and deadly positivism, which are no longer capable of an awareness of anything more than facts and which are therefore incapable of culling the energy to create new inter-relationships of vital or living forces.[3]

Many of Sloterdijk's books are accompanied by reproductions of paintings, photographs, sketches, diagrams, or architectural designs, which serve to illustrate a point or to make one, but notwithstanding his extensive reliance on the visual arts, literature holds a privileged place in his philosophical writings. The author of *Sphären* is an avid reader of poetry and narrative fiction; he wrote a doctoral thesis on the poet Heinrich Heine; a considerable number of his philosophical reflections involve the commentary of literary works; he published *Der Zauberbaum* (1985), a novel in which he began to explore ideas that came into focus in later books; his writings adopt and adapt various kinds of literary modalities in order to develop or present philosophical ideas, such as the imaginary dialogue between a historian, a theologian and a literary critic with which the *Sphären* trilogy comes to a close; and on numerous occasions he has sought insights in imaginative writings – not just literary exemplifications of concepts or insights that have already been expressed or worked out by himself or others – to address problems where the philosophical tradition has had little, or perhaps less to offer. Sloterdijk is persuaded that a work of literature can surpass, not just the form in which ideas are presented, but even the conceptual sophistication of certain philosophical schools, especially in the domain that matters to him the most, a domain in which even Nietzsche and Heidegger – the philosophers to whom he has devoted more commentary than any others – have fallen short, namely, the philosophical exploration of life as it is actually lived:

> Existentialist philosophies are in the rearguard of a literature about lived experience with which creative writers went beyond the wisdom of philosophers, including Heidegger's audacious academicism. Philosophical theories of everyday-life – whether they deal with labor, politics, or communicative action – pale in comparison to the great explorations of subjectivity, from Shakespeare to Joseph Conrad, Camões to Gabriel García Márquez, and Machiavelli to Dostoyevsky; not only on account of their superior representational adroitness, but even from a conceptual point of view. (WK 113–14)

In a series of lectures on the connections between language, literature and life, Sloterdijk argued that life and literature are closely bound: 'If literature were just literature and life just life, it would be impossible to make connections between the problems of literature and those of life. [. . .] In the final analysis, a strict demarcation between literature and life can not be made so easily' (ZWK 35–36).[4]

In his philosophical meditations on human existence, Sloterdijk draws on literature and literary conceits to illustrate his own insights, but he often also draws on literature and literary conceits to work through and to unearth them. A pun on Heidegger's *Sein und Zeit* (*Being and Time*) in the title of *Zorn und Zeit* (*Rage and Time*, 2006) allows Sloterdijk to suggest the substantive point that resentment may be a more productive concept to account for human projects in time than the Heideggerian emphasis on a human being's concern with respect to their own death; and even though Sloterdijk had explored the notion of resentment in his meditations on Nietzsche, and in other writings on the dynamics of rancor and violence, it is not until he engages with a work of literature – in this case with Homer's *Iliad* – that Sloterdijk is able to transform inchoate insights into a vigorous psychological theory with anthropological and historical implications.[5]

In *Zorn und Zeit* Sloterdijk's exploration of the angry, wounded pride of Achilles is the starting point of his corrective to psychological theories which reduce a constellation of feelings including pride and ambition to underlying libidinal forces or death impulses. According to Sloterdijk, feelings which can generate vengefulness and resentment when they are not satisfied amount to 'a second fundamental force in the psychic realm' (ZZ 28) which co-exists and interacts with the erotic drive.

In his attempt to set the ground-work for a philosophical theory of globalization, in *Im Weltinnenraum des Kapitals. Für eine philosophische Theorie der Globalisierung*, Sloterdijk does not hesitate to underscore a philosophical dimension in Jules Verne's depiction, in *Around the World in Eighty Days*, of a traveller whose main reason for travelling is to address the logistics of travel itself: 'Phileas Fogg . . . did not have to pretend that there was anything essential to be learnt about the world during his travels. Jules Verne is the best of Hegelians, therefore, because he had understood that in an organized world substantive heroes are no longer possible, but only heroes of a secondary kind' (WK 67). Sloterdijk is not simply claiming that Jules Verne's novel resonated with concepts that were available in the philosophical literature, his point is that the novelist was able to express a philosophical understanding that was ahead of, and in some ways beyond, the current philosophical discourse on globalization: 'It was not, however, a philosopher who was able to formulate the true concept of the ambitions of the subject in the age of mobilization, but a novelist, Jules Verne, who in the motto of his Captain Nemo: MOBILIS IN MOBILI (mobility in the mobile element), had articulated the formula for the era' (WK 145–6).

In Sloterdijk's philosophical writings literary terms, concepts, and practices such as fiction, narrative and metaphor play a central rather than decorative role in his mode of philosophical exposition and analysis. It would take a monograph to explore the full dimension of Sloterdijk's philosophical engagements with literature. My aim here is limited: to discuss three topics which exemplify Sloterdijk's engagements with narrative in general, and some narrative fictions in particular, which will also serve as an introduction to two of his central philosophical concerns: his views on psychology which disavow the illusion of the autonomous individual, and his views on our 'post-historical' moment in which the work of deconstructionists has come to closure because the task at hand is to understand how the world has changed. The three topics are (1) Sloterdijk's inclination towards narrative as a tool of philosophical investigation; (2) his fictional account of the discovery of the unconscious in his only novel *Der Zauberbaum*, in which its protagonist has intimations that his sense of self is an illusion; and (3) his use of Thomas Mann's biblical novel *Joseph and his Brothers* to situate the legacy of Jacques Derrida – in the context of post-metaphysical philosophy in the 'post-historical' moment – as the metaphysician whose philosophy signals the end of the historical period, and the beginning of the post-humanist phase which is our own.

The prism through which I will discuss these three topics is Sloterdijk's 'Theory of the Spheres', one of the most vigorous attempts to pay homage, and to reach beyond the post-modernist disavowal of formalist and universalist paradigms, not only because these vulnerable paradigms are susceptible to political critique or to conceptual deconstruction, but also because the world has changed dramatically since the 1970s, and we are in a situation in which, as Sloterdijk has put it in different meditations: 'it is no longer possible to understand the future as a continuation of the past' (ZB 115). It is also not enough to criticize the paradigms of the past, if one is indifferent to the changes that have taken place.[6]

The presupposition that we are still living in a social or artistic universe of pre-set perennial human values, a hardened reality of the human condition, is no longer tenable. The relativism of some post-modernist, post-colonial, gender, and identity theorists may or may not be persuasive to some, and it may be irritating to others, but it is neither trivial nor arbitrary: it is symptomatic of transformations that have already taken place. As the French philosopher Yves Michaud – who has written a book about Sloterdijk – has argued, 'we have entered a new era. Modernity came to an end two or three decades ago, and post-modernity was a convenient name . . . to acknowledge the passing of modernity.'[7]

There is no reason to be nostalgic about the past, or bitter about changes that have taken place, but it is no longer enough to question, unmask, debunk, or deconstruct the bankrupt paradigms of the past. It is time to acknowledge that we have entered a new era, and Sloterdijk's philosophical project is an impressive attempt to reconsider the past, giving pride of place to its discontinuities with respect to the present; to consider contemporary predicaments of a globalized world informed by new media and new technologies that have evolved with human life itself; and to work towards new ways of social co-existence and co-operation with an understanding of the world as it is, without feelings of melancholy or resentment about historical narratives that are no longer relevant; but without fear of experimenting with new narratives that may tell us how we have arrived where we are. And if some of the historical narratives that guided the way in which many humans lived were fictions or fantasies that were taken all too seriously – and which therefore had an impact on the course of history, or in the way historical moments have been experienced or understood – then it makes sense to study the consequences of having taken these fictions as guiding paradigms. There is an acknowledged Nietzschean and Heideggerian underpinning in Sloterdijk's critique of the ease with which humanity can delude itself about life as it is lived.

Sloterdijk's fundamental insight involves a concentrated critique of individualism (or the illusion of the self-sufficiency of the individual), inspired by Heidegger's notion of a horizon of shared intersubjective experience.[8] For Sloterdijk co-existence is the key to a proper understanding of the complexities of micro and macro historical situations, psychological processes, and our relationship to space. But if for Heidegger – who privileged time over the spaces in which intersubjective experience unfolds – there was a single horizon of human experience against which inauthentic experiences or idle philosophical chatter can be measured, Sloterdijk conceives of a plurality of horizons associated to the spatial configurations of lived experience, some of which can be more ephemeral or enduring than others. Sloterdijk is concerned with the effects of inauthenticity (as opposed to Heidegger's derision of it) in as much as it impoverishes the possibility of gregarious human co-existence. Sloterdijk distances himself from Heidegger's Romantic attraction to death as the ultimate gauge of a human project. He offers a correction to the Heideggerian turn in the Hermeneutical tradition, and its central metaphor of a horizon of human experience, as he adopts a metaphor better suited to capture both the temporal and spatial dimensions of life as it is lived: the metaphor of a sphere (and related metaphors such as the globe, foam, and bubbles) to suggest a plurality of possibilities of intersubjective constructions of space. The sphere is the most salient example of the centrality of a metaphor in Sloterdijk's thinking, as it is also the title and organizing principle of his most important philosophical work.

On Narratives and Spheres

For Sloterdijk the notion of self-contained or self-sufficient individuals who negotiate their existence with others, with objects and with their natural environment is an illusion akin to the illusion that individuals are best understood in terms of their place in a single, all-encompassing cosmos; but to the extent that individuals and peoples (and philosophers) have held these views, narrative is a privileged approach to philosophical enquiry. Narrative is an effective means to explore the vicissitudes of an illusion. Sloterdijk has sometimes spoken about *Sphären II* as a philosophical novel, perhaps because the book focuses on the effects of a fiction, which was taken seriously over centuries in Western culture in the period that Sloterdijk has referred to in different contexts as either the metaphysical or the historical age, namely the fiction that human-ity is at the literal or metaphorical centre of the universe. It makes sense that tools of literary analysis, such as narrative and fiction, are part of Sloterdijk's philosophical repertoire.

Sloterdijk defines his fundamental concept of the 'sphere' as 'a world formatted by its inhabitants',[9] or as 'the spaces where people actually live. I would like to show that human beings have, till today, been misunderstood, because the *space* where they exist has always been taken for granted, without ever being made conscious and explicit.'[10] From this perspective the fundamental microcosm is not the self-contained individual but that which takes place

when at least two bodies interact in a relation of co-existence
which is both spatial and psychological, and which includes the
objects, machines in our negotiations with physical and cultural
environments from which we seek protection or immunization. If, for Marshal McLuhan, the medium is the message, for
Sloterdijk the medium is us, at least as metonymy, as we are a
component of the medium: along with other beings, objects, and
architectural spaces with which we shelter and protect ourselves.
The first volume of his trilogy *Sphären I (Blasen. Mikrosphärologie)*
is devoted to the dynamic space of the couple as the minimal unit
of psychological and sociological reflection, as he summarized the
fundamental idea of this volume: 'Where is the individual? The
sphereological answer would be: it is first and mostly a part of a
couple, where what is important is not just the discernible couple,
but above all, the invisible or virtual dual structure' (ST 146). The
second volume of the trilogy *Sphären II (Globen. Macrosphärologie)*
is devoted to the processes whereby this fundamental microcosm
expands, giving place to political, theological, architectural and
other attempts to fashion literal and metaphorical visions of a globe
or a cosmos that can encompass the totality of human experience.
For Sloterdijk the attempt to create such an all-encompassing
globe or cosmos corresponds to the great monotheistic religions,
to metaphysical and imperial projects; all of which were doomed
to instability and failure: if the sphere is excessively large it will
leave many unprotected and it will also become a space susceptible
to abuse. In Sloterdijk's view there was an intrinsic self-destructive
mechanism in the totalizing projects of culture since these are
'attempts to force an impossible equivalence between home and
the cosmos against the evidence of imperial alienation' (S II 229).
On the political level the all-encompassing sphere is a metaphor for
totalitarianism, the great temptation of what Sloterdijk has labelled
the 'historical period'. It is with a measure of irony and provocation
– and a sense that his pronouncement must be nuanced in order to
fine-tune an important insight – that Sloterdijk has made the bold
claim that we may be living in a 'post-historical' world:

the only event which can properly be called historical is the journey
that starts in the mid fifteenth century with the conquest of the

ocean by Portuguese navigation and the first voyage of Christopher Columbus and culminates around the middle of the twentieth century with the founding of a post-colonial world system marked on the one hand by the institution of a global monetary system [. . .] and on the other hand by the process of decolonization during the 1950s. The final chapter of this series of events was in 1974 with the Portuguese retreat from their overseas possessions after the famous Carnations Revolution. So history in this precise sense of the term lasted from 1492 to 1974.[11]

The proper abode for human co-existence, for Sloterdijk, is not the totalizing sphere, which was the grounding illusion of the historical period, but other spaces in which solidarity and co-operation can flourish. Sloterdijk makes his point with eloquence in *Sphären II*, in his suggestive interpretation of Dante's *Inferno* as a phenomenology of negativity: a realm without immunity intended for the dissidents of the universal order. In Sloterdijk's analysis Dante's Satan is a melancholic genius, a depressive rebel unable to find an alternative to the universal order, who has excluded himself from communion or community, and as such he is the *a priori* of the individualism presupposed by the illusion of a self-contained individuality. In Dante's afterlife, Satan is literally at the very centre of the universe, and the other denizens of the *Inferno* are worthy of him:

> If the supreme devil can count on partisans, and subjects it is because negation is infectious and because the splendorous image of evil mobilizes great retinues of adepts who are enclosed in themselves. Dante's *Inferno* represents the first wave of individualism: each one for himself and all for the devil. The integration of all individual egotisms into a great kingdom with its own style is the meaning of this image of hell which amazes for its meticulousness. [. . .] Dante investigates with heroic patience, an 'end of the world' in which all sharing of psychic space and all complementation of one by another has ceased. (S II 610)

In the third volume of the trilogy, *Sphären III (Schäume. Plurale Sphärologie)* Sloterdijk explores the heterogeneity of spheres of human co-existence – some of which are more ephemeral and others more enduring – in the pluralistic contemporary period whose complexities, utopias and dystopias are no longer those of the unified sphere, but whose dynamic needs to be taken into account, in order to move beyond the deconstructive gestures towards the past.

Sloterdijk is especially concerned about the fantasies and the illusions of those who are unable to see things for what they are, especially when these fantasies and illusions are taken as realities, and have dire consequences, precisely because they are taken seriously. From this perspective narrative can be a fruitful method for cultural critique. Narrative can offer an account of what happens when a fantasy or an illusion is taken seriously; and it can also offer accounts of how the illusions and fantasies are dissolved in the minds of individuals and collectivities; in historical processes, or through the intervention of those who can face the world without subterfuges, resentments, and whose investigations and narrations are not clouded by their personal or collective will to power. From these considerations a theory of narrative emerges with an anthropological dimension. In a corrective to Aristotle's notion that 'man' is the animal who thinks, Sloterdijk has argued that 'man' is the animal who narrates (ZWK 39). From this perspective, phenomenology, for Sloterdijk, is not just an intensified form of observation with the senses, but a theory grounded in narrative:

> Phenomenology is the narrative theory that makes explicit that which, at the beginning can only be given implicitly. Here to be implicit means: not revealed; in a state of cognitive rest; exonerated from the pressure of development and detailed exploration; given as an obscure proximity which is not yet mobilized in a discursive regime; and not yet participating in a process. To become explicit means, on the other hand to be moved by the current that moves from Lethe to the clearing of the forest, from the fold to the unfolding. (S III 74)

If structuralists and post-modernists were particularly drawn to the stories and essays of Jorge Luis Borges of the 1940s and 1950s, which underscored the arbitrary, it is symptomatic that Sloterdijk would be more attracted to the later period, when Borges elaborated his most daring conceits without subterfuges. Sloterdijk draws on Borges' story 'The Book of Sand' as a parable for the role that narrative fiction necessarily plays in any narrative about the self. Borges' 'book of sand' has an infinite number of thin pages, but lacks a first or a last page. The book's pagination is random, but once a reader turns a page, she will never be able to find it again. The narrator of the story, an Argentine rare book collector purchases the book from a Scotsman who had acquired it from an illiterate man in India. The original owner makes a connection between the book of sand and the metaphor in its name, 'because neither sand nor this book has a beginning or an end'.[12] According to Sloterdijk, Borges' 'book of sand' is a searching philosophical image, which suggests that 'to begin and to begin from the beginning are two very different things' (ZWK 38). For Sloterdijk, our entry into any narrative of our own life is as belated as our entry into Borges' book of sand because the most acute memory cannot account for its own beginnings, and Borges' story becomes a cautionary tale according to which we need to be aware that there is always room for deception and self-deception when beginnings must necessarily have an imaginative component. Sloterdijk's view about the fiction of the biography of the self-contained individual resonates with *Der Zauberbaum*, his philosophical novel, which can be read as an early step towards his theory of the spheres to the extent that it explores a crucial milestone in contemporary thought: the moment in which developments in psychology begin to shatter the illusion of the self-contained autonomous individual.

Der Zauberbaum

Sloterdijk praises the Greek philosopher Xenophon for developing his thought process in 'histories of the spirit or in pedagogical philosophical novels' (S III 74). Many of Sloterdijk's philosophical investigations take the form of narratives, and his novel, *Der Zauberbaum* published in 1985, fourteen years before the first volume of the *Sphären* trilogy, is precisely a pedagogical philosophical novel in this sense. The full title of the novel makes it clear that Sloterdijk is experimenting with a form in which fiction, intellectual history and philosophy are all at play: *Der Zauberbaum. Die Entstehung der Psychoanalyse im Jahr 1785. Ein epischer Versuch zur Philosophie der Psychologie.*

The tree to which the title of the novel refers is the one under which the Marquis de Puységur developed and practised hypnotism, and other psychological experiments in which groups of individuals in trances revealed their inhibitions. These experiments may have been the starting point of our contemporary notion of the unconscious and, in the novel, Sloterdijk underscores the therapeutic potential of collective experiences that can also be dangerous, and he draws a parallel between the release of unconscious forces, and the unleashing of the forces that led to the French revolution.

The novel's central concerns about psychology were incorporated and nuanced in *Sphären I*, most particularly in chapters 3 and 5, in which he argues that the birth of modern psychology in the eighteenth century involved intimations of intersubjective processes, that psychology took a wrong turn when it ignored intersubjectivity, and that a psychological theory in our time should redress this inadequacy: 'The fundamental consistency of intersubjectivity is not in the objective relations between subject and object, nor in the affective transactions between subject and object, but only in those subject–object units which, like resonating cells of a psychical metabolism, precede all other material and communicative activities' (S II 474). Sloterdijk's weariness of psychological approaches that do not pay sufficient attention to intersubjective social dimension continue to inform his most recent writings: 'It is more important now than ever to beware of psychology, which tends to attribute even the greatest projects to small mechanisms in those carrying out the projection' (GZ 135).

The novel is a fictional re-enactment of Sloterdijk's views – buttressed, in part, by Henry F. Ellenberger's findings in *The Discovery of the Unconscious* – that the psychological experiments of Mesmer and of the Marquis de Puységur offered intimations of both psychotherapy and of the sort of historization of psychic space, which are the most important antecedents to Sloterdijk's post-Heideggerian project, and his move from the phenomenological metaphor of the horizon to his own metaphor of the spheres.[13]

Der Zauberbaum is a work of fiction based on the same kind of research that informs Sloterdijk's philosophical writings. The novel was inspired by the life of Jan Van Leyden – a young Viennese medical doctor interested in psychological phenomena, and who witnessed the psychological experiments of de Puységur. Sloterdijk did archival work and discovered writings by Van Leyden, which he incorporated into the novel. But he was just as interested in the creation of a literary character in a process of personal and intellectual discovery of the kind Sloterdijk himself had experienced in his own personal and intellectual trajectory, and he drew on other literary works in his creative process. He dialogues with Diderot's philosophical novel, *Rameau's Nephew*, in the creation of his novel's French atmosphere (he even borrows some characters from Diderot's novel), and with Thomas Mann's *The Magic Mountain* to engage with the German literary tradition of the post-Nietzschean novel. Sloterdijk's Van Leyden's most relevant literary antecedent is the engineer Hans Castorp, the protagonist of *The Magic Mountain*. Like Hans Castorp, Van Leyden is not a particularly extraordinary individual, he is not a public hero of his time; and like Hans Castorp, the protagonist of *Der Zauberbaum* happens to be in the right place at the right time to observe, and to be caught up in a critical intellectual and historical transformation that only the narrative voice of a novelist with a philosophical power of synthesis can bring into focus to a reading public whose perspective includes the fact that the transformation the character is experiencing – and was in no position to assess – has already taken place. In the case of Hans Castorp, the transformation involves the crisis of European thought as the Great War is about to break out; and in the case of Van Leyden, the crisis involves the unravelling of the religious and aristocratic order as the French revolution is about to transform the European political landscape, a historical event whose analogue, according to Sloterdijk, is the move from the metaphysical to the post-metaphysical age.

When he wrote *Der Zauberbaum*, Sloterdijk had not yet come upon the metaphor of a sphere to replace the phenomenological metaphor of a horizon, but some of the central concerns of

Sphären, are anticipated in the novel: it is set in a period in which the compensations of religion are breaking down, in which history takes revenge on some idealists and utopians by allowing them to become witnesses to horrors committed in the name of universal ideals, and in which its protagonist has intimations of a transformation that is taking place at the psychic level, which resonates with the historical events of the moment, and which also resonates with the creation of the concept of the unconscious, with its contemporary secular and clinical inflections, many years before Sigmund Freud engaged with it in his epoch-making psychological investigations. There are several passages of the novel that Sloterdijk reworked into the first volume of *Sphären*. Indeed, some of the observations by the main character prefigure Sloterdijk's investigations in the trilogy, as when he says 'I often have the idea of not knowing what I mean when I say I' (ZB 139). As the protagonist gains poetic intimations of the dissolution of his individual self, he gains intimations of a co-existence which transcends the notion of Cartesian subjectivity and which amounts to a cosmic parody of Descartes' *cogito ergo sum*: 'Man is a thinking meteorite. Only in contact with what exists does his surrounding catch fire. Through my incandescence appears what exists and makes sense as a surrounding. I burn, and therefore, it can't be that there is nothing. If I burn, it is because I am here to co-exist with the rest of what is here' (ZB 282). The notion of a burning atom was a metaphor that was useful to Sloterdijk to suggest the intimation that the subjective self was being dissolved in order to experience a sense of co-existence. This metaphor was no longer useful to Sloterdijk when he developed his theory of the spheres for which a more searching response would be the acknowledgement that humans participate in relations of co-existence that already exist, or in the construction of new ones. When he transposed sections of *Der Zauberbaum* into *Sphären I*, Sloterdijk eliminated the metaphor of the burning ego along with its Buddhist suggestions that the annihilation of the ego makes it possible to experience feelings of ecstasy and of communion with a cosmic order. Instead he developed his more nuanced view that human beings participate in spheres of various kinds. That being said, Sloterdijk's impulse to critique the illusion of the autonomous individuality in *Der Zauberbaum* is consistent with the main theme of *Sphären I*, and with his move from an adherence to deconstructive gestures, such as the deconstruction of the individual, to his critique of deconstruction as an endpoint for philosophical analysis.

Derrida, an Egyptian

For Sloterdijk, psychoanalysis takes a wrong turn if it fails to pay sufficient attention to the intersubjective, but the birth of psychology – as he had explored it in *Der Zauberbaum* and in *Sphären I* – had the potential to unearth an intersubjective component and psychic forces other than libidinal ones. His critique of the self-contained autonomous individual amounts to a deconstruction, but Sloterdijk is weary of deconstruction as the main thrust of a philosophical method which is unable to go beyond the unravelling of illusions. This is why *Sphären I* is not just a deconstruction of the notion of the autonomous subjectivity, it is also an attempt to map out the dynamics of the couple as the minimal anthropological unit. Sloterdijk also addresses Derrida's deconstructive project in as much as it resonates with his own views of the historical period as the one explored in *Sphären II*; but he is not simply interested in identifying illusions, he is also interested in exploring the consequences of taking those illusions seriously. For Sloterdijk, Derrida's main limitation, was his inability to move beyond the renewal of deconstructive gestures, or more precisely his sense of comfort with endless deconstruction, and his reluctance to describe and explain the human spaces in which we live, which is also a limitation Sloterdijk attributes to Heidegger. Sloterdijk agrees with Niklas Luhmann's view that Derrida's deconstruction 'is a rigorous but dated theoretical behaviour' (DE 6).

In *Derrida, an Egyptian* Sloterdijk argues that the father of deconstruction lived at a time in which it was no longer tenable to develop a holistic theory that would integrate metaphysical thinking into a coherent whole. The instructive paradox of Derrida is that the last chance of a theory of integration was a general theory of disintegration. The movement from stability and centre to stability of sorts by way of flexibility and decentring reflects the bankruptcy of totalizing views at a time when they have lost their explanatory force, or the illusion that they ever had it. Deconstruction may well be the last 'holistic' philosophy, and Derrida's philosophical legacy may well be the last general theory as a theory of disintegration.

In a bold gesture, which recalls Derrida's own daring juxtaposition of philosophical and literary figures (such as Hegel and Jean Genet in *Glas*), Sloterdijk argues that Derrida's trajectory had been prefigured in Thomas Mann's monumental novel, *Joseph and His Brothers*. Mann's novel – which Sloterdijk considers to be 'the secret main text of modern theology' (DE 21) – famously expands a few pages of *Genesis* into a narrative of over 1,500 pages. Its ironic, fictional account of the birth of monotheism and the invention of the unique God is informed by a post-Nietzschean sensibility, as when the narrator outlines

> a tremendous fact, which had to do with the outward side of God as well as with the inward greatness of Abraham, whose own actual creation it probably was: the fact that the contradiction in terms of a world which should be living and at the same time just resided in God's greatness itself; that He, the living God, was not good, or only good among other attributes, including evil, and that accordingly His essence included evil and was therewith sacrosanct; was sanctity itself and demanded sanctity.[14]

In the novel Abraham is presented ambiguously as the creator of a monotheistic God whose metaphysical dimensions would be worked out by the theologians of the future. If God in the novel is Abraham's invention, Joseph's own encounters with the divine take place mostly in the form of dreams; and, following the biblical story with post-Freudian irony, Joseph's prestige depends on his ability to investigate the content of dreams.

In Sloterdijk's analysis *Joseph and his Brothers* is 'a psychoanalytical and novelistic subversion of the Exodus story' (DE 21). There is an ambiguity in the novel (and here Sloterdijk offers a nod to Derrida's famous analysis of the ambiguity in the word 'pharmakon', which means both remedy and poison, in his meditation on the pharmacy of Plato) in which a crime is the best thing that could have happened to its victim. Joseph is sold by his brothers as a slave to a rich Egyptian, but as Sloterdijk points out – in a commentary that presupposes Freud's assumption that Moses was an Egyptian – 'a sharp-witted hetero-Egyptian brought into Egypt through a second distortion could indeed have the ability to understand the homo-Egyptians better than they understood themselves. This hermeneutical superiority was the gift of his marginality' (DE 23).

For Sloterdijk, Joseph's interpretation of Pharaoh's dreams in Thomas Mann's novel is a 'subtle parody of psychoanalysis' because the novel is set up to make the following analogy: Joseph is to the Egyptians what Freud was to his patients: 'What Thomas Mann had in mind was the career of Sigmund Freud, who, by suggesting a science of dream analysis, had succeeded in making the late feudal society of the Habsburg Austro-Egyptians dependent on his interpretations' (DE 24). To situate Derrida's hermeneutical interventions, Sloterdijk cites Ernst Bloch and Walter Benjamin as a second wave of dream interpretation after Freud in as much as they give a political dimension to Freud's approach to interpretation. If Joseph is to the Egyptians what Freud is to the Habsburgs, then Bloch and Benjamin are to the dreams of the masses what Freud was to the dreams of the wealthy bourgeoisie.

In this line of thinking, Derrida's deconstructive enterprise is the third wave of interpretation of dreams. In Derrida's radical semiology

> the signs of being never provide the wealth of meaning that they promise – in other words: being is not a true sender, and the subject cannot be a place of complete collection. Derrida interpreted Joseph's fate by showing how death dreams in us – or, to put it differently – how Egypt works in us. 'Egyptian' is the term for all constructs that can be subjected to deconstruction – except for the pyramid, that most Egyptian of edifices. (DE 27)

Sloterdijk concludes this reflection by pointing out that the Pyramid is the ideal architectural embodiment of deconstruction: 'It stands in its place, unshakeable for all time, because its form is nothing other than the undeconstructible remainder of a construction that, following the plan of its architect, is built to look as it would after its own collapse' (DE 27). To put it in Sloterdijk's metaphorical terms, the limitation of deconstruction is its inability to move beyond the pyramidal shape. In this spirit, Sloterdijk is also careful to point out that for all of his reliance on architectural metaphors, Derrida was not engaged with the practices of contemporary architecture:

[Derrida] always remained distant from the world of modern architecture, and used such terms as constructing/deconstructing purely metaphorically, without ever developing a material connection between the practice of building truly contemporary, i.e. demystified buildings free of historical baggage.) He apparently had the same tendency, symbolically speaking, as people who are condemned always to live in old houses – or even haunted castles, even if they think they are residing in neutral buildings of the present. (DE 36)

This observation brings us back in full circle to Sloterdijk's post-Heideggerian project, which involves an engagement with our contemporary dwellings, the central concern in Sloterdijk's thinking. Sloterdijk is a philosopher who takes seriously both the metaphors of construction and deconstruction, but also the architectural realities of the dwellings that shape the heterogeneous patterns of our current psycho-social co-existence, for better and for worse; and in this process Sloterdijk is unwilling to move away from a zone of philosophical mediation, in which he has chosen to give literature, and literary practices, a central role:

As long as I can, I will always resist the pressure to chose between philosophy and poetry. Philosophy has every reason to consider with more precision the virtual realm of rationality in poetic languages, and the wisdom of poetic discourse, in order to develop fruitful theoretical models. (ST 157–8)

10

The Time of the Crime of the Monstrous: On the Philosophical Justification of the Artificial

Peter Sloterdijk
(translated by Wieland Hoban)

As we approach the bimillennium, we begin to look upon the Modern Age as a period in which monstrous things are achieved by human perpetrators – entrepreneurs, technicians, artists and consumers. This monstrous is neither sent by the old gods nor represented by classical monsters; the Modern Age is the era of the man-made monstrous. To be modern, one must be touched by the awareness that, beside the inevitable fact of being a witness, one has been drawn into a sort of complicity with the newer form of the monstrous. If one asks a modern person, 'Where were you at the time of the crime?', the answer is: 'I was at the scene of the crime' – that is to say, within that totality of the monstrous which, as a complex of modern criminal circumstances, encompasses its accomplices and accessories. Modernity means dispensing with the possibility of having an alibi.

The monstrous in a cross-section of modern deeds cannot be summed up in any single term or restricted to a particular field – it is a work of art, but far more than a work of art; it is great politics, but far more than great politics; it is technology, but far more than technology; it is illness, but far more than illness; it is crime, but far more than crime. It is a project, but far more than a project. For this reason, all juridical, aesthetic, politological, technological and pathological discourses are only of limited use in describing the modern world, because these languages serve to check phenomena and document states, but cannot express the supra-phenomenal monstrous of modernity. So the moderns, when they drop their alibis, can be found where this multiple *far more* is premeditated, committed and attested. Modernity is something that can sooner be expressed in confessions than described in programmes. One is involved in it like a fever that provokes its victims into a new mode of being beyond healthy and sick. Complicity with and cognizance of the monstrous in our time is more likely to be confessed in works than recorded at symposia.

From this perspective, theory of modernity is always already, and only ever, possible as a reflection on the sublime in the man-made; it is itself a echo from the monstrous in the sum of the new actions carried out in the time of the crime; its object can be no other than the supra-objective man-made or man-mediated immeasurable. That is why theory, insofar as it explicates the new monstrous, becomes a sublime form. This reveals the decisive reason why thought in modernity can no longer be a metaphysics in the old style – but no mere academic research either. The former was committed to the mission – immemorial even for itself – of interpreting the existent in total as the greatest of all possible domestic spaces; its passion was to carry out the equation of the cosmos and the home; classical metaphysics was sworn into the project of trivializing humans as the temporary inhabitants of a timeless world house. When it did mention the monstrous, it interpreted it directly as the God who makes us, the mortals, suffer whenever He shows Himself or takes action. In classical metaphysics, the monstrous is possible only for God, which is why, in the metaphysical age, sublime theory could only appear as theology. Modern theory, on the other hand, begins from the monstrousness of the humanly possible. It deals, in an anthropological form, with the supra-anthropological content of the newest history of power. For it, humans are the beings that have abandoned their houses – even if only under the pretext of settling into them better. Essentially, the Modern Age is the era of the exit from the house of being. It is the time of the crime of the monstrous.

The man-made monstrousness of the Modern Age has three

faces, three areas of appearance; these reveal themselves as the monstrous in man-made space, the monstrous in man-made time and the monstrous in the man-made thing. Accordingly, I shall begin by speaking of the earth as the represented gathering-place of the human species; then of the millennium as the represented duration of the Modern Age human; and finally of art and technology as the represented power of humans. The decisive representation of the earth in the Modern Age is the European-made and European-used globe as geodicy; the decisive interpretation of history as the realm of human actions is the post-historical millennium as end time without end; and the decisive projection of the coming human possibilities is the future as the advent of power in its threefold quality as the future of organization, the future of apparatus and the future of art.

Geodicy

Today we can face the fact that Jacob Burckhardt's famous Renaissance formula in its principle concept contains an erroneous description, because the event of the fifteenth century that pushed open the door to the Modern Age was not 'the discovery of the world and of humans' but the connection of a human routine structure to the spatial and technological monstrous. What we call the Modern Age is the explosion of the Old European space of possibility through experimenting technologies and arts. That is why Europeans of the late fifteenth century were the model moderns of the Old World, less discoverers than experimenters; expansion routines were their profession; their world-space grew because they knew how to include new space in new routines of reaching out. So the essential quality of the Modern Age is not so much the discovery of unexplored spaces – as if unknown continents had wanted to be woken by Europeans from the slumber of their undiscovered state. The distinctive characteristic of the Modern Age is rather the opening of extended operational spaces by means of new procedures. The nautical routines of the Portuguese and the Spanish brought forth the two Americas as their concrete by-product;[1] the manufacturing routines of architects, doctors and painters in the fifteenth century revealed new horizons of feasibilities as their material result. The world is not everything that is to be discovered; it is everything that can be incorporated into routines of action. In that sense, 'Modern Age' is a name for the execution of the operativistic revolution. It leads to a new state of the world in which mastering higher-degree artificialities will become the norm.

The most important testament to Modern Age routines in reaching out for the cosmic foundation of the species is the production of globes; from the late fifteenth century on, they spread among European earth-users as the primary medium of geological enlightenment. Originating from Greek and Arab prototypes, globes became the dominant signifiers of the operable earth idea from the start of the Modern Age onwards. They not only represented the earth as a geological monad before the eyes of European expansionists with varying accuracy; in a sense, they were what produced the earth as a foil of action for Modern Age mankind in the first place. The earth and the globe form the paradigm of modern semiotics; representational geography marks the start of the 'age of the world picture'.[2] Because the earth was depicted 'accurately enough' on the globe, the truth of meaning for modern users of iconic systems was established; whatever was no more inaccurate in its depictive power than a globe in relation to the earth could be considered sufficiently true.

The oldest surviving globes from the early period of European representations of the complete earth, the Behaim Globe from Nuremberg and the Laon Globe – both from the final decade of the fifteenth century – still show the pre-Columbian outlines of the continents; in graphic terms, they are pre-modern and pre-American. Nonetheless, both offer a perfect demonstration of the new access to the earth's totality among scholars, merchants and ministers in the early Modern Age. They made the earth ready-to-hand [*zuhanden*] for Europeans; with their left hands, the Nuremberg councillors could turn this globe, made in 1492 by the young merchant Martin Behaim, who had just returned from Lisbon with new geographical insights; with a diameter of 50.7 cm, the image of the earth had been reduced to a scale of

1:25,000,000. The metal Laon Globe – with a diameter of 17 cm – could even be held in one hand; at first glance, it might have been mistaken for an imperial orb from the Middle Ages. Nonetheless, the imperial orb and the globe belong to fundamentally different eras: if the imperial orb, as an image from the holy sphere, represents the ball of the existent in the left hand of the German Caesars, this is a feudal symbol of the world that shows how the cosmos lies in a single human hand as a divine fief.[3] The globe, on the other hand, is the profane world-signifier of an age in which all points of the earth were imagined with the central assumption of equal accessibility and exploitability for Europeans – it was no longer a metaphysical symbol, but rather a medium of earthly traffic that had become routine. Even if semanticists felt obliged to remind people that the map is not the land, the majority of Modern Age Europeans did believe that the globe was the earth. This carefree equation expresses the fact that we represent and produce the earth and the globe in the same spirit. The globe is the earth insofar as it reveals the complete use of the earth for human history upon it. The total use of the earth is preceded by the globe lesson, which teaches that all points on the earth's surface can be described through the postulate of homogeneous accessibility and availability for Euro-American interventions.

Consistently with this, the result of the globe era is the acute globalization of human interventions on the earth. Here the man-made monstrous becomes visible. No one can still miss the fact that, in the half-millennium between Columbus's voyage and the first journey into space, the neo-European habit of practical earth-use established itself in the real earthly space. The use of the earth for history takes on – corresponding to the threefold basic definition of history – three different meanings: firstly a dramatic one, insofar as history means a campaign or struggle for supremacy between economic and political empires; here the earth is used primarily as a stage for a play that absolutely must be enacted. Secondly, an economic-alchemical one, insofar as history primarily constitutes an undertaking to acquire wealth; here using the earth means interpreting it as a resource and framework for all fabrications. Thirdly, a reading of history as exodus and emancipation; here everything narrow, local and rooted is liberated into the boundless, into the Promised Land of the everywhere; here using the earth means applying it as a foil for world traffic – as a background for messages, a terrain for crossings and a carrier for transports.

The monstrous in geodicy via the European globe manifests itself in two ways: as a shallow monster, to the extent that the globe provides the model uniform for our cosmic place – with the image of earth as a guide for everyday titanism; or as a deep monster, if we look through the globe to observe the geological monad. This latter – because it is a singularity – can by its nature not be understood, only meditated upon in its uniqueness. As the only encompassing and uncanny house of life, it is an unspeakable individual. Modernity is the time of the crime of the geological monstrous because it carries out the process of geological enlightenment in global operative routines. Thus the twentieth century plays a culminating part in the time of the crime of modernity because, in its course, historical and regional alibis were increasingly eliminated so that all contemporaries could potentially be acquired as witnesses and accomplices to the man-made monstrous. In the twentieth century, the pictorial world exploded primarily in the sense of shallow monstrousness: the image of the earth now provided the frame for the space through which all other images must be transported. The earth became the illustrated magazine on which all other illustrations circulate.

Certainly one also finds works appearing in the great art of modernity which reply to the deep monster that is the earth. Only rarely, however, do they reach the level of equal monstrousness alongside the geological monad. In great works of art, the monstrous of the Modern Age comes to itself as a time of the crime. In this sense, all significant works of thought and form in our age are indirect monuments to our geodicy. They show the state of what is possible on earth. They attest that the humanly possible now always means the monstrous, whether in routine or singular actions. It is of this earth, illuminated by its artistic outbursts, that Heidegger wrote in one of his greatest texts: 'The earth appears as the un-world of errancy. In being-historical terms, it is the errant planet.'[4] Two questions formulated by Deleuze and Guattari answer as if from a different planet: 'Who does the earth think it is?' and 'Who does man think he is?'[5]

Millennium

On the eve of the bimillennium, six world languages have established themselves on what Heidegger, around 1945, termed the 'errant planet': English, the dollar, multinational brands, popular music, the news and abstract art. Their functional commonality is the synchronization of intra-species traffic. Through the effects of the Eurocentric age from 1492 to 1945, there developed on the earth a system of interactions that is realized in economic, diplomatic and informatic routines. The necessity of bringing the 'partners' scattered across the earth into a shared world time takes effect on the basis of all globalization routines. The purpose of all cultural revolutions is synchronization – meaning the initiation of humans into the simultaneity of the earthly present. Hence the Modern Age is always also the age of mankind *en marche*. By annulling the original scattered mode of being among the human species that had prevailed for millions of years and throughout the old regional empires, globalization forced the un-united together in the hazardous form of the current world traffic commune. European expansions and the world market bring the age-old anthropological diaspora to an end. From 1492 onwards, the monstrous in time is the 'world society' squeezed together into a new, simultaneously existing unity. The mental trauma of the Modern Age is not the loss of the middle, but rather the loss of distance from the many others. As a result, modernization takes place as an establishment of temporal communism for the species as a whole. Where humans interpret their position in space and time according to modern standards, they must view themselves as members of a forced commune that no longer permits any escape – whoever has seen globes and the news can scarcely have any illusions about belonging together with the rest of the species; we have now become chrono-communists and bio-communists against our will, as it were, dismayed members of a genetic universal church that surrounds us with relatives on all sides. The modern ones are those who must wonder what the Chinese and the Icelanders are up to today. Robert Walser already found a formula for this at the start of the twentieth century:

> Running around with the problem of nations in one's head – doesn't
> this mean falling prey to disproportion? Dragging in *millions of people*
> willy-nilly, what a burden on the brain! [. . .] In the jumble comprised
> of the sentences above, I think I *hear* in the distance the *Minotaur*, who
> represents, it seems to me, nothing more than the shaggy difficulty of
> making sense of the problem of nations [. . .][6]

The problems of nations are the small change of the question
of mankind, where we view the monstrous as the norm. The
depiction of earth actionism in the 'world picture' is necessarily
followed by a world clock system and a world news system. The
use of both is as far from being harmless as the observing of globes
was in former times; its ultimate consequence is to separate people
from their local histories, their ethnic rhythms and their national
calendars to incorporate them in the homogeneous, synchronous
world time. This makes them active players in the game of the
disproportionate. What we call modernity is complicity with
the synchronous world form; modernization is the adaptation of
forms of life to synchronous world routines; and modernism is the
ethos of this adaptation as the existentialism of synchronization.
It implies the ultimate form of egalitarianism as the equality of all
before the homogeneous earthly present, which realizes itself as
the equality of humans before the news. For news is not simply a
world-language genre in the aforementioned sense among others,
but simultaneously the adjustment from historicism to actualism.
The news systems of today only become possible in a globalized
world form where a homogeneous event space is probed for differences from previous states. The result of such probings is fed into
the pipelines of the synchronous world media; these are, as it were,
the performative of the eternal present of homogenized humanity
with itself. Their only task is to inform the synchronized world of
its synchronization.

There are always some heads of state meeting somewhere
for some world summit on some subject; there are always some
troops advancing, under some pretext and in some numbers, on
some enemy who is accused of some crime; there are always some
currencies falling below some previously unthinkable minimum
levels; there are always some major firms merging with some

others in some joint ventures. There are always some commemorations of some events in some past time taking place on some day with the sympathy of the general public; something is always so-and-so-many years ago and can act as material for some generally consumed memory. There are always some works by some artists being somehow honoured in some retrospectives.

The staging of simultaneity takes place in two ways in the synchronous world: as a culture of currentness, the synchronous culture combs daily through the threads of events in global events to find those knots and differences that stand out sufficiently to attract attention; as an anniversary culture, it ensures that we maintain the same distance from all regionally powerful events from the past. It asserts the rule that all things which once advanced history as potencies and events are now transformed into homogeneous anniversary material. In this sense, the information system of the synchronous world guarantees our incipient post-historicity. We are living in a constant state of transition into it.

Whenever we have reason to think that this transition is irreversible, we also have reason to confirm modernization. Then we count each one of our steps into modernity. It is not implausible that we today, at a very conservative estimate, are located in the fifth modernity, because the Modern Age, as a modernization process, has progressed through at least four crises or major reactions: Counter-Reformation, Romanticism, vitalism and fascism; consequently we are presently in transition to the sixth modernity, as the triumph of constructivism over regionalism and anti-globalism is becoming apparent before our eyes as the – for now – last anti-modernisms.

The persistent final event in the historical world is the current globalization as the production of the constant earthly present. For the current generations, this major man-made event runs through the middle of their lives. It is the monstrous in time. We can tell from it that Modern Age humans are – contrary to the claims of philosophies of history – essentially uninterested in making history, but more concerned with concluding history and bringing about post-historical conditions. The continuous movement towards the eternal present, in which the sum of all events would be zero, was the true project of modernity. In this sense, the idea of the Third

Reich was not simply a fascistoid parody of Christian millenarism as it had developed from Joachim von Fiore to Lessing, Schelling and Saint-Simon; at the same time, it remains the latent matrix for all demanding modernisms, because it was the first to grasp the logical form of a potentially final age with sufficiently formal standards. In order to be modern, perhaps even final, an age must be a third – at least structurally. An age is final if its constitution is such that no matter how much might happen in it, nothing during or after it could be epoch-making. Because of the temporal logic of its design, modernity is actually a constant dawning of a third or millenary age, an incessant crossing-over from history into post-history, a continuous transition into an end time without end. This cannot be any other way, because modernity's ambition to be an age of penetrating self-reflexivity is formally unsurpassable.

The soundness of this claim can be verified by means of a thought experiment in which we ask how, from the perspective of modernity, one might imagine a subsequent epoch. There are two kinds of answer to this: the catastrophic and the continuous. With catastrophic answers, one has to assume that modernization as a whole would be broken off through a completely incommensurable event and diverted in an unpredictable direction – either through a biosystemic disaster or a theological epiphany, or through an extraterrestrial intervention. If we exclude the catastrophic variants from the discourse of modernity and post-modernity on account of their excessive and irrational implications, that leaves only the continuous form of response. According to this, the only thing that could possibly succeed modernity would be a further, later, heightened aggregate state of modernity. Located within its own continuum, modernity is an enduringly accumulative process, and only keeps moving through continuous self-upgrade. That is why the 'project of modernity' futurizes itself. A world process that produces its own futures, however, corresponds to the concept of the millennium or of end time without end. In that sense, the non-excessive version of a theory of modernity is forced at least to admit to the millenarist aspect of the current world form. That is already far more than a conventional theory, one that is committed to a balanced middle ground and proclaims itself as critical, could grant. This concession would bring the monstrous character of modernity's temporal structure alarmingly into view. The conventional forms of modernism, pragmatism and populism, resolutely turn a blind eye to the monstrous to which they belong; they are fanaticisms of normality.

Nonetheless, time has shown that in its temporal structure too, the nature of the Modern Age as the time of a crime is so disproportionate that it cannot be fully formulated in conventional theoretical or programmatic texts. There is no theory of the monstrous, only hyperbolic projections. One can utter them, just as the feeling of going insane can be articulated; one can confess to them as one confesses to sensing that one has committed a crime of an indeterminable nature in a dream. Participation in modernity can only be admitted to like a radical suspicion towards oneself.

Art History and Nothingness History

Having discussed the monstrous as a spatial and temporal form of modernity, we should now speak of the monstrous in the object-forms of modernity. Any contemporary can easily convince themselves of the increasing presence of the artificial in Modern Age lifeworlds. Modernity as a campaign for the increase of comfort and routines of competence implies furnishing 'subjects' with ever more effective equipment for self-enhancement: we have long existed in technologized lifeworlds where classical and cybernetic machines are the leading factor in our shaping of existence. In the light of these evident phenomena, it is easy to assert the interpretation of modernization as artificialization. The law of modernity is the increasing employment of artificiality in all essential dimensions of existence. What is more difficult is defending this finding against the widespread and growing unease in modernness.[7] For the grammars of advanced civilizations are, for the time being, no help to us in the attempt to state the place of the artificial in the real.[8]

All traditional thought forms agree that they stir up a certain suspicion of nihilism towards artefacts; since Plato, the private parts of technology and the world of images have been considered deficient forms of being; at least the self-assured monisms of the Indians let Samsara and Nirvana converge. Within the tradition of thought on being, as embodied in the high forms of Western metaphysics, unease about the artificial is a solid constant. It expresses the fact that a language of being is inadequate for articulating what machines, sign systems and works of art are 'according to their nature'. It seems to be their nature to break with what nature typically is. For everything that is a work claims to negate substantial being through representation and to augment it with invented additions. If anything in the Western tradition is exempt from the suspicion of being mere illusion and nothingness, it is the 'great works' of art, to which even classical thought – reluctantly, as it were – grants a preferred participation in substance and the soul, despite their extreme artificiality.

It is not without significance that some have attempted in recent art history to show that images are based more fundamentally on cult than artifice. Cult too is a derivative of being; it cloaks the images in a gestural, religious, indeed physiological meaning; it wants the foam of signs to begin from the flesh of things, from ritually harnessed life itself. This is easy to understand: if one presupposes the primacy of being, artificialities can only be viewed as ontological bastards in which part of being's wealth had unrightfully been seized by nothingness. Aesthetics and technology theory under the sign of being always and inevitably lead to more or less explicit denunciations of the 'illusory world' as a sphere comprising unnecessary additions to an older stock. Works of art, like those of technology, are really the children of nothingness – at best, half-siblings of the truly existent; they are constructs of ontological injustice, devoid of archetypes and only comprehensible as dilutions of opulence, uncovered in their origins and insubstantial in the strong sense of the word. In them, a supplementary nothing tricks its way into the dense world of natural and essential orders.

One can understand how, with the fundamental growth of the artificial factor in modernity, this line of thought would have to result in a totalizing criticism of the artificial worlds' abandonment by being [*Seinsverlassenheit*]. The last thinkers of being inevitably view themselves as the last ones alive in an environment of colourful death – that is, machines, simulacra and streams of signifiers. For them, the most recent phase of art history is a *danse macabre* illuminated by lost leftovers of souls. The artificial world, viewed with the eyes of the faithful ancients, putrefies as nihilistic voluntarism. At the centre, the curator sits enthroned as the pope of abandonment by reason (or alternatively the director, features editor, cultural consultant or festival director). Heidegger countered this artificial and ontologically secondary world with a first nature still backed by the opulence of origin:

> The birch never exceeds its possibilities. The colony of bees dwells within its possibilities. It is only the will, which established itself in technology with universal validity, that drags the earth into the exhaustion, exploitation and alteration of the artificial. It forces the earth beyond the developed circle of its possibilities into something that is no longer the possible, and is therefore the impossible.[9]

Anyone who wants to read the history of art and technology as a history of being will – as Heidegger's case illustrates – find nothing but terminations everywhere: forgetfulness of being, the end of art history as an interpretation of substance, the fall of humanity into the impossible and multimedial for dead souls. One cannot escape the necessity of admitting to oneself that the history of the artificial can no longer be developed in the style of the history of being. The artificial thing – if conceived from the perspective of being – will never shake off the suspicion of a betrayal of an initial wealth of sense and the soul. The thinking of being is not sufficient for an understanding of what constitutes modernity: de-animism in action and redistribution of subjectivity among humans *and* things. While the advanced civilizations were founded on the discovery and development of the difference between subject and object or soul and thing, modernity destabilized these time-honoured distinctions along with their over-simplifying power. This sets in motion a progressive redistribution in which what were things of the soul are shifted to the sphere of things and the previously subjective into the scope of the objective. Gotthard Günther, to whom we owe the most advanced theory of technology in the twentieth century, points to the world-historical purpose of these shifts:

In the history of technology until now, the relationship between subject and object has been mistakenly described, in so far as traditional thought assigns to the realm of the soul an overflowing wealth of qualities that actually belong on the side of things, where they can be understood as mechanisms of a higher order.[10]

This leads to an unlimitedly far-reaching programme of corrections to the image of themselves that humans fashioned in the period of advanced civilizations.

The process of this correction is to be the central issue in the next major period of world history.[11]

Modernity as the millennium of progressive artificialization then has its substance in the technical as the 'progressive conquest of nothingness'. The depth of the future can only be thought today as a complex of growth dimensions of the artificial. Such an increase, however, can no longer be viewed as a phase in the history of being; if one is to deal with it conceptually, it must be treated as the unfolding history of nothingness. Nothingness is increasingly transpiring as the true element of progressive capacity. If thought must correspond to being, then correspondences with nothing are daring leaps into the operation: wanting, acting and composing are then adequate responses to the realization that in nothingness, although nothing can be identified, anything can be achieved. In this sense, one can say that nothingness is the element of modernity; its beginning was, and shall ever remain, the deed – or, in modern parlance, the undertaking. Through the operatively capable will, enormous steps can be taken in nothingness to increase artificialization; these will provide later thought with the blueprints for reflection on the existent.

If, almost three thousand years ago, classical thought developed under the overwhelming impression of a supposedly ever-complete nature with a seemingly insurmountable headstart on all human action (which provides the logical basis for religious feeling), this thought, already precise, also articulates – despite feeling overwhelmed by the being before it – a mental deed with its own ontological weight whose most distant consequences would only reveal themselves in modernity. By seeking to contemplate the nature of natures, classical reason produced the characteristically metaphysical semblance of sublime calm. Its elements were spirit or stone, both understood as the extreme substantialities that were above all action and made the respective other seem meaningless beside them.[12] Modern thought, on the other hand, is dazed from its own might; it notices itself as power, consummation and capability; increasingly disconcerted, activated and attentive to its own acts, it follows man-made history, which must finally be carried out systematically. It interferes to a constantly growing extent in 'that which is'. In the course of its elevation, it had to approach a point from which the human will would become sufficiently powerful to become a rival of classical substance. Non nature and being lost their ontological monopoly: they found themselves provoked and replaced by successions of artificial creations out of nothingness and the rise of a post-natural world of the will.

It is hardly surprising that the strongholds of being in the age of advanced civilizations always saw a dark shadow creeping around them – it was that same nothingness which could initially (under the predominance of a monovalent concept of being in which only being is, and nothingness is not) only be imagined as that which goes against being, as the void that fools humans with illusions and phantoms. With modern nihilism, however, the power of humans to commit unprecedented and fathomless acts and invent new things, a prime characteristic of the Modern Age, was officially recognized and presented generally under a striking, albeit still defamatory name: nothing now became something – the ontological field presented itself as multivalent. Since then, the malignant appearance of the nothingness of nihilism has peeled away. As we now know, the nothingness of nihilism represents the reverse of creativity – and what modernity would allow itself to be deprived of its birthright to creative life and projections of the will? For the entire world time of coming states of modernity, no doubts are possible about the primacy of the will to artificiality over the willingness to submit to a defined nature or a normative antiquity. No neo-Catholic trends can change that. At the core of modernity, once its conception has been taken further, only inventors, artists and entrepreneurs can play a key role in shaping themselves – and no longer thinkers, in the strict sense of the philosophical tradition. It is obvious that 'thought' per se, as a correlate to the existent, is becoming a merely partial function of the culture of will and projects. The shepherds of being – trapped in the beautiful dream of pure extra-technological existentiality and a purely obedient reflection – move towards the side-lines; in fact, being itself, as the realm of past freedom, now seems like a narrow ontological province – it has been pushed to the periphery of the nothing-'based' empire of will, creations and projects.

One can now observe a flight from being, just as there was a rural flight to the cities; the new entrepreneurs in the project space, the artists, the organizers, the writers of programmes and also the entrepreneurs in the traditional sense are constantly emigrating from the old world of contemplatively sheltered being to settle dynamically in the new world of the nothingness that is open for projects. The typical gesture of these escapees of being is the assumption of leadership by a constructivity reaching for a power that is based on capably continuing. Entrepreneurs and artists do not guard or conserve what 'there is'; they unleash and create works from what has never existed in that form, constantly repulsing the given. Old being and its entity find themselves overgrown with an increasingly powerful supplement of new realizations whose results spread as acts of artificialization in cultures of apparatus and images. What was once called being already resembles a chapel standing amidst skyscrapers – or a proof of God's existence on a computer printout. Out of glass and steel, new working materials and new writing systems, grows an unclosable in-between world that cannot be controlled by any synthesis, and is neither nature nor a will to novelty still incubating unrealized, but rather a crystallized world of apparatus as past will, along with technical refuse as waste from the mass of devalued artefacts; giant cities, museums and rubbish heaps are typical contemporary products of the monstrous as an industry.

Since the seventeenth century, the activation revolution has developed into a self-motivating escalation system. Its consistent success ensures that an end of art history is no more the case than an end of technological history or an end of state history. There is no reason not to believe that the best is being created at this moment or is yet to come. Anyone who thinks they are seeing the imminent end of whatever ahead is drawing mistaken conclusions about world events on the basis of fatigue. What genuinely ends is the possibility of thinking over the histories of art, technology and the will from the perspective of a history of being. Modernity as a world process escalates further, reaching the time of the crime of the openly monstrous; for it remains the form of consummation for an unreconsiderable history of nothingness that primarily has power over reality. The realization that the old natures still require nurturing within it leads, in our time, to the growth of an idea – a historically unprecedented type of conservatism as a space of green concern. Configuring the latter productively with the freedom-historical results of modern forms of society and life: such a task now marks the foremost frontline of the thought that was once called philosophical.

Mankind, therefore, where it extends its horizons of will in constantly expanded routines, can look out into a broadly arranged depth of temporal layers. In this era, whoever relies purely on being will experience wear on all fronts. The power of continuous modernity is the impossibility of exhausting nothingness.

Notes

1 Worlds, Engagements, Temperaments

1 Despite his claim (SV 16) this was not his first book: a version of his doctoral thesis was published as *Literatur und Lebenserfahrung: Autobiographien der Zwanziger Jahre*, München: Hanser Verlag, 1978.

2 Slavoj Žižek, *First as Tragedy, Then as Farce*, London: Verso, 2009, p. 131.

3 Slavoj Žižek, *Living in the End Times*, London: Verso, 2010, p. 236. See pp. 236–41 for a discussion of his views on taxation.

4 Slavoj Žižek, *The Parallax View*, Cambridge, MA: MIT Press, 2006; *Violence*, New York: Picador, 2008. See also Alberto Toscano, *Fanaticism: On the Uses of an Idea*, London: Verso, 2010, pp. 31ff; and his 'Review: Sloterdijk, Sloterdijk and Sloterdijk'; *TPM. The Philosopher's Magazine*, No. 48, 2010, http://www.philosophypress.co.uk/?p=1006

5 Translations of the titles of Sloterdijk's books can be found at the beginning of this volume. Throughout, a title in English means the book is already translated; a title in German means that there is no existing English version.

6 Wouter Kusters, 'Peter Sloterdijk; a Psychonaut in Outer Space',

2000. The original link to this piece is dead, but it has been archived at http://www.bloggers.nl/obelisk

7 For a discussion, see WF 213–33.

8 Michel Foucault, *Le courage de la vérité: Le gouvernement de soi et des autres II: Cours au Collège de France, 1984*, edited by Frédéric Gros, Paris: Gallimard/Seuil, 2009, p. 165.

9 For generally positive appropriations, see William Chaloupka, *Everybody Knows: Cynicism in America*, Minneapolis: University of Minnesota Press, 1999; and Wilber W. Caldwell, *Cynicism and the Evolution of the American Dream*, Washington, DC, Potomac Books, 2006.

10 Alain Finkielkraut and Peter Sloterdijk, *Les battements du monde: Dialogue*, Paris: Pauvert, 2003, p. 23.

11 On this book and their relation, see Dalie Giroux, 'Nietzsche et Sloterdijk, corps en resonance', *Horizons philosophiques*, Vol. 17 No. 2, 2007, pp. 101–22; and Keith Ansell-Pearson, 'The Transfiguration of Existence and Sovereign Life: Sloterdijk and Nietzsche on Posthuman Futures', *Environment and Planning D: Society and Space*, Vol. 27 No. 1, 2009, pp. 139–56.

12 For a discussion, see Elliot Jarbe, 'Impolitical Kinetics: A Brief Sketch on Peter Sloterdijk's "Mobilization of the Planet from the Spirit of Self-Intensification"', forthcoming.

13 Small parts of the *Sphären* books have appeared in English translation, including a variant of the text that Sloterdijk published separately as *Luftbeben* (Terror from the Air) (LB; TA); and 'Foam City: About Urban Spatial Multitudes', *New Geographies: Design Agency Territory*, translated by Antonio Petrov, Vol. 0, pp. 136–43; 'Geometry in the colossal: the project of metaphysical globalisation', translated by Samuel A. Butler; and 'Airquakes', translated by Eduardo Mendieta, in *Environment and Planning D: Society and Space*, Vol. 27 No. 1, 2009, pp. 29–40, pp. 41–57. See also Jean-Christophe Royoux and Peter Sloterdijk, 'Foreword to the Theory of the Spheres', in Melik Ohanian and Jean-Christophe Royoux (eds), *Cosmograms*, New York: Lukas and Sternberg, 2005, pp. 223–40; and 'Atmospheric Politics', in Bruno Latour and Peter Weibel (eds), *Making Things Public: Atmospheres of Democracy*, Cambridge: MIT Press, pp. 944–51. Wieland Hoban, a contributor to this volume and translator of GZ and DE, is preparing a translation of *Sphären* for Semiotext(e).

14 Slavoj Žižek, *Living in the End Times*, London: Verso, 2010, p. 266.

15 Didier Franck, *Heidegger et le problème de l'espace*, Paris: Les Éditions de Minuit 1986; Edward S. Casey, *Getting Back into Place: Toward a Renewed Understanding of the Place-world*, Indianapolis: Indiana University Press, 1993; Stuart Elden, *Mapping the Present: Heidegger, Foucault and the Project of a Spatial History*, London: Continuum, 2001; Theodore Schatzki, *Heidegger: Theorist of Space*, Stuttgart: Steiner Verlag, 2007; Jeff Malpas, *Heidegger's Topology: Being, Place, World*, Cambridge: MIT Press, 2007; Andrew J. Mitchell, *Heidegger Among the Sculptors: Body, Space, and the Art of Dwelling*, Stanford: Stanford University Press, 2010; Mikko Joronen, *The Age of Planetary Space: On Heidegger, Being, and Metaphysics of Globalization*, Turku: University of Turku, 2010.

16 For a discussion, see Marie-Eve Morin, 'Cohabiting in the globalised world: Peter Sloterdijk's global foams and Bruno Latour's cosmopolitics', *Environment and Planning D: Society and Space*, Vol. 27 No. 1, 2009, pp. 58–72; and her chapter in this volume.

17 See Stuart Elden, *Speaking Against Number: Heidegger, Language and the Politics of Calculation*, Edinburgh: Edinburgh University Press, 2006.

18 For Heidegger's rejection of reading 'in' as spatial, as opposed to existential, see SZ 53–4. For an extended discussion, see S I 336–45.

19 Henk Oosterling, 'Interest and Excess of Modern Man's Radical Mediocrity: Rescaling Sloterdijk's Grandiose Aesthetic Strategy', *Cultural Politics*, Vol. 3 No. 3, 2007, pp. 357–80, p. 372. This is picked up by Bruno Latour, 'A Cautious Prometheus? A Few Steps toward a Philosophy of Design with Special Attention to Peter Sloterdijk', in Sjoerd van Tuinen and Koenraad Hemelsoet (eds), *Measuring the Monstrous: Peter Sloterdijk's Jovial Modernity*, Brussels: KVAB, 2008, pp. 61–71, p. 66. Sloterdijk's principal writings on art and design are collected in AI; see also TB.

20 'Against Gravity: Bettina Funcke talks with Peter Sloterdijk', *Book Forum*, 2005, http://www.bookforum.com/archive/feb_05/funcke. html

21 Gaston Bachelard, *Poetics of Space*, translated by Maria Jolas, New York: Orion Press, 1964; see WK 308.

22 Funcke and Sloterdijk, 'Against Gravity'.

23 The diagram is reproduced in Martin Heidegger, *Zollikoner Seminare:*

Protokolle – Gespräche – Briefe, edited by Medard Boss, Frankfurt am Main: Vittorio Klostermann, 1987, p. 3.

24 Francisco Klauser, 'Splintering Spheres of Security: Sloterdijk and the Contemporary Fortress City', *Environment and Planning D: Society and Space*, Vol. 28 No. 2, 2010. pp. 326–40, p. 330.

25 Eric Morse and Peter Sloterdijk, 'Something in the Air', *Frieze Magazine*, No. 127, 2009, http://www.frieze.com/issue/article/something_in_the_air/. For a critique, see Nigel Thrift, 'Different Atmospheres: Of Sloterdijk, China, and Site', *Environment and Planning D: Society and Space*, Vol. 27 No.1, 2009, pp. 119–38.

26 This is the title of Chapter 33 of WK. The French translation takes this as its title: *Le palais de cristal: l'intérieur du capitalisme planétaire*, translated by Olivier Mannoni, Paris: Maren Sell, 2008.

27 See John Carroll, *Break-out from the Crystal Palace: The Anarcho-Psychological Critique: Stirner, Dostoevsky, Nietzsche*, London: Routledge and Kegan Paul, 1974.

28 Morse and Sloterdijk, 'Something in the Air'.

29 Oosterling, 'Interest and Excess of Modern Man's Radical Mediocrity, p. 361.

30 Heik Afheldt and Bernd Ulrich, 'Animal Rights, Gene Technology, and Human Breeding: A Conversation with Peter Sloterdijk', *Logos: A Journal of Modern Society and Culture*, Vol. 6 No. 3, 2007, http://www.logosjournal.com/issue_6.3/sloterdijk.htm. For Sloterdijk's further reflections on the notion of *das Ungeheure*, the monstrous, see NG 367–87; this volume chapter 10; and on this as a measure of the world, see also S II 47–72.

31 Homer, *Iliad*, I, 1.

32 See Mario Wenning, 'The Return of Rage', *Parrhesia*, No. 8, 2009, pp. 89–99.

33 Sloterdijk's juxtaposition of Derrida with a range of other thinkers, including contemporaries such as Niklas Luhmann and Boris Groys and the long-dead Thomas Mann, Freud and Hegel can be seen as a staging of just such encounters in the republic of letters.

34 See Andrew Fisher, 'Flirting with Fascism - The Sloterdijk Debate', *Radical Philosophy*, No. 99, 2000, pp. 8–10; and the discussion in LHTC and NSND.

35 Žižek, *The Parallax View*, p. 179.

36 Žižek, *Living in the End Times*, p. 134 n. 53.

37 Peter Sloterdijk, *Die Großen Erzählungen – Ein Lesebuch*, Suhrkamp Verlag, Frankfurt am Main, 2011; *Lesen in den Eingeweiden des Zeitgeistes*, Suhrkamp Verlag, Frankfurt am Main, 2011.
38 Sjoerd van Tuinen, *Peter Sloterdijk: Ein Profil*, München: Wilhelm Fink, 2006.
39 The text can be found online at http://www.petersloterdijk.net/ agenda/artikel/die-revolution-der-gebenden-hand An expanded edition of these arguments has appeared as NHGS.
40 For a selection of pieces sparked by the debate, see Jan Rehmann and Thomas Wagner (eds), *Angriff der Leistungsträger? Das Buch zur Sloterdijk-Debatte*, Hamburg: Argument, 2010.
41 Sjoerd van Tuinen (ed.), 'Special Issue on Peter Sloterdijk', *Cultural Politics*, Vol. 3 No. 3, 2007; Stuart Elden, Eduardo Mendieta, and Nigel Thrift (eds), 'The Worlds of Peter Sloterdijk', *Environment and Planning D: Society and Space*, Vol. 27 No. 1, 2009. There have also been works in other languages, including H. von Dobeneck, 2006, *Das Sloterdijk-Alphabet: Eine lexikalische Einführung in Sloterdijks Gedankenkosmos*, Würzburg: Königshausen and Neumann, 2006; Marc Jongen, Sjoerd van Tuinen and Koenraad Hemelsoet (eds), *Die Vermessung des Ungeheuren: Philosophie nach Peter Sloterdijk*, München: Wilhelm Fink, 2009; Hans-Jürgen Heinrichs, *Peter Sloterdijk: Die Kunst des Philosophierens*, München: Hanser, 2011.

2 Sloterdijk's Cynicism: Diogenes in the Marketplace

1 Slavoj Žižek, *The Sublime Object of Ideology*, London: Verso, 1989, see pp. 27ff.
2 Žižek, *The Sublime Object of Ideology*, p. 31.
3 Žižek, *The Sublime Object of Ideology*, p. 31.
4 Diogenes Laertius, *Lives of Eminent Philosophers*, trans. R. D. Hicks, Cambridge: Harvard University Press, 1925, Vol. II, p. 23.
5 Percy Gardner, 'Diogenes and Delphi', *The Classical Review*, Vol. 7, No. 10 (Dec., 1893): 437–9, here 437.
6 According to Swift, 'Epicurus, Diogenes, Apollonius, Lucretius, Paracelsus, Des Cartes, and others; who, if they were now in the world, tied fast, and separate from their followers, would in this, our undistinguishing age, incur manifest danger of *phlebotomy*, and *whips*, and *chains*, and *dark chambers*, and *straw*.' Swift, *A Tale of a Tub:*

Written for the Universal Improvement of Mankind, London: Thomas Tegg, 1911 [1697], p. 192.

7 Soren Kierkegaard, 'Attack upon "Christendom"', in: Robert Bretall, ed., *A Kierkegaard Anthology*, Princeton: Princeton University Press, 1946, p. 448. Here and throughout.

8 Žižek, *The Sublime Object of Ideology*, p. 29.

9 Cited in Third Essay of Northrop Frye, *The Anatomy of Criticism*, Princeton: Princeton University Press, 1957.

10 'Read my books' as Mary Daly would say, a female kynic if ever there was one. See Babich, 'Great Men, Little Black Dresses, and the Virtues of Keeping One's Feet on the Ground', *MP: An Online Feminist Journal*, Vol. 3, Issue 1 (August 2010): pp. 57–78, esp. 60–5 for a discussion of Daly who 'pissed against the wind' in academe – with the disastrous results that usually follow.

11 Cited by Seymore Papert in his introduction to Warren S. McCulloch, *Embodiments of Mind*, Cambridge, Massachusetts: MIT Press, 1965, p. xx.

12 Set off as an epigraph, Sloterdijk emphasizes his debt to Heinrich Niehues-Pröbsting's magisterial *Der Kynismus des Diogenes und der Begriff des Zynismus*, Frankfurt am Main: Suhrkamp, 1988.

13 Troublesomely, alas, Eldred renders Sloterdijk's *'die verlorene Frechheit'* as 'cheekiness' which we are accordingly advised to follow à la Proust, CCR 101ff.

14 Sigmund Freud, 'On Narcissism: An Introduction'. *Standard Edition*, [1914], Vol. 14, pp. 81–105; p. 19.

15 See, for example, the chapter 'How We Learned to Stop Worrying, and Love the Bomb' in Gerard J. De Groot, *The Bomb: A Life*, Cambridge: Harvard University Press, 2005, pp. 272ff.

16 See Richard Perkins, 'A Giant and Some Dwarves: Nietzsche's Unpublished Märchen on the Exception and the Rule', *Marvels and Tales: Fairy-Tale Studies*, 11/1–2 (1997), pp. 61–73.

17 See Swift, *Gulliver's Travels*, London: Jones and Company, 1826, 11. See further, for an analysis and discussion, Frank Boyle, *Swift as Nemesis: Modernity and its Satirist*, Palo Alto: Stanford University Press, 2000, pp. 34ff.

18 Gulliver's charges concern 'The Emperor's Apartments set on fire by accident, the author instrumental in saving the rest of the palace' Swift, *Gulliver's Travels*, p. 51, cf. p. 59.

19 Northrop Frye, *Educated Imagination and Other Writings on Critical Theory, 1933–1962*, Toronto: University of Toronto Press, 2006, p. 85.

20 Sloterdijk also discusses thinking on the philosophy of technology in Rathaus, Freyer, Turel, Jünger, Dessauer, etc., in the latter pages of *Critique of Cynical Reason*.

21 The 'singularity' term as applied to technology was arguably used for the first time by the computer scientist and science fiction author, Vernor Vinge who himself attributes it to John von Neumann. See Vinge's 'The Coming Technological Singularity: How to Survive in the Post-Human Era', presented at NASA Lewis Research Center and the Ohio Aerospace Institute, March 30–1, 1993. By far the greatest attention has been paid to Kurzweil's re-animation of the term, *The Singularity is Near: When Humans Transcend Biology*, New York: Viking, 2005.

22 Günther Anders, *Die Antiquiertheit des Menschen: über die Seele im Zeitalter der zweiten industriellen Revolution*, Munich: Beck, 1980, p. 40.

23 See for a further discussion, Babich, 'Nietzsche's Will to Power: Politics and Destiny', in: Tracy B. Strong, ed., *Friedrich Nietzsche*, London: Ashgate, 2009, pp. 282–96.

24 Nietzsche also speaks of 'Politik und Geldgier', KSA IX, 213.

25 Friedrich Dessauer, *Philosophie der Technik. Das Problem der Realisierung*, cited in CCR 455.

26 Here the translator's rendering 'Anyone' is misleading.

27 Heidegger, *Introduction to Metaphysics*, trans. Ralph Manheim (New Haven: Yale University Press, 1979), p. 45. Heidegger's lectures date from 1935.

28 Regler, *Das Ohr des Malchus*, 1933, cited in CCR 530.

29 See Bruno Latour, 'Reflections on Etienne Souriau's *Les différents modes d'existence*', in: Levi Bryant, Nick Srnicek and Graham Harman, eds, *The Speculative Turn* (repress: Melbourne, 2011), pp. 304–33, here p. 304 but also throughout.

30 Thus even as restrained a scholar as Andreas Huyssen can be moved, however mildly he is moved, to observe that Sloterdijk 'clearly has the rational, reified, male subject in mind. The question of women's subjectivity and its relationship to the cynicism-kynicism constellation is never really explored.' Andreas Huyssen, *Twilight Memories: Marking Time in a Culture of Amnesia*, London: Routledge, 1995, p. 169.

31 Some will, so we are told, qualify, in some way, for some assistance, say, if one is completely indigent. The relevant point is that the insurance company will get paid no matter what.
32 Nietzsche, KSA III, 565. What Sloterdijk calls an 'Other History', Nietzsche calls incipient or 'Future "Humaneness"'.

3 From Psychopolitics to Cosmopolitics: The Problem of Ressentiment

1 Gilles Deleuze, *Nietzsche and Philosophy*, translated by Hugh Tomlinson, New York: Columbia University Press, 2006, p. 111.
2 Deleuze, *Nietzsche and Philosophy*, p. 89; Deleuze and Félix Guattari *Anti-Oedipus. Capitalism and Schizophrenia*, translated by Robert Hurley, Mark Seem, and Helen R. Lane, London: Continuum, 2003, p. 247. I offer a defense of Sloterdijk's recent work against criticisms by Slavoj Žižek and Alberto Toscano that reject any clinical focus on affect, in 'A Thymotic Left? Peter Sloterdijk and the Psychopolitics of *Ressentiment*', *Symploke*, 18(1/2), 217–34. I demonstrate why for Sloterdijk later German critical theory has the same weight as freudomarxism for Deleuze and Guattari, since not only do both currents germinate in and around the revolution of 1968 only to dissolve in counterrevolution, they also both tend to organize *ressentiment* in the same priestly manner (i.e. by cultivating bad conscience and a pious belief in lack).
3 Hannah Arendt, *The Human Condition. A Study of the Central Dilemmas Facing Modern Man*, New York: Double Day, 1958.
4 'Die wahre Irrlehre. Über die Weltreligion der Weltlosigkeit', in Peter Sloterdijk and Thomas H. Macho (eds), *Weltrevolution der Seele. Ein Lese- und Arbeitsbuch der Gnosis von der Spätantike bis zur Gegenwart*, Mannheim: Artemis and Winkler, 1991.
5 Sloterdijk defines gnosis as 'the hermeneutics of *Fehlgeburt* into a hostile world' (SV 64–6). Just as with Adorno, critical theory became 'a gnostic George-circle of the left' ('Die Kritische Theorie ist tot', *Zeit*, 37, 1999, pp. 35–6; NG 244–55), he discovers in Hardt and Negri's *Empire* a 'gnosis of militancy', since although our world is now without a clearly identifiable enemy, 'the affect "against"' has to suffice in itself. (S III 825–7)
6 For a further development of Sloterdijk's media ecology, see my 'Breath of Relief: Peter Sloterdijk and the Politics of the

Intimate', in D. Hoens, S. Jottkandt and G. Buelens (eds) *Tickle your Catastrophe: On Borders, Cuts and Edges in Contemporary Theory*, Palgrave Macmillan: Basingstoke, 2009, pp. 53–81.

7　Alain Badiou, *Saint Paul: The Foundation of Universalism*, translated by Ray Brassier, Stanford: Stanford University Press, 2003, p. 61.

8　Both cited in Badiou, *Saint Paul*, p. 62.

9　For a further development of this theme in terms of Sloterdijk's 'monogeism', see my 'Air Conditioning Spaceship Earth: Peter Sloterdijk's Ethico-Aesthetic Paradigm', *Society and Space*, 27 (1), 2009, pp. 105–18.

10　Elsewhere, Sloterdijk therefore contrasts Nietzsche's ethics of generosity to Girard's counter-ressentimental apologetism of deca-logue-religions, see 'Erwachen im Reich der Eifersucht. Notiz zu René Girards anthropologischer Sendung', in René Girard, *Ich sah den Satan vom Himmel fallen wie einen Blitz. Eine kritische Anthropologie des Christentums*, München: Hanser Belletristik, pp. 241–54, pp. 251–2.

11　See Dalie Giroux, 'Nietzsche et Sloterdijk, corps en resonance', *Horizons philosophiques*, 27 (2), 2007, pp. 109–32.

12　Michael Foucault *The Use of Pleasure: The History of Sexuality Volume II*, translated by Robert Hurley, London: Penguin, 1992, p. 9.

13　See also ET 174–209 for a Heideggerian approach to self-birth *(Selbstgeburtliche)* or autopoietical positions.

4　A Letter on *Überhumanismus: Beyond Posthumanism and Transhumanism*

1　Don Ihde, *Heidegger's Technologies: Postphenomenological Perspectives*. New York, Fordham University Press, 2010.

2　Felix Duque, *En Torno al Humanismo: Heidegger, Gadamer, Sloterdijk*, Madrid, Technos, 2002, p. 125.

3　Cary Wolfe, *What is Posthumanism?* Minneapolis, University of Minnesota Press, 2010.

4　Nick Bostrom 'A History of Transhumanist Thought', *Journal of Evolution and Technology*, Vol. 14 No. 1, 2005, pp. 1–25.

5　Stefan Lorenz Sorgner, 'Beyond Humanism: Reflections on Trans- and Posthumanism', *Journal of Evolution and Technology*, Vol. 21 No. 2, 2010, pp. 1–19.

6 Werner Jaeger, *Paideia: The Ideals of Greek Culture*, 3 vols, New York: Oxford University Press, 1939.

7 For a major study of this theologem and philosopheme of Imago Dei see Herschel Baker, *The Image of Man: A Study of the Idea of Human Dignity in Classical Antiquity, the Middle Ages, and the Renaissance*, New York: Harper Torchbooks, 1947.

8 Ernst Cassirer, Paul Oskar Kristeller, John Hermann Randall, Jr, *The Renaissance Philosophy of Man*, Chicago and London, Phoenix Books, 1948, p. 19.

9 For excellent profiles of these and other Renaissance thinkers see Paul Oskar Kristeller, *Eight Philosophers of the Italian Renaissance*, Stanford, Stanford University Press, 1964.

10 Ernesto Grassi, *Heidegger and the Question of Renaissance Humanism. Four Studies*, Binghampton, New York, Medieval and Renaissance Text and Studies, 1983, p. xix

11 Grassi, *Heidegger and the Question of Renaissance Humanism*, p. 17.

12 Grassi, *Heidegger and the Question of Renaissance Humanism*, p. 19.

13 Grassi, *Heidegger and the Question of Renaissance Humanism*, p. 29.

14 KSA I, 875; F. Nietzsche, *The Birth of Tragedy And Other Writings*, Cambridge, Cambridge University Press, 1999, p. 141.

15 KSA, I, 880–1; *The Birth of Tragedy*, p. 146.

16 I have benefited greatly from Duque's wonderful book *En Torno al Humanismo*, based on a series of lectures delivered in 2002 in Murcia, Spain, but I arrive at different conclusions, and of course, coming eight years later, I have the benefit of a more expansive reading of Sloterdijk's work, in particular *Spheres*, and the follow ups to RHZ, namely NG and MT, which Duque did not know or did not directly address in his analysis.

17 The debate in Germany involved mostly journalists and a rather unfortunate, and in retrospect embarrassing, pronouncement from Sloterdijk. Some refer to this polemic as the Habermas–Sloterdijk, which is surely a misnomer as Habermas did not respond to Sloterdijk, nor did he write one of his customarily thorough essays. Sloterdijk, on the other hand, wrote a rather hysterical letter entitled, 'Critical Theory is Dead' (*Die Zeit*, No. 37, September 9, 1999), in which he accuses Habermas of censoring and vilifying him. As far as I know, and in accordance with the published record, Habermas did neither. In any event, no debate took place. Only recently, a decade

later, has a colleague directly associated with the Frankfurt School, and Habermas in particular, responded in press to Sloterdijk. And this is Axel Honneth. In this case, the debate has to do with the future of the welfare state and nothing to do with biotechnology. At the most, one could engage in a hypothetical polemic, in which one could theorize what either Habermas or Sloterdijk would say to the other. In any event, even such a hypothetical exchange would require much mediation and translation. See my essay 'Habermas on Cloning: The debate on the future of the species' *Philosophy and Social Criticism*, Vol. 30, no. 5–6 (2004): 721–43. See also Max Pensky, *The Ends of Solidarity: Discourse Theory in Ethics and Politics* (Albany: SUNY Press, 2008), chapter 7.

5 The Coming-to-the-World of the Human Animal

1 A shorter version of this chapter was presented at IAPL 2009 conference. I thank Kieran Aarons for inviting me to the Sloterdijk panel as well as the participants for their challenging questions. A draft of this chapter was also presented at the Continental Philosophy Workshop in Montreal. I thank Iain Macdonald, Christine Daigle, Antonio Calcagno, Bettina Bergo, and Martine Béland for their comments and questions. They were very useful in revising this chapter.

2 On Heidegger's position toward anthropology, see SZ § 10. Of course, Sloterdijk is not the first to challenge the inflexibility of the ontico-ontological difference and use the Heideggerian insights into existence to develop an anthropology or developmental psychology: during Heidegger's time among others Scheler, Plessner, Gehlen, later Merleau-Ponty, and most recently Stiegler.

3 Martin Heidegger, *Introduction to Metaphysics*, New Haven: Yale University Press, 2000, p. 166.

4 See Martin Heidegger, *The Fundamental Concepts of Metaphysics: World, Finitude, Solitude*, Bloomington: Indiana University Press, 2001.

5 See G. W. F. Hegel, *Aesthetics: Lectures on Fine Art, Volume I*, translated by T. M. Knox, Oxford: Oxford University Press, 1973, p. 31.

6 Even though Heidegger could accept the first part of this statement since for him dwelling is not merely occupying a lodging, but the essential way in which humans are on earth in proximity to being,

he would never speak of a 'space' (a housing) prior to the standing-out into the clearing of being or the space of intelligibility. See Martin Heidegger, *Poetry, Language, Thought*, translated by Albert Hofstadter, New York: HarperCollins, 1971, p. 213. The point of contention concerns the meaning of 'priority', as either 'historical priority' (that one event must have happened before the other) or 'ontological priority' (that there must be the correlation of being and Dasein for the first kind of priority to *appear*).

7　Again, speaking of a positive or primitive *Ge-Stell* is a contradiction in terms from the Heideggerian point of view. *Ge-Stell* is the way in which entities are revealed for wilful subjects; it is the way of being of modern technology and synonymous with all forms of doing.

8　Here we would find a direct connection to Sloterdijk's controversial discussion of anthropo-technological forms of taming and breeding in *Rules for the Human Zoo*.

9　See the discussion of various kinds of islands in S III Chapter 1.

10　Whether we see this double movement as a movement in the being of Dasein between thrownness [*Geworfenheit*] and resolute projection [*Entwurf*] or as a movement in the Ereignis itself: opening on the basis of a concealing/withdrawal, is irrelevant.

11　Heidegger, *Poetry, Language, Thought*, pp. 163–4.

12　Of course Heidegger's point regarding these movements would be that they are merely focused on the presence of what is at-hand and forget that this presence is made possible by a potentiality or an absence at the heart of existence and which Heidegger analyses under the concept of temporality.

13　In the 'Introduction to "What is Metaphysics?"' Heidegger insists that the most fitting word to think of existence is 'in-standing' or 'in-abiding' [*Inständigkeit*]. Ex-sisting as in-standing means resisting the inertia of falling, resisting restlessness and coming to stand so that one can stand free towards beings (including oneself) and let them be (W 203). See also Heidegger, *Mindfulness*, London: Continuum, 2006, § 33 and § 41.

14　From § 47 of the *Tao Te Ching*.

15　For a detailed discussion of these three phases, see my 'Cohabiting in the globalised world', *Environment and Planning D: Society and Space*, Vol. 27 No. 1, 2009, pp. 58–72.

16　Heidegger, *Introduction to Metaphysics*, p. 217.

17 Martin Heidegger, *The Question Concerning Technology and Other Essays*, trans. William Lovitt, Harper and Row, New York, 1977, p. 28.

18 Heidegger, *The Question Concerning Technology*, p. 180–1, trans. mod.

19 Heidegger, *The Question Concerning Technology*, p. 35. See also Martin Heidegger, *Nietzsche Volume 4: Nihilism*, San Francisco: Harper and Row, 1982, p. 227.

20 Sloterdijk, 'Du centrisme mou au risque de penser', *Le Monde*, 8 October 1999. See also NG 233, 301.

21 Martin Heidegger, 'What Calls for Thinking?', in *Basic Writings*, edited by David Farrell Krell, London: Routledge, 1993, p. 379.

6 A Public Intellectual

1 I would like to thank Alex Del Duca for providing a great deal of assistance in the writing of this chapter.

2 Jean-Paul Sartre 'A Plea for Intellectuals', *Between Existentialism and Marxism*, London: New Left Books, 1974, p. 244.

3 Richard A. Posner, *Public Intellectuals: A Study of Decline*, Cambridge, MA: Harvard University Press, Cambridge, 2001, p. 35.

4 Posner, *Public Intellectuals*, p. 388.

5 Posner, *Public Intellectuals*, p. 29.

6 While being applauded as a major German scholar, Sloterdijk also appears regularly on national television with his own show, *Das Philosophische Quartett*, in addition to numerous appearances in cultural and public affairs programmes. The most prestigious German newspapers and magazines, such as *Die Welt, Frankfurter Allgemeine Zeitung, Süddeutsche Zeitung* or *Der Spiegel*, are also constantly soliciting Sloterdijk's views on national and international issues.

7 U. J. Schneider 'The Situation of Philosophy, the Culture of the Philosophers: Philosophy in the New Germany', *Social Research*, Vol. 64 No. 2, 1997, p. 294.

8 During the months following his *Regeln für den Menschenpark* lecture, Sloterdijk was brusquely attacked by journalists from *Die Zeit* and *Der Spiegel*. Interestingly, the beleaguered philosopher asserted throughout the scandal, with evidence, that Habermas himself sponsored and organized this vendetta against him. While the latter strongly denied any such cloak and dagger activity, it was

not long before the press intervened to blow Habermas' cover: the few notes he truly sent to Thomas Assheuer (see his instrumental/ized position in figure 1 above), one of the key journalists at the origin of this national controversy, were published for all to read. In light of this course of events, Sloterdijk did not miss the opportunity to deliver returning fire, proclaiming 'critical theory is dead' and that 'the time of sons with bad or good conscience is over'.

9   Axel Honneth, 'Fataler Tiefsinn aus Karlsruhe', *Die Zeit* No. 40, 24.09.2009.

10 Heinz U. Nennen *Philosophie in Echtzeit. Die Sloterdijk-Debatte: Chronik einer Inszenierung*, Würzburg: Königshausen and Neumann, 2003, p. 74.

11 Nennen, *Philosophie in Echtzeit*, p. 116.

12 Rudolf Walther and Martin Halter quoted by Nennen, *Philosophie in Echtzeit*, p. 74.

13 Pierre Bourdieu and Loic Wacquant, *An Invitation to Reflexive Sociology*, Chicago: University of Chicago Press, 1992, p. 101.

14 Randall Collins, *The Sociology of Philosophies. A Global Theory of Intellectual Change*, Cambridge, MA: Harvard University Press, 1998, p. 621.

15 Collins, *The Sociology of Philosophies*, p. 621.

16 Peter Sloterdijk, 'Die Revolution der gebenden Hand', *Die Zukunft des Kapitalismus*, F. Schirrmacher and T. Strobl (eds), Suhrkamp, Berlin, 2010, pp. 69–70. Originally published in *Frankfurter Allgemeine Zeitung*, 13.6.2009.

17 Sloterdijk, 'Die Revolution der gebenden Hand', p. 70.

18 Honneth, 'Fataler Tiefsinn aus Karlsruhe'.

19 Peter Sloterdijk, 'Wider der Verteufelung der Leistungsträger', *Süddeutsche Zeitung*, 6.1.2010.

20 Honneth, 'Fataler Tiefsinn aus Karlsruhe'.

21 Peter Sloterdijk, 'Das elfte Gebot: die progressive Einkommenssteuer', *Frankfurter Allgemeine Zeitung*, 27.9.2009.

22 Axel Honneth, 'Nach neuen Formen suchen', *Kölner Stadt-Anzeiger*, 16.12.2009.

23 Peter Sloterdijk, 'Aufbruch der Leistungsträger', *Cicero*, November 2009.

24 Sloterdijk, 'Wider der Verteufelung der Leistungsträger'.

25 Rob Sharp, 'Guy Laliberté: The first clown in space?', *The Independent*, 22.09.2009.

26 According to the official numbers of the German Federal Republic quoted by Sloterdijk, no more than 10 per cent of the whole German population can be considered as relatively poor. Even if this proportion is double in the US, Sloterdijk firmly asserts that, in the light of this fact, 'we are still facing here a historical and unprecedented space of prosperity' (S III 683).

27 Sloterdijk, 'Aufbruch der Leistungsträger'.

28 Robert Pfaller, 'Disinhibition, Subjectivity, and Pride. Or: Guess Who is Looking?', S. van Tuinen and K. Hemelsoet (eds), *Measuring the Monstrous. Peter Sloterdijk's Jovial Modernity*, Brussels: KVAB, 2009, pp. 47–8.

7 *The Language of Give and Take: Sloterdijk's Stylistic Methods*

1 Christoph Menke, 'Wahrheit, nicht Stil', in *Die Zeit* 43/2009.

2 'Eingeweide des Zeitgeistes', interview with Peter Sloterdijk, in *Der Spiegel* 44/2009, pp. 172f.

3 The figure of Narcissus is afforded a slightly more differentiated treatment in volume 1 of *Sphären*, where he is placed in a more historical context: 'We should precisely *not* read the myth of Narcissus as evidence of a natural relationship between humans and their own faces in the mirror, but as an indication of the disturbingly unaccustomed nature of burgeoning facial reflection' (S I 201). This is an example of the conceptual and contextual layers whose absence makes his more publicly oriented work lack the depth of his books.

4 Robert Pape, *Dying to Win: The Strategic Logic of Suicide Terrorism*, New York: Random House, 2005, p. 4.

5 Pape, *Dying to Win*, p. 208.

6 Pape, *Dying to Win*, pp. 212f.

7 Pape, *Dying to Win*, p. 213.

8 Pape, *Dying to Win*, p. 214.

9 Pape, *Dying to Win*, p. 220.

10 Both Honneth's article and Sloterdijk's response call to mind the latter's remark: 'As in every dispute over opinions, the parties are actually fighting over the truth of the persons involved' (KMPA 120).

11 Petra Kuhnau, '*Masse und Macht*' *in der Geschichte*, Würzburg: Königshausen and Neumann, 1996, pp. 1f.

12 For example the term *Sklavensprache* [slave language], recalling Nietzsche's *Herrenmoral* (and, regrettably, the appropriations of such terminology in the Third Reich), with which Sloterdijk refers to conventions of political correctness which ensure that those who speak their mind on matters such as social inequality are punished if they offend democratic sensibilities. See Sloterdijk, 'Aufbruch der Leistungsträger', in *Cicero*, November 2009.

13 One notes a slightly different tone six years later in *Weldfremdheit*, where Sloterdijk invokes Kafka's figure of the hunger artist as a parallel to what he sees as gratuitous self-flagellation among modern composers: 'While Kafka's parable of the hunger artist has not applied to painters, sculptors or writers for one or two generations, it will retain its significance among composers for the time being' (WF 303).

8 Peter Sloterdijk and the Philosopher's Stone

1 Bruno Latour, 'Coming out as a philosopher' *Social Studies of Science*, August 2010, 40: 599–608, p. 9,

2 Eric Hazan, *The Invention of Paris. A History in Footsteps*, London: Verso, 2010, p. 369.

3 Thus philosophy comes to live an 'excessive, artificial existence' (Alain Badiou, *Second Manifesto for Philosophy*, Cambridge: Polity, 2011, p. 68). 'What worries some philosophers . . . is that this process of diffusion is proliferating at an alarming rate in what is an apparent philosophization of everything, one that threatens to leave philosophy nowhere precisely because it is everywhere. Philosophy will have lost its own identity' (John Mullarkey, *Philosophy and the Moving Image. Refractions of Reality*, London: Palgrave Macmillan, 2010, p. xvii). It is the where in this concern that I want to address in this chapter as precisely a problem of address.

4 Alain Badiou and Slavoj Žižek, *Philosophy in the Present*, Cambridge: Polity, 2009, pp. 66–7.

5 It is difficult to see how Foucault's thoughts on Iran could ever be taken as seriously now in France as they were in the 1980s. Even there, philosophers' stock as somehow thinkers with a privileged access to the world has declined.

6 See, for example, Alberto Toscano, 'Review: Sloterdijk, Sloterdijk and Sloterdijk', *TPM. The Philosopher's Magazine*, No. 48, 2010.

7 Ian Morris, *Why the West Rules – For Now. The Patterns of History and What They Reveal About the Future*, London, Profile Books, 2010.

8 Emmanuel Faye, *Heidegger. The Introduction of Nazism into Philosophy*, New Haven: Yale University Press, 2009.

9 Christine Buci-Glucksmann, *L'Oeil Cartographique de l'Art*, Paris: Galilee, 1996.

10 Mary Douglas, *Thinking in Circles. An Essay on Ring Composition*, New Haven: Yale University Press, 2010

11 Timothy Morton, *The Ecological Thought*, Cambridge, MA: Harvard University Press, 2010.

12 Nigel Thrift, 'Halos: Finding Space in the World for New Political Forms', in Bruce Braun and Sarah J. Whatmore (eds), *Political Matter. Technoscience, Democracy and Public Life*, Minneapolis, University of Minnesota Press, 2010, pp. 139–74.

13 Chandra Mukerji *Impossible Engineering. Technology and Territoriality on the Canal du Midi*, Princeton, Princeton University Press, 2009.

14 This and the next paragraph are modified from my 'Different Atmospheres: Of Sloterdijk, China and Site', *Environment and Planning D. Society and Space*, Vol. 27 No. 1, 2009, pp. 119–38.

15 See, for example, the work of John Shotter or that strand of work inspired by the discovery of mirror neurons.

16 'Nietzsche . . . is in my opinion the first and has been up to now the only psychologist' (Otto Rank, *Truth and Reality*, New York: W. W. Norton, 1964 [1936], p. 18).

17 Thus nature becomes ever more conscious of herself through birth and rebirth, a motif which threads throughout the pages of *Sphären* as a view of the world as womb.

18 Adam Phillips, *On Balance*, London: Hamish Hamilton, 2010, p. 30.

19 John Knechtel (ed.), *Air*, Cambridge, MA: MIT Press, 2010.

20 Graham Harman, *Towards Speculative Realism*, Winchester: Zero Books, 2010; *Circus Philosophicus*, Winchester: Zero Books, 2010.

21 François Laruelle, *Philosophies of Difference: A Critical Introduction to Non-Philosophy*, translated by Rocco Gangle, London: Continuum, 2010.

22 John Mullarkey, *Post-Continental Philosophy: An Outline*, London: Continuum, 2006.

23 Mullarkey, *Philosophy and the Moving Image*, p. 192.

24 Bruno Latour, *Reassembling the Social. An Introduction to Actor-Network Theory*, Oxford: Oxford University Press, 2007.

25 Mullarkey, *Post-Continental Philosophy*.

26 Peter Howlett and Mary S. Morgan (eds), *How Well Do Facts Travel? The Dissemination of Reliable Knowledge*, Cambridge: Cambridge University Press, 2010.

27 Morris, *Why the West Rules*.

28 To provide just one example. No doubt there is a problem that, with a few exceptions, French philosophers 'say practically nothing about economics' (Bernard Stiegler, *For a New Critique of Political Economy*, translated by Daniel Ross, Cambridge: Polity, 2010, p. 19). Unfortunately, when they do, they fall back on the old ways of proceeding which simply assert that this is the way the world is, a fault that Marx could never have been accused of. For example, as a philosopher making his way into the domain of economics, Stiegler legislates the world by insisting that the grammatization of perception and of the nervous system (a tendency for which there is ample evidence) inexorably leads to the proletarianization (not pauperization) of consumers (a tendency for which the ethnographic evidence from social science is, to put it kindly, patchy and often flatly contradicted). Any social scientist would want to unpick such claims and could easily produce counter-examples. It is an endemic problem of critique that it assumes that accusation, a continuous process which is somewhere between analysis and action, and which automatically includes often rather satisfying affects like blame and guilt and anger, is the only intellectual mode of proceeding worth the effort and is somehow self-justifying.

29 See my *Non-Representational Theory: Space, Politics, Affect*, London: Routledge, 2007; 'Different Atmospheres'; 'Halos'; and 'Lifeworld Inc. and what to do about it', *Environment and Planning D. Society and Space*, Vol. 29 No. 1, 2011, pp. 4–25.

30 Peter Sloterdijk, 'Atmospheric Politics' in Bruno Latour and Peter Weibel, (eds) *Making Things Public. Atmospheres of Democracy*, Cambridge, Mass., MIT Press, 2005, pp. 944–51.

31 The emphasis on understandiang how small differences can produce large changes is founded in Tarde and Deleuze but can also be located in classical Chinese thought (François Jullien, *The Silent Transformations*, Chicago: University of Chicago Press 2011).

32 Landscapes of thought/mediums of growth that can bring different worlds into existence which productively combine various concepts, percepts and affects.

9 Literature in Sloterdijk's Philosophy

1 R. G. Collingwood, *Outlines of a Philosophy of Art*, Oxford University Press, 1925, p. 11.

2 Collingwood, *Outlines of a Philosophy of Art*, p. 100.

3 Interview with Peter Sloterdijk by Stephan Schmidt-Wulffen, in Jean Baudrillard, Hans-Georg Gadamer, et al, *Art and Philosophy*, Milan: Giancarlo Politi Editore, 1991, pp. 117–18.

4 It would be instructive to compare Sloterdijk's views on literature and life with those of Kenneth Burke, the American literary critic who devoted his life to this question; and who shares a number of literary instincts with Sloterdijk, including the conceit of creating dialogues with fictional characters to ponder over philosophical matters.

5 Sloterdijk's concern with rancour and resentment, for example, is touched upon in the final pages of *Die Verachtung der Massen*; and in sections of *Die Sonne und der Tod* (ST 302–3).

6 It might be instructive to note that this time-line is similar to Zygmunt Bauman's view regarding a shift that takes place around the 1970s from that which he calls a 'solid' modern period to our 'liquid modern' times. See Bauman, *Liquid Modernity*, Cambridge: Polity, 2000.

7 Michaud, Yves, *L'art à l'état gazeux* Paris: Stock, 2003, p. 18. Michaud's book on Sloterdijk is called *Humain, Inhumain, Trop Humain: Réflexions philosophiques sur les biotechnologies, la vie et la conservation de soi à partir de l'oeuvre de Peter Sloterdijk*, Paris: Micro-Climats, 2002. For Sloterdijk the label 'postmodernism' is not an indication of an era but an invitation to reflect on new circumstances. See the chapter 'Nach der Modernität' in *Eurotaoismus*, in particular the discussion in ET 266–93.

8 Heidegger's insight is a radical version of Dilthey's view that intersubjective experience is the key to understanding the social sciences and to distinguishing them from the natural sciences. For Heidegger the intersubjective experience is also the grounding for both scientific and non-scientific thought.

9   Peter Sloterdijk, 'Foreword to the Theory of Spheres' (Interview with Jean Christophe Royoux), in Melik Ohanian and Jean Christophe Royoux, (eds) *Cosmograms*, New York: Lukas and Sternberg, 2005, p. 232.

10 http://www.petersloterdijk.net/

11 Sloterdijk, 'Foreword to the Theory of Spheres', pp. 227–8. Sloterdijk develops this idea in WK 243–64.

12 Jorge Luis Borges, 'The Book of Sand', translated by Andrew Hurley, *Collected Fictions*, New York, Penguin, 1998, p. 481.

13 Sloterdijk pays homage to Henry F. Ellenberger in S I 412–13.

14 Thomas Mann, 'How Abraham Found God', *Joseph and his Brothers*, translated by H. T. Lowe-Porter, New York: Knopf, 1948, p. 286.

10   The Time of the Crime of the Monstrous: On the Philosophical Justification of the Artificial

1   See Sloterdijk, S II, Chapter 8: 'Zu einer philosophischen Geschichte der terrestrischen Globalisierung', pp. 801–1005.

2   See Martin Heidegger, 'The Age of the World Picture', in *Off the Beaten Track*, ed. and trans. Julian Young and Kenneth Haynes, Cambridge University Press, 2002, pp. 57–85.

3   See Percy Ernst Schramm, *Sphaira. Globus. Reichsapfel: Wanderung und Wandlung eines Herrschaftszeichens von Caesar bis Elisabeth II; ein 'Beitrag' zum 'Nachleben' der Antike*, Stuttgart: Hiersemann, 1958.

4   Heidegger, 'Überwindung der Metaphysik', in *Vorträge und Aufsätze*, Stuttgart: Klett-Cotta, 2009, p. 93. See 'Overcoming Metaphysics', in *The End of Philosophy*, trans. Joan Stambaugh, Harper and Row, 1973, pp. 108–9, translation Wieland Hoban.

5   Gilles Deleuze and Félix Guattari, *A Thousand Plateaus: Capitalism and Schizophrenia*, New York: Continuum, 2004, trans. Brian Massumi, pp. 44 and 71.

6   Robert Walser, *Masquerade and Other Stories*, trans. Susan Bernofsky, Baltimore: Johns Hopkins University Press, 1990, p. 180.

7   Translator's note: the phrase *Unbehagen in der Modernität* is almost certainly meant to recall Freud's *Das Unbehagen in der Kultur*, which, though published in English as *Civilization and Its Discontents*, would be more accurately translated as 'Unease in Culture'.

8   See Hans Blumenberg's essay 'Nachahmung der Natur.

Zur Vorgeschichte der Idee des schöpferischen Menschen', in *Wirklichkeiten, in denen wir leben,* Stuttgart: Reclam, 1981, pp. 55–103.

9 Heidegger, 'Überwindung der Metaphysik', p. 94. See 'Overcoming Metaphysics', p. 109, translation Wieland Hoban.

10 Gotthard Günther, *Beiträge zur Grundlegung einer operationsfähigen Dialektik,* Vol. 3, Hamburg: Felix Meiner, 1980, pp. 224f.

11 Gotthard Günther, *Beiträge zur Grundlegung einer operationsfähigen Dialektik,* pp. 224f.

12 The old ontology of things makes reflection unreal; the old ontology of spirit makes material unreal. Both reductions (conditioned by ontological monovalence) are in effect to this day, massively guided by the former (positivistic) mode.

Index